T0305285

PLANTATION SLAVERY, JAMAICA
AND ABSENTEE OWNERSHIP

Plantation Slavery, Jamaica and Absentee Ownership

The Burtons of Norfolk, 1788–1846

Richard C. Maguire

THE BOYDELL PRESS

First published 2024
The Boydell Press, Woodbridge

ISBN 978 1 83765 124 5

The Boydell Press is an imprint of Boydell & Brewer Ltd
PO Box 9, Woodbridge, Suffolk IP12 3DF, UK
and of Boydell & Brewer Inc.
668 Mt Hope Avenue, Rochester, NY 14620–2731, USA
website: www.boydellandbrewer.com

A CIP catalogue record for this book is available
from the British Library

For my beloved mother, Patricia Rodenhurst Maguire (1938–2023)
Requiescat in pace

Contents

Illustrations

Maps

Tables

ACKNOWLEDGEMENTS

I would like to thank the staff at the Norfolk Record Office, the Bodleian Library, Oxford, the William & Mary Library, Virginia, the National Library of Jamaica, Kingston, and the Jamaica Archives and Records Department, Kingston, for their help in making the research for this book possible. Their patience and helpfulness in dealing with the problems of access was invaluable. I would also like to thank the two anonymous readers, whose kind and helpful comments were vital in the final shaping of the manuscript. All errors in the book are, of course, my own.

I have modernised and simplified spelling and capitalisation, for ease of reading. Often, the original sources contain their own variant spellings. In referring to the proprietors of Golden Grove, I have used Arcedeckne (pronounced 'Archdeacon') rather than Arcedekne. In referring to England, Wales, Scotland, and Ireland, I have sometimes used 'Great Britain' to comprehend the total, though England and Scotland were not constitutionally united until 1707 and the union of 'Great Britain and Ireland' occurred only in 1801. In relation to Jamaica currency, I have assumed throughout that the exchange rate was steady at 140 current money to 100 sterling money, as per John J. McCusker, *Money and Exchange in Europe and America, 1600–1775* (Chapel Hill, NC, 1978).

NOTE TO THE READER

This book had its beginnings when I was working in the Norfolk Record Office archives and came across the letters of a Norfolk farmer William Wright, written from Jamaica in the mid-1820s, which described the agricultural processes of the Chiswick sugar estate in detail. His discussion of the business operations of a Jamaican sugar estate seemed to me to be something worth following up, and I originally intended to write a journal article based around the letters, looking at the transfer of agricultural techniques between England and the colonies.

As I did my research, however, I came across the three volumes of letters held in the Bodleian Library Oxford. These were sent between the Burton family, their solicitor, London factor, and their Jamaican attorneys, between 1829 and 1846. It became clear to me that a monograph could be written using them. These records are excellent, but were predominantly focused, as were those of Wright, on the commercial aspects of growing sugar in Jamaica, and the business challenges faced by the owners and managers of the Chiswick estate over the tumultuous years from 1829 to 1846 as the system of slavery upon which those operations were based was dismantled. To understand these records properly, it was clear that I had to try to piece together the story of the previous decades of ownership of the Chiswick estate by the Burton family and, once again, the only records that had survived were focused on commercial operations. Hardly anything personal had survived, and the Burton family members remain something of an enigma as individuals.

The nature of the historical records with which I have been working has, therefore, determined the type of book I have written. If one wanted to categorise it, this monograph should be seen, first and foremost, as a contribution to business history, since it is a socio-economic study of the operation of a Jamaican sugar estate and the challenges posed by the absentee ownership of such an estate in the late eighteenth and early nineteenth century. By extension, however, the story of the estate's enslaved workers can be gleaned from these historical records. Their story illuminates the economic data and managerial letters brought together here.

Introduction

'A VERY CONSIDERABLE FORTUNE': THE BURTON FAMILY, PLANTATION SLAVERY AND ABSENTEE OWNERSHIP IN JAMAICA AND NORFOLK

In the spring of 1788 Mr Thomas Burton of Bracondale Hill, Norwich, in Norfolk – a wealthy and successful financier – was informed that a family acquaintance, John Vernon Esquire, had recently died at his sugar estate on the island of Jamaica.[1] The death notice in the *Gentleman's Magazine* described Vernon as a 'considerable person' and the news presented Thomas Burton with a remarkable windfall that would have significant effect on the rest of his life and upon the lives of his brothers, wife, and children for the next sixty years. This was because in a will dated 6 July 1786, Vernon had left Thomas Burton two-thirds of his Jamaican sugar estate, which was named Chiswick, and the two hundred and seventy or so enslaved people who lived and worked there. Vernon had then bequeathed the remaining one-third of Chiswick to Burton's brother, John, who lived in Jacobstowe, Devon.[2] Why Vernon had done this will be explored later but this bequest provided the Burton family with a substantial new element to their 'very considerable fortune'.[3]

The island of Jamaica lies about 4,000 miles south-west of the Burton brothers' homes in Norfolk and Devon. It is situated about ninety miles to the west of St

---

[1] *The Gentleman's Magazine, and Historical Chronicle*, Volume 58, Part 1 (1788), p. 465.

[2] Vernon's will had been lost by the 1830s when the family sought to check its provisions. It is not listed in Madeleine Enid Mitchell, *Alphabetical Index to Early Wills of Jamaica, West Indies, 1655–1816: PCC Wills, 1655–1816, Registrar General's Office, Spanish Town, 1662–1750* (Pullman, WA: M. E. Mitchell, 2000), nor in 'Names of Persons whose Wills are Registered in Jamaica Previous to 1700', *Caribbeana*, Vol. 1 (1910), pp. 103–14; nor at Inventories | Legacies of British Slavery (ucl.ac.uk). Neither is it at the National Archives, Kew. The will's details have been reconstructed from Bodleian Library Oxford, MSS. W. Ind. s.17, 1815–1831, MSS. W. Ind.s.18, 1832–1835, and MSS. W. Ind. s.19, 1836–1847, Letters, documents, and reports to its English owners from the agents in Jamaica managing the Chiswick sugar plantation, 1825–1847. 3 volumes (hereafter BLO/MSS.W.Ind.s.17, s.18, or s.19), s.17, fol. 17, Pitcairn & Amos to Thomas Mayhew (hereafter Mayhew), 21 January 1829, and the wills of Thomas Burton and his brother, The National Archives of the United Kingdom (hereafter NA) PROB/11/1411/154, Will of John Burton of Jacobstowe, Devon, 13 July 1804 and NA/PROB/11/1426/242, Will of Thomas Burton of Norwich, Norfolk, 12 June 1805.

[3] Charles John Palmer, *Perlustration of Great Yarmouth Vol. II* (Great Yarmouth: Nall, 1874), p. 393.

Domingo, almost the same distance to the south of Cuba, and 435 miles to the north of Cartagena in South America. A relatively small island, Jamaica is 150 miles in length, and on a medium of three measurements, at different parts, about forty miles in breadth. According to Robertson's survey of 1801, the island contains 2,724,262 acres of land.[4] In the eighteenth-century Jamaica was divided into three counties – Cornwall, Middlesex, and Surrey – which had been subdivided into parishes in 1758 to facilitate the British county court system. In the county of Surrey, at the south-eastern edge of the island was the parish of St Thomas-in-the-East, and it was here that the Chiswick sugar estate was situated.

There is no evidence that the Burton brothers were involved in trade with Jamaica or in plantation ownership before 1788.[5] As an educated and successful businessman, however, Thomas Burton would have known that the economy of Jamaica was founded on the production of sugar, the market for which – along with other the crops of the New World, such as cotton, tobacco, coffee, molasses, and rum – had grown rapidly during the eighteenth century.[6] In 1700, the British Isles imported 23,000 tons of sugar; one hundred years later this amount had grown tenfold, to 245,000 tons.[7] In consequence, the value of British Caribbean plantation produce doubled from 1700 to 1770, a growth rate of 1 per cent per annum, slightly more than the growth rate of British national income in the same period, which was 0.7 per cent.[8]

Jamaica was a crucial part of this economy providing, on average, 42 per cent of the sugar imported into Britain.[9] In 1750, per capita output in Jamaica was roughly £8.0 sterling in current money, more than half which came from exports. This had

---

[4]   National Library of Scotland, Shelfmark, EMAM.s.4, 'Maps of Jamaica by James Robertson, 1804'.

[5]   There is no mention of any such activity in their papers or, for example, in the list of directors of the Royal African Company, William A. Pettigrew, *Freedom's Debt: The Royal African Company and the Politics of the Atlantic Slave Trade, 1672–1752* (Omohundro Institute of Early American History and Culture, Williamsburg, Virginia) (Chapel Hill, NC: University of North Carolina Press, 2013), pp. 237–39.

[6]   Jordan Goodman, *Tobacco in History: The Cultures of Dependence* (London: Routledge, 1993), pp. 59–67; Sidney Mintz, *Sweetness and Power; The Place of Sugar in Modern History* (New York: Viking, 1985), pp. 37–38, 74–150; Christopher J. French, 'Productivity in the Atlantic Shipping Industry: A Quantitative Study', *Journal of Interdisciplinary History* Vol. 17 (1987), pp. 613–38; David Hancock, *Citizens of the World: London Merchants and the Integration of the British Atlantic Community, 1735-1785* (Cambridge: Cambridge University Press, 1995); B. W. Higman, 'The Sugar Revolution', *Economic History Review* (2000), pp. 213–36.

[7]   Mintz, *Sweetness*, p. 73; Richard S. Dunn, *Sugar and Slaves: The Rise of the Planter Class in the English West Indies, 1624–1713* (Chapel Hill, NC: University of North Carolina Press, 1972), p. 203.

[8]   David Eltis and Stanley L. Engerman, 'The Importance of Slavery and the Slave Trade to Industrializing Britain', *The Journal of Economic History* Vol. 60 (2000), pp. 123–44.

[9]   T. G. Burnard, '"Prodigious Riches": The Wealth of Jamaica before the American Revolution', *The Economic History Review*, New Series Vol. 54 (2001), pp. 506–24; Richard B. Sheridan, *Sugar and Slavery: An Economic History of the British West Indies, 1623–1775* (Kingston, Jamaica: Canoe Press, 1994), pp. 467–71.

increased to £13.2 by 1770, which was higher than the estimated £10.7 for the thirteen mainland colonies of North America, and £10.0 for England and Wales. This performance continued into the period that the Burton brothers became members of the island's plantation-owning class. From 1770 to 1800, Jamaica's per capita product doubled, to £29.2 in current money by 1800 – as sugar prices and production increased.[10] The result of this remarkable growth was that by the end of the eighteenth century Jamaica had become an economic powerhouse in the British Empire, exporting 80 per cent of its sugar output.[11] This made the island one of the wealthiest of eighteenth-century Britain's many colonial possessions.[12] Men living in South Carolina and the British Caribbean were thirteen times wealthier than those in the south of British America and twenty-two times wealthier than those in the north, and successful Jamaican planters were among the richest subjects of Britain's empire; in 1774, their wealth averaged £4,403, in contrast to that in England and Wales of £421.[13]

The industry that provided this economic growth and personal wealth relied, however, on slavery. The most recent research indicates that, between 1501 and 1875, 36,000 slaving voyages transported a total of 12,521,337 Africans to the Americas, with 2,763,411 coming to the British colonies in the Caribbean. Of this British portion some 1,212,352 enslaved people – around 44 per cent – arrived in Jamaica.[14] This massive level of slave imports to the island meant that eighteenth-century

[10] B. W. Higman, *Slave Population and Economy in Jamaica, 1807–1834* (Cambridge: Cambridge University Press, 1976), pp. 17, 215, 255–56; James A. Rawley and Stephen D. Behrendt, *The Transatlantic Slave Trade: A History* (Lincoln, NE: University of Nebraska Press, 2005), pp. 1–7; William Darity, 'British Industry and the West Indies Plantations', in *The Atlantic Slave Trade: Effects on Economies, Societies, and Peoples in Africa, the Americas, and Europe*, ed. J. E. Inikori and Stanley L. Engerman (Durham, NC: Duke University Press, 1992), pp. 247–79; J. E. Inikori, 'Slavery and the Development of Industrial Capitalism in England', in *British Capitalism and Caribbean Slavery*, ed. Barbara Solow and Stanley Engerman (Cambridge: Cambridge University Press, 1987), pp. 79–101; Eric Williams, *Capitalism and Slavery* (New York: G. P. Putnam, 1966).

[11] Noël Deerr, *The History of Sugar* (London: Chapman and Hall, 1949–1950), Volume 1, pp. 59–60 and 198; J. H. Galloway, *The Sugar Cane Industry: An Historical Geography from its Origins to 1914* (Cambridge: Cambridge University Press, 1989), pp. 198–208.

[12] Richard Pares, *Merchants and Planters*, Econ. Hist. Rev. Supplement. no. 4 (Cambridge: Cambridge University Press, 1960), p. 91; R. B. Sheridan, 'The Wealth of Jamaica in the Eighteenth Century', *The Economic History Review* (1965), pp. 292–311; Richard Sheridan, 'The Formation of Caribbean Plantation Society, 1689–1748', in *The Oxford History of the British Empire: The Eighteenth Century*, ed. P. J. Marshall and Judith M. Brown (Oxford: Oxford University Press, 1998), pp. 394–414, at p. 395; Andrew Jackson O'Shaughnessy, *An Empire Divided: The American Revolution and the British Caribbean* (Philadelphia, PA: University of Pennsylvania Press, 2000), pp. xi–xii.

[13] Burnard, 'Prodigious', p. 522; Sheridan, *Sugar*, pp. 467–71.

[14] See the summary statistics table in the Trans-Atlantic Slave Trade Database Estimates (slavevoyages.org). For earlier estimates, see Philip D. Curtin, *The Atlantic Slave Trade: A Census* (Madison, WI: University of Wisconsin Press, 1969), p. 268; David Eltis, 'The Volume and Structure of the Transatlantic Slave Trade: A Reassessment', *William & Mary Quarterly* (2001), pp. 35–37, 45.

Jamaican culture, politics, and economics were dominated by the facts and consequences of enslavement. Along with the land on which they worked, these enslaved men, women, and children were the major component of Jamaican wealth, and their exploitation was crucial for sugar production. When the Burton brothers inherited Chiswick from John Vernon in 1788, the estate's enslaved workers were a critical element of its value.

Historians have shown that the circumstances that resulted in Jamaica becoming a slave-based economy were not inevitable, and that it was only at the start of the eighteenth century that Jamaica's planting elite accepted the integration under imperial authority that permitted its subsequent economic and social development.[15] Edward Rugemer points out that Jamaican planters developed their businesses in consequence of a system made possible by a strong state, imperial troops, and the pervasive culture of violence.[16] The unhappy fact was that the enslaved workers who produced Jamaica's wealth were subject to 'poor diet, debilitating work regimes and brutal treatment'. These factors combined with ever-present diseases, such as yellow fever, to mean that the life expectancy of enslaved people in the island was poor, especially among those newly arrived and young children.[17] Consequently, the enslaved workers on the island failed to create a naturally reproducing population, requiring a constant new flow of replacements from the slave trade. This was different to the situation in North America. By 1807, the 2.3 million Africans imported to the British Caribbean islands had engendered a slave population of about 775,000, of whom 355,000 lived in Jamaica. In contrast, the 388,000 Africans taken to North America over the same period had grown to a population of 1.4 million.[18]

[15] For discussion of the sixteenth century, see Carla Gardina Pestana, *The English Conquest of Jamaica: Oliver Cromwell's Bid for Empire* (Cambridge, MA: The Belknap Press of Harvard University Press, 2017); Dunn, *Sugar*; Sarah Barber, *Disputatious Caribbean: the West Indies in the Seventeenth Century* (New York: Palgrave Macmillan, 2014); John Robert McNeill, *Mosquito Empires: Ecology and War in the Greater Caribbean, 1620–1914* (New York: Cambridge University Press, 2010); Richard S. Dunn, 'The Glorious Revolution and America', in *The Oxford History of the British Empire. Volume I, The Origins of Empire*, ed. Nicholas Canny (Oxford: Oxford University Press, 1998), pp. 463–65.

[16] Edward B. Rugemer, *Slave Law and the Politics of Resistance in the Early Atlantic World* (Cambridge, MA: Harvard University Press, 2018).

[17] Douglas Hall, *In Miserable Slavery: Thomas Thistlewood in Jamaica, 1750–86* (Mona, Jamaica: University of the West Indies Press, 1999), pp. 186–87, 189, 195, 208, 212; Richard B. Sheridan, *Doctors and Slaves: A Medical and Demographic History of Slavery in the British West Indies, 1680–1834* (Cambridge: Cambridge University Press, 1985), pp. 200–01, 236–39.

[18] Trevor Burnard, *Mastery, Tyranny, and Desire: Thomas Thistlewood and His Slaves in the Anglo-Jamaican World* (Chapel Hill, NC: University of North Carolina Press, 2004), pp. 5–16, 31–34; Lorena S. Walsh, 'Liverpool's Slave Trade to the Colonial Chesapeake: Slaving on the Periphery', in *Liverpool and Transatlantic Slavery*, ed. David Richardson, Suzanne Schwarz, and Anthony Tibbles (Liverpool: Liverpool University Press, 2007), p. 101; Michael Tadman, 'The Demographic Cost of Sugar: Debates on Slave Societies and Natural Increase in the Americas', *American Historical Review* 105 (2000), pp. 1534–75; Richard S. Dunn, *A Tale of Two Plantations: Slave Life and Labor in Jamaica and Virginia* (Cambridge, MA: Harvard University Press, 2014), p. 24; Trevor Burnard and Kenneth Morgan, 'The

Mortality rates amongst European migrants on the island were also terrifyingly high; on average, even lucky migrants could expect to live only for twelve and a half years after their arrival.[19] The combination of such high levels of death and huge slave importation meant that the planters found themselves vastly outnumbered by their enslaved workers. Estimates provided to the British government in 1774 suggested that 12,737 planters held 192,787 slaves on the island.[20] The perceived threat posed by so many enslaved Africans 'fundamentally conditioned the planters' thinking' meaning that Jamaica's planters operated through a 'control mechanism of terror, repression and punishment.'[21] As the commentator Charles Leslie put it in the 1740s, 'No country excels them in a barbarous treatment of Slaves, or in the cruel methods they put them to death.'[22]

Most of the enslaved population were held on a variety of 'plantations' spread across Jamaica. 'Plantation' was a general term used to describe properties producing a wide variety of produce, including coffee, pimento, ginger, cotton, arrowroot, and other minor staples. There were also 'pens', which were like British breeding farms, for horses, mules, and cattle.[23] The term 'estate' was synonymous with the production of sugar, and although it was acceptable to refer to an estate as a 'sugar plantation', in general the term 'sugar estate' was preferred.[24] By 1789 there were at nearly 800 sugar estates spread around the island, including the Burton family's new acquisition of Chiswick. Between them these estates accounted for nearly half of the sugar output of the British Caribbean.[25]

Dynamics of the Slave Market and Slave Purchasing Patterns in Jamaica, 1655–1788', *The William and Mary Quarterly* Vol. 58 (2001), pp. 205–28.

[19] Trevor Burnard, '"The Countrie Continues Sicklie": White Mortality in Jamaica, 1655–1780', *Social History of Medicine* (1999), pp. 45–72.

[20] Norfolk Record Office (hereafter NRO) WLS/XVII/31, 'Queries Relative to the state of His Majesty's Island of Jamaica with answers thereto in 1774'.

[21] M. J. Steel, 'A Philosophy of Fear: The World View of the Jamaican Plantocracy in a Comparative Perspective', *The Journal of Caribbean History* (1993), pp. 1–20, at p. 17; G. K. Lewis, *Slavery, Imperialism, and Freedom: Studies in English Radical Thought* (New York: Monthly Review Press, 1978), p. 147; Claudius K. Fergus, '"Dread of Insurrection": Abolitionism, Security, and Labor in Britain's West Indian Colonies, 1760–1823', *William and Mary Quarterly* (2009), pp. 757–80.

[22] Charles Leslie, *A new and exact account of Jamaica* (Edinburgh, c. 1741), p. 41.

[23] Philip D. Morgan, 'Slaves and Livestock in Eighteenth-Century Jamaica: Vineyard Pen, 1750-1751', *The William and Mary Quarterly* (1995), pp. 47–76; B. W. Higman, 'The Internal Economy of Jamaican Pens, 1760–1890', *Social and Economic Studies* (1989), pp. 61–86.

[24] Higman, *Slave*, pp. 30–31.

[25] M. Craton and Garry Greenland, *Searching for the Invisible Man: Slaves and Plantation Life in Jamaica* (Cambridge, MA: Harvard University Press, 1978), pp. 39 and 48; Sheridan, *Sugar*, p. 223; Deerr, *The History*, vol. 1, pp. 193–202.

No member of the Burton family had been to Jamaica before they inherited Chiswick and the family members remained ensconced in Norfolk's county town of Norwich and the port of Great Yarmouth after receiving their inheritance. Only one Burton would visit the Chiswick estate during nearly sixty years of ownership. Such non-attendance was not unusual. As Bryan Edwards wrote in the late eighteenth century:

> Many persons there are, in Great Britain [...], who, amidst the continual fluctuation of human affairs, and the changes incident to property, find themselves possessed of estates in the West Indies which they have never seen.[26]

This meant that, upon inheriting the Chiswick estate, Thomas Burton and his family became members of an important group of people in the story of Jamaica – the absentee plantation owners – those people who lived in Britain but owned a plantation in the colonies.[27] The family would own Chiswick as absentees from 1788 to 1846, and it is the letters that allowed them to run a Jamaican plantation from Norfolk that form the core primary sources for this study. These letters are held at the Bodleian Library, Oxford, and have not been evaluated in detail previously. They consist of three volumes written by the Burtons, their London agents, and Jamaican managers between 1829 and 1846 to the family's solicitor, Thomas Mayhew, after he was appointed to help the Burtons deal with a major problem on the estate.[28]

Chosen because he was trusted by the family, rather than because he had any experience of working in the sugar economy, Mayhew was an ordinary provincial solicitor who lived in the Suffolk market town of Saxmundham all his life and freely admitted that 'on a Thursday [...] I do not like leaving home being a market day'.[29] Mayhew's participation in the affairs of the Chiswick estate dragged him away from the familiar and dependable domain of local agriculture, business, and domestic legal affairs in rural Suffolk, and threw him headlong into the exotic realm of Jamaican slavery. With no prior involvement in the world of sugar and slavery, for around seventeen years Mayhew acted as the hub of a business operation that linked

---

[26] Bryan Edwards, *The History, Civil and Commercial, of the British Colonies in the West Indies: Volume II* (London: J. Stockdale, 1793), p. 75.

[27] For discussion of absentees from various perspectives, see B. W. Higman, *Plantation Jamaica, 1750–1850: Capital and Control in a Colonial Economy* (Kingston, Jamaica: University of the West Indies Press, 2008); Trevor Burnard, 'Passengers Only: The Extent and Significance of Absenteeism in Eighteenth-Century Jamaica', *Atlantic Studies* (2004), pp. 178–195; Douglas Hall, 'Absentee Proprietorship in the British West Indies, to about 1850', *The Jamaican Historical Review* (1964), pp. 15–35; David Beck Ryden, *West Indian Slavery and British Abolition, 1783–1807* (Cambridge: Cambridge University Press, 2009); Lowell Joseph Ragatz, 'Absentee Landlordism in the British Caribbean, 1750–1833', *Agricultural History* (1931), pp. 7–24.

[28] The letters have been mentioned in Kathleen Mary Butler, *The Economics of Emancipation: Jamaica & Barbados, 1823–1843* (Chapel Hill, NC: University of North Carolina Press, 1995), pp. 74, 155 n. 21, 162 n. 1; Vincent Brown, *The Reaper's Garden: Death and Power in the World of Atlantic Slavery* (Cambridge, MA: Harvard University Press, 2010), p. 296.

[29] BLO/MSS.W.Ind.s.17, fol. 6; Mayhew to John Lee Farr (hereafter Farr), Letter is damaged but internal evidence suggests May 1829.

the Burton family via his office in tiny Saxmundham to the metropolis of London and, from there, across the Atlantic Ocean to Kingston and Port Morant in Jamaica, and finally to a sugar estate on the far eastern edge of the island itself. This role required Mayhew to become closely involved in the management of Chiswick and the surviving correspondence, although partial, provides a wealth of information about the estate's agricultural practices, sugar refining operations, the shipping and sale of its sugar and rum, and the lives of the enslaved people upon whose shoulders the fortunes of Chiswick, and its proprietors, ultimately depended.

These letters help us to piece together the story of an East Anglian family – whose members had no connection to the plantations before the 1780s – as they became involved in the singular and brutal world of Jamaican slavery. To enable us to examine the period before 1829, these records have been augmented by estate crop returns and maps held in the Jamaican Archives and National Library, by letters and documents held in the Norfolk and Suffolk Record Offices, others in the National Archives of the United Kingdom, and by more deposited at the William and Mary Libraries, Virginia. Used together, these primary sources help us to unravel the story of how the Burton family tried to navigate the vicissitudes of absentee plantation ownership in Jamaica, and how they responded to the unique characteristics and history of the island over the sixty or so years they owned Chiswick.

In following their story this book utilises the insights of, and seeks to add to, an 'outpouring' of literature on the history of Jamaica in the last decade which has confirmed 'the importance of the island in a regional and global context'.[30] This recent work, of course, has built upon the excellent research of previous historians, such as David Eltis and his collaborators, who have provided superb quantitative data regarding the slave trade, the business of slavery, and the place of Jamaica in the Atlantic World.[31] Likewise, Barry Higman has used registration data to analyse the composition of the enslaved population in the British West Indian colonies between 1807 and 1833, and also provided major works on plantation layouts, the economy, and the labour force, which are of immense help in unravelling the data from Chiswick.[32] In more recent years historians have examined the world of slavery in Jamaica from a cultural perspective: for example, Vincent Brown has looked at the cultural impact of high mortality rates on its populace, Trevor Burnard has used Thomas Thistlewood's diaries to explore the mentality of the slave-owner, and Sasha Turner has explored enslaved women's contrasting ideas about maternity and raising children.[33] This study touches on all these areas, and uses their findings to interrogate the Chiswick paperwork.

[30] Trevor Burnard, "'Wi Lickle but Wi Tallawah": Writing Jamaica into the Atlantic World, 1655–1834', *Reviews in American History* (2021), pp. 168–86, pp. 168–69.

[31] For example, David Eltis, *Economic Growth and the Ending of the Transatlantic Slave Trade* (New York: Oxford University Press, 1987); *The Rise of African Slavery in the Americas* (Cambridge: Cambridge University Press, 2000).

[32] For example, B. W. Higman, *Jamaica Surveyed: Plantation Maps and Plans of the Eighteenth and Nineteenth Centuries* (Kingston, Jamaica: University of the West Indies Press, 2001).

[33] Burnard, *Mastery*; Brown, *Reaper's*; Sasha Turner, *Contested Bodies: Pregnancy, Childrearing, and Slavery in Jamaica* (Philadelphia, PA: University of Pennsylvania Press, 2017).

Most directly, this work adds to the excellent studies of individual sugar estates on the island that have been published in the last few decades. In 1970 Michael Craton and James Walvin set the bar very high, with their work on the Worthy Park estate, and their work has been expanded on by Craton and Greenland, among others.[34] Other examples include Higman's work on the Montpelier estate, which has provided a long-term study of a sugar estate over nearly two centuries, and his work on absentee ownership before and after the abolition of slavery.[35] Most recently, Dunn's comparative study of the Mesopotamia sugar estate in Jamaica and Mount Airy in Virginia has provided a wealth of detail about the life of the enslaved.[36] Insights from all of these studies, and others, have been used here to illuminate the information gleaned from the Chiswick documents and expand our understanding of the operations and thinking of absentee estate owners.

As we shall see, the records concerning the enslaved people of Chiswick are sparse since the Burtons did not require their managers to collect detailed records about the numbers, make-up, health, and welfare of their workforce. In consequence, we cannot do extensive quantitative analysis to reveal the details of their world as has been possible in relation to sugar estates like Worthy Park and Montpelier.[37] Neither do we have detailed probate inventories for Chiswick of the type used so successfully by Burnard and Alice Hanson Jones.[38] Nonetheless, taking a leaf from the work of historians such as Marisa Fuentes and Stephanie Smallwood, we can 'read against the grain' and look at the records that we do possess to find the presence of enslaved people in the archive, even when they are 'not explicitly mentioned'.[39] This important element of the book has, consequently, been squeezed from between the lines of letters, accounting records, and the British government's censuses. I hope that it provides some inkling of the important role of Chiswick's working people in the estate's history. Indeed, there are a few places in the papers where we hear the direct voice of the workers; it is a faint one and mediated through reports written by their managers, but is a voice, nonetheless.

[34] Michael Craton and James Walvin, *A Jamaican Plantation. The History of Worthy Park, 1670–1970* (London; New York: W. H. Allen, 1970); Craton and Greenland, *Searching*.

[35] B. W. Higman, *Montpelier, Jamaica: A Plantation Community in Slavery and Freedom, 1739–1912* (Barbados, Jamaica, Trinidad, and Tobago: The University of the West Indies Press, 1998); Higman, *Plantation*.

[36] Richard S. Dunn, *A Tale of Two Plantations: Slave Life and Labor in Jamaica and Virginia* (Cambridge, MA: Harvard University Press, 2014). For some early, and very useful, examples, see Ulrich B. Phillips, 'An Antigua Plantation, 1769–1818', *The North Carolina Historical Review* (1926), pp. 439–45; Noël Deerr and H. W. Dickinson, 'Sugar Planting in The West Indies at the Beginning of the Nineteenth Century', *Negro History Bulletin* (1947), pp. 20–21.

[37] As exemplified in Higman, *Slave Population*; Craton, *Searching*.

[38] Alice Hanson Jones, *Wealth of a Nation to Be: The American Colonies on the Eve of the Revolution* (New York: Columbia University Press, 1980); Burnard, 'Prodigious', pp. 506–24; Burnard, *Planters*, especially pp. 157–210.

[39] Marisa J. Fuentes, *Dispossessed Lives: Enslaved Women, Violence, and the Archive* (Philadelphia, PA: University of Pennsylvania Press, 2016), pp. 11, 156; Stephanie E. Smallwood, 'The Politics of the Archive and History's Accountability to the Enslaved', *History of the Present* Vol. 6, No. 2 (2016), pp. 117–32, pp. 118, 126.

Because the period under examination covers the times of enslavement, apprenticeship, and full freedom, I have tended to describe the members of the worker population of the Chiswick sugar estate as 'the people', a term used for them in the correspondence from 1829 onwards.[40] I have sometimes used the phrases 'working people' or 'the enslaved workforce', or 'enslaved workers', or variants thereof. This choice reflects my preference not to define the working people of Chiswick primarily by their enslaved condition but, rather, to see them primarily as individual human beings possessing their own innate dignity and having their own agency, who had the misfortune to be enslaved.

Alongside augmenting our understanding of the lives of absentee owners and the enslaved, this book uses the information from Chiswick's papers to contribute to the wider discussion of the question of 'the decline of the planter class' more generally.[41] The spectacular growth of the plantation economy from the sixteenth to eighteenth centuries, outlined above, was followed by a period of challenges that culminated in the ending of slavery in the British Empire in 1833, and in the Americas by the end of the nineteenth century, a process Curtin calls 'the rise and fall of the plantation complex'.[42] At the mid-point of the eighteenth century, sugar planters in the British Caribbean were among the wealthiest people in the British Empire, and some of its most influential.[43] As Petley puts it, at this historical moment planters 'had many good reasons to feel confident about their place at the cutting edge of British imperial development'.[44] Yet, in 1807 the planter class suffered a body blow to its mode of operation, in the abolition of the slave trade, which was the first step in a process lasting that would dismantle the system of slavery on which planter wealth and power depended.

The issue of the 'decline of the planter class' is central to our understanding of the history of the Chiswick estate, the institution of slavery, and of Jamaica itself. Yet, the driving forces behind this decline remain a matter of discussion. Through much of the nineteenth century the historiographical emphasis was on the success

[40] For the first written use of the term 'the people', see BLO/MSS.W.Ind.s.17, fol. 98, James Forsyth (hereafter Forsyth) to Pitcairn & Amos, 22 August 1829.

[41] Christopher Leslie Brown, 'The Politics of Slavery', in *The British Atlantic World, 1500–1800*, ed. David Armitage and Michael J. Braddick (Basingstoke: Palgrave, 2009), pp. 232–50, at p. 249. See also a useful survey by Petley: Christer Petley, 'Rethinking the Fall of the Planter Class', *Atlantic Studies* (2012), pp. 1–17.

[42] Philip Curtin, *The Rise and Fall of the Plantation Complex: Essays in Atlantic History* (Cambridge: Cambridge University Press, 1990).

[43] See B.W. Higman, 'The West India "Interest" in Parliament, 1807–1833', *Historical Studies* (1967), pp. 1–19; Andrew J. O'Shaughnessy, 'The Formation of a Commercial Lobby: The West India Interest, British Colonial Policy and the American Revolution', *The Historical Journal* (1997), pp. 71–95; M. W. McCahill (ed.), *The Correspondence of Stephen Fuller, 1788–1795: Jamaica, the West India Interest at Westminster and the Campaign to Preserve the Slave Trade* (Oxford: Oxford University Press, 2014); Perry Gauci, *William Beckford: First Prime Minister of the London Empire* (New Haven, CT: Yale University Press, 2013).

[44] Christer Petley, 'Slaveholders and Revolution: The Jamaican Planter Class, British Imperial Politics, and the Ending of the Slave Trade, 1775–1807', *Slavery & Abolition* (2018), pp. 53–79, at p. 53.

of abolitionism and its religious underpinnings. Abolitionists tended to consider that the sin of slaveholding held within in it the seeds of its destruction, as it spawned degenerate societies.[45] The emphasis on the triumph of Christian virtue lessened in the early twentieth century and was discarded dramatically in the work of historians such as Lowell Ragatz and Eric Williams, who focused on economics and the idea that the second half of the eighteenth century was a period of economic 'decline', driven especially by the American War of Independence. In this view, it was this economic shift that undermined the power of the planters and so led to their downfall, in a dialectical struggle between a declining mercantile economy and emerging industrial capitalism.[46]

While the idea of 'decline' has been proposed most recently by Selwyn Carrington, in general historians no longer accept that there were any more than temporary economic difficulties caused by the American Revolution.[47] Drescher interrogated the trade figures and argued that the slave economy had, in fact been in good health when the British decided to end the slave trade. He suggested, therefore, that British abolition had been a case of *econocide* – the destruction of a healthy economic sector for non-economic motives.[48] Recent research has supported this idea and, as Burnard and Garrigus argue, the economic decline of Jamaica 'gets pushed back closer and closer to the eve of emancipation with major economic difficulties occurring only in the early 1830s'.[49] The blame for decline has been placed increasingly on the ending

[45] See, for example, Robert Isaac Wilberforce and Samuel Wilberforce, *The Life of William Wilberforce*, 5 vols (London: J. Murray, 1838); Joseph John Gurney, *Familiar Sketch of the Late William Wilberforce* (Norwich: Josiah Fletcher, 1838). This approach has been revisited in recent years, see, for example, Eric Mataxas, *Amazing Grace: William Wilberforce and the Heroic Campaign to End Slavery* (Oxford: Monarch 2007). Key works in the discussion of abolitionism include David Brion Davis, *The Problem of Slavery in the Age of Revolution, 1770–1823* (Ithaca, NY: Cornell University Press, 1975); Roger Anstey, *The Atlantic Slave Trade and British Abolition, 1760–1810* (Atlantic Highlands, NJ: Humanities Press, 1975); J. R. Oldfield, *Popular Politics and British Anti-Slavery: The Mobilisation of Public Opinion against the Slave Trade, 1787–1807* (Manchester: Manchester University Press, 1995).

[46] Ragatz, 'Absentee', p. 7; Frank W. Pitman, *The Development of the British West Indies, 1700–1763* (New Haven, CT: Yale University Press, 1917), pp. 334–60; Lowell Joseph Ragatz, *The Fall of the Planter Class in the British Caribbean, 1763–1833* (New York: Octagon Books, 1963), pp. vii–viii; Eric Williams, *Capitalism and Slavery* (New York: G. P. Putnam, 1966), pp. 132, 135–36, 149–52, 169, 178.

[47] Selwyn H. H. Carrington, *The Sugar Industry and the End of the Slave Trade, 1775–1810* (Gainesville, FL: University Press of Florida, 2002); John McCusker, 'The Economy of the British West Indies, 1763–1790: Growth, Stagnation, or Decline?', in *Essays in the Economic History of the Atlantic World* (London: Routledge, 1997), pp. 310–31 at p. 330.

[48] Seymour Drescher, *Econocide: British Slavery in the Era of Abolition*, 2nd edn (Chapel Hill, NC: University of North Carolina Press, 2010), pp. 5–7 and 186.

[49] Trevor Burnard and John Garrigus, *The Plantation Machine: Atlantic capitalism in French Saint-Domingue and British Jamaica* (Philadelphia, PA: University of Pennsylvania Press, 2016), p. 220; Nicholas Draper, *The Price of Emancipation: Slave-Ownership, Compensation and British Society at the End of Slavery* (Cambridge: Cambridge University Press), pp. 100–01; James Walvin, 'Why Did the British Abolish the Slave Trade? Econocide Revisited', *Slavery and Abolition* Vol. 4 (2011), pp. 583–88; Ryden, *West Indian*, p. 237; David Eltis,

of the supply of labour from Africa, which made it difficult for planters to expand, or even maintain, production. This was followed by further problems resulting from the abolition of slavery itself, which were then compounded by difficulties in transitioning to a free-labour economy.[50] As we shall see, the data from Chiswick provide support for this interpretation.

The emphasis has shifted to, what has been proposed as, a period of opportunity for abolitionists to act successfully, that was consequent upon economic and social upheavals. Christopher Leslie Brown has suggested that several factors came into play at the time of the American Revolution, a crisis that led to debates about colonial reform and the impact of slavery on the empire and allowed the ideas of abolitionists to gain purchase.[51] This can be linked to a wider re-evaluation of the idea of empire in the period, which linked corruption in the West Indies with that elsewhere in the empire, such as in India.[52]

Recent work on the Caribbean has also eyed the negative political consequences for planters that flowed from the American Revolution, situating the dismantling of slavery in the context of a complex struggle over the future of the British Empire and connecting colonial histories with those of British political culture and the nature of the British state during the eighteenth century.[53] In relation to Jamaica, Burnard identifies a strong thread in the recent literature which argues that settler Jamaica reached a peak of importance and wealth around the time of the Seven Years' War, before the regime was undermined by the consequences of the Haitian Revolution and British abolitionism.[54] Excellent studies of slaveholder politics have been augmented by work which has emphasised the political impact in the colonies and Britain of rebellion by enslaved people, especially that in Haiti.[55] There has, perhaps, been a tendency to see the fate of the planter class as sealed in the 1780s, not so much

---

Frank D. Lewis, and David Richardson, 'Slave Prices, the African Slave Trade, and Productivity in the Caribbean, 1674–1807', *The Economic History Review* Vol. 58, No. 4 (2005), pp. 673–700.

[50] Drescher, *Econocide*, p. 148.

[51] Christopher Leslie Brown, *Moral Capital: Foundations of British Abolitionism* (Chapel Hill, NC: University of North Carolina Press, 2006), pp. 458, 461–62.

[52] Nicholas B. Dirks, *The Scandal of Empire: India and the Creation of Imperial Britain* (Cambridge, MA: Harvard University Press, 2006); Tillman W. Nechtman, *Nabobs: Empire and Identity in Eighteenth-Century Britain* (Cambridge: Cambridge University Press, 2010).

[53] Steve Pincus, 'Rethinking Mercantilism: Political Economy, the British Empire, and the Atlantic World in the Seventeenth and Eighteenth Centuries', *William and Mary Quarterly* Vol. 69, No. 1 (2012), pp. 3–34.

[54] Burnard, '"Wi Lickle"', pp. 168–86 at 168–69.

[55] Examples include Michael Craton, *Testing the Chains: Resistance to Slavery in the British West Indies* (Ithaca, NY: Cornell University Press, 1982); Trevor Burnard, *Planters, Merchants, and Slaves: Plantation Societies in British America, 1650–1820* (Chicago, IL: University of Chicago Press, 2015); Ryden, *West Indian*; Fergus, '"Dread"'; David Lambert, *White Creole Culture, Politics and Identity During the Age of Abolition* (Cambridge: Cambridge University Press, 2005); Christer Petley, *Slaveholders in Jamaica: Colonial Society and Culture during the Era of Abolition* (London: Pickering & Chatto, 2009); Srividhya Swaminathan, *Debating the Slave Trade: Rhetoric of British National Identity, 1759–1815* (Farnham: Ashgate, 2009); Claudius K. Fergus, *Revolutionary Emancipation: Slavery and Abolitionism in the British*

because of the economics identified by Ragatz and Williams, but rather because these other factors created a political situation that prevented planters from responding effectively to the nationwide British abolitionist campaign that started in 1787.[56]

The story of Chiswick and the Burtons touches on many of these issues and reveals how both high politics and local factors combined to affect a Jamaican sugar estate which was, on the face of things, rather ordinary. At 1,148 acres Chiswick was a relatively large estate, which produced sugar of an average quality. It was owned by a middle-class family from provincial England, who were not involved in the field of sugar estate management before they inherited it and possessed no other land outside England. The managers trusted to run the estate were not the major managers of multiple sugar estates whose operations have been studied elsewhere, rather they were small-scale Jamaican businessmen – of widely varying abilities. Chiswick's workforce was large, but not as large as some estates, and numbered perhaps 280 at its peak. According to the letters written from Jamaica, at first glance it might seem that the enslaved people on Chiswick behaved in a generally calm and orderly fashion.

By undertaking a careful analysis of the economic data regarding Chiswick and combining it with a close reading of the letters concerning the estate, we can situate these data in the wider currents of Jamaican history and the research of other historians to follow the story of this, apparently ordinary, sugar estate from 1788 to 1846 and see a rather different picture. Instead of an ordinary, uninteresting, and unimportant sugar estate, these data help us to uncover the turmoil, tension, and conflict that marked its existence. Moreover, when interrogated thoroughly, the papers provide information about the profitability, economics, and operations of sugar planting more generally, the challenges of absentee ownership, and the resistance of the workers on the estate.

As we shall see, the Burton family's Jamaican story began at an historical moment when sugar estates could provide significant profits for their owners. The family made excellent profits from their estate for many years and ran it effectively during the first decade and a half of ownership. Their story runs from that high point, however, to a period when that profitability and successful management had evaporated – partly because of changes beyond their control, partly because of their own poor decision-making and partly, it will be suggested, because of the ongoing impact of poor moral choices – to be replaced with a miasma of debt, regret, acrimony, and financial disaster.

Our tale begins in Chapter 1, 'A very sensible good sort of man', with a discussion of the Burton family and Chiswick sugar estate from around 1700 to 1788. It

West Indies (Baton Rouge, LA: Louisiana State University Press, 2013); Petley, 'Slaveholders', pp. 70–72.

[56] See Christopher Leslie Brown, *Moral Capital: Foundations of British Abolitionism* (Chapel Hill, NC: University of North Carolina Press, 2006); O'Shaughnessy, *An Empire*; Trevor Burnard, 'Powerless Masters: The Curious Decline of Jamaican Sugar Planters in the Foundational Period of British Abolitionism', *Slavery & Abolition* Vol. 32, No. 2 (2011), pp. 185–98; Trevor Burnard, 'Harvest Years? Reconfigurations of Empire in Jamaica, 1756–1807', *Journal of Imperial and Commonwealth History* Vol. 40, No. 4 (2012), pp. 533–55.

explores how a family from Norfolk came to own a sugar estate in the Caribbean, recounts what little we know about the previous history of the estate and establishes its geographic boundaries and size. Having laid this foundation, Chapter 2, 'Judicious management', analyses the period from 1788 to 1797, as the Burtons began managing the estate as absentee owners. Using data gleaned from later letters and the crop records held at the Jamaican Archive to reconstruct the accounts of Chiswick, this chapter argues that the Burton family's first decade of ownership was successful, as they improved Chiswick's productivity and profitability while reducing its debt burden. It also attempts to reconstruct the Burton family's ideas about the ownership of enslaved people and suggests this was a subject they sought to avoid considering in any detail. The essential idea proposed is that their geographic distance enabled them to concentrate purely on the situation's financial rewards and the logistics of absentee management, while ignoring the moral implications of their choice to become slave-owners.

Chapter 3 examines a shift in management strategy by following the story of the only member of the Burton family who ever visited the estate. By considering his experiences, and using information gathered from other visitors to Chiswick in this period and later, the chapter studies the operations of the estate as it produced its sugar, rum, and molasses. In the absence of any maps of the estate, this chapter uses contemporary documents and archaeological evidence, along with recent historical research, to reconstruct Chiswick's internal physical layout. It is in this period that, for the first time, we consider the lives of the enslaved workforce.

The management, productivity, and operations of the estate in the period from 1802 to 1815 are scrutinised in Chapter 4, which looks at how the ownership of the Chiswick estate came to be distributed among Thomas Burton's seven children – including the four Burton sisters. It also examines the effect on Chiswick of the global economic challenges created by the Napoleonic Wars, and the impact of the 1807 decision to abolish the slave trade in British ships upon operations. The period from 1816 to 1822 is covered in Chapter 5, which investigates the reasons for a sudden decline in production on the estate. Crucial in this was the impact of declining worker numbers which was a direct consequence of the abolition of the slave trade. The chapter analyses the composition of the population of the estate and assesses the degree to which the Burton family engaged with the process of amelioration. Chapter 6 considers the harsh economic policies pursued as the family attempted to revitalise Chiswick from 1823 to 1828, the lives of the enslaved workers in the 1820s, and the beginning of a financial crisis caused by the fraud of a family member.

Chapter 7 focuses on final years of slavery. As the family struggled to deal with the consequences of the fraud, their managers attempted to change operations at Chiswick but were constantly stymied by the declining numbers of enslaved workers. The chapter reveals how the fraud crisis offered an opportunity for those enslaved workers to influence the actions being taken in Norfolk and London through low-level resistance. It then surveys how these difficulties were compounded by the emancipation of the enslaved workers in the British Empire. The years 1834–1838 are the subject of Chapter 8, which considers the stresses and strains placed upon the operation of the estate, its people, and its management, both in Jamaica and in England, by the creation of the system of 'apprenticeship' in the aftermath of emancipation. In exploring the increasingly rapid decline in the fortunes of the Chiswick estate, the importance of the actions of the apprentices on Chiswick's operation and profitability are revealed.

The final chapter looks at the situation after 1838, as the Burtons and their managers grappled with the collapse of operations on Chiswick following the end of the system of apprenticeship. From August 1838, for the first time, the family had to deal with a fully emancipated set of workers who were able to engage with their employers are 'free labourers'. In this period the historical role of the people of Chiswick becomes far clearer, as does their fundamental importance to the estate's story and to our analysis. The chapter argues that the people of Chiswick responded to emancipation by calmly asserting their rights, to the chagrin of their managers.

The Postscript reviews the story of the Burtons, the people of Chiswick, and the estate itself, and asks what we can learn from their tale. The overall suggestion made is that the story of Chiswick shows that the cultivation of sugar there could have remained profitable into the 1840s but did not because of a variety of factors. Viewed purely as a business, the Chiswick estate was run efficiently, and extremely profitably, up to the start of the nineteenth century and the family were able to deal with the impact of war and politics on their business. The greatest external challenge to the family's business operations was provided in 1807 by the decision to abolish the slave trade. The underlying argument is that even this event could have been dealt with between 1807 and 1833 by engaged and innovative management. It was the commercial disinterest of the second generation of Burton owners which prevented the necessary action being taken to save the estate. This outcome was exacerbated by the negative impact of the Burtons' absentee status on their commercial understanding. When slavery ended and was replaced by apprenticeship, the Burtons remained uninterested in commerce and were still unable to provide the innovative responses required to deal with the economic and social consequences of the new era. After apprenticeship finished, the estate collapsed quickly because the family had not attempted to deal with the changing commercial environment since 1807.

Moving beyond a purely commercial analysis, however, the wider proposal made here is that the history of Chiswick was contextualised by high politics but decided by individual choices, both commercial and ethical. As we shall see, the underlying suggestion is that the Burton family made a choice for, what we can term, avarice in 1788, which coloured everything relating to Chiswick and its people thereafter. The family inherited a sugar estate and its enslaved people and chose to keep them when they did not have to. The Burtons could have sold Chiswick, as other men in Norwich faced with a similar situation chose to, but avarice dictated, and then framed, the family's actions.[57] It appears that this became the primary motivation that drove the next six decades of their ownership; the Burton family held onto

---

[57] Throughout this book 'avarice' or 'greed' is understood in its traditional sense as one of the seven capital sins, 'the desire to amass earthly goods without limit', see the *Catechism of the Catholic Church* (London: Catholic Truth Society, 2016), paragraphs 2534–2540, at paragraph 2536.

the estate and chose to be slave-owners purely because doing so earned them large sums of money.

Seeking profits is not problematic in itself; the generation of wealth for wider society depends upon the incentive provided by profit which encourages and rewards entrepreneurial activity. The pursuit of profit does, nonetheless, open us to a danger. That is when an individual's focus, or that of a group of people, becomes overly focused on that one goal, and morphs the legitimate aim of making profit, into an unhealthy love of monetary gain, which is avarice.[58] Philosophers and theologians have recognised this problem for centuries. Aquinas explained that the issue with avarice is that, unchecked and incorrectly ordered, it percolates through every aspect of a life, shaping the activity of those who yield to it.[59] As we shall see, this is what appears to have happened with the Burton family in relation to Chiswick, its people, and the issue of slavery. Driven by avarice from the first moment of their owner-ship, the Burtons largely ignored the people of Chiswick and did not address the ethical implications of slavery. There is no overt evidence of deep-seated racism in the Burton family prior to their ownership of the Chiswick estate, and it appears that their willingness to become slave-owners was a consequence more of greed than any other factor. Had the plantations of Jamaica been populated by indentured servants, as had those of seventeenth-century Barbados, it seems probable that the prospect of large profit would have still caused the Burtons take ownership of Chiswick.[60] The fundamental issue in understanding the history of the Chiswick plantation is that of greed, rather than race. This interpretation draws on my previous argument that the culture of East Anglia was not defined by racism during the early modern period and that the racialist ideas imported from the highly racialised colonial environment only gradually percolated into the region's consciousness, without ever becoming

---

[58] For discussion of this issue, see Pope Leo XIII, *Rerum Novarum: Encyclical on the Rights and Duties of Capital and Labour* (London: Catholic Truth Society, 2002); Saint John Paul II, *Centesimus Annus* (London: Catholic Truth Society, 1991).

[59] Aquinas explained 'Now as has been explained (q. 117, a. 3), exterior goods have the nature of being useful for an end. Hence, a man's good with respect to them must consist in a certain measure, viz., that a man should seek to possess exterior riches in a given measure, viz., insofar as those riches are necessary for his life given his own situation. And so sin consists in exceeding this measure, viz., when someone wants to acquire or to hold on to exterior riches in a way that exceeds the appropriate manner. This is what the nature of avarice involves with avarice being defined as an immoderate love of possessing'. Saint Thomas Aquinas, *Summa Theologiae II–II, 118, 1. ad 2 New English Translation of St Thomas Aquinas's Summa Theologiae (Summa Theologica)*, trans. Alfred J. Freddoso (Notre Dame, IN: University of Notre Dame), st2-2-ques118.pdf (nd.edu).

[60] See, for example, John Donoghue, '"Out of the Land of Bondage": The English Revolution and the Atlantic Origins of Abolition', *The American Historical Review* (2010), pp. 943–74; Hilary McD Beckles, 'Plantation Production and White "Proto-Slavery": White Indentured Servants and the Colonisation of the English West Indies, 1624-1645', *The Americas* (1985), pp. 21–45; Jerome S. Handler and Matthew C. Reilly, 'Contesting "White Slavery" in the Caribbean: Enslaved Africans and European Indentured Servants in Seventeenth-Century Barbados', *New West Indian Guide* (2017), pp. 30–55.

dominant. Ironically, it was the involvement of people such as the Burtons in the colonial economy that provided the means for such ideas to travel to the region.[61]

In the long run, this unbalanced focus on profit alone was at the root of the undoing of the Burton family. The result of their tendency to avarice was that, especially after 1805, the Burtons paid little attention to the sugar estate's commercial operations and the enslaved people working there. The Burton family's greed meant that they never engaged with the estate as farmers in any meaningful sense. Rather, they merely chose to own and exploit both the land and its people. Because of this narrow viewpoint, after the abolitionists had managed to change the operating environment for the sugar estates in 1807, the Burtons failed to respond effectively to the political and economic changes they faced. This failure to act in Norfolk meant that Chiswick's fate, and the economic fortunes of the Burton family, was not ultimately decided in England, but in Jamaica. Throughout the period that the Burton family owned the sugar estate, and treated it purely as a money-making machine, the people of Chiswick worked hard because they were forced to and were treated purely as an asset class on the Burtons' balance sheets. As time progressed, while the Burtons were blinded by avarice, the situation changed by increments. Chiswick's people resisted as best they could, when the opportunity arose, and these protests were ignored. Finally, from 1834 onwards, the ending of the system of slavery meant that Chiswick's people could, finally, assert their dignity and rights and, in doing so, they ensured Chiswick's commercial demise.

[61] Richard C. Maguire, *Africans in East Anglia, 1467 to 1833* (Woodbridge: Boydell Press, 2021), especially pp. 15–21, 40–48, 93–111.

1

'A VERY SENSIBLE GOOD SORT OF MAN': THE BURTON FAMILY AND THE CHISWICK ESTATE, 1700–1788

The clue to why John Vernon left the Chiswick estate to the Burton family can be found in a Leeds marriage licence from 1735.[1] Thomas Burton's father, John, came from Knaresdale, Northumberland, and became a successful merchant in Leeds and London. In 1735 he married Sarah Reveley in Leeds and the marriage register entry was expanded to recount the, clearly notable and admirable, fact that on their marriage Burton gave his new wife's 'fortune' to her sister – Mrs Rachel Reveley. The reason given for this action was that John Burton was already wealthy since his uncle was 'one of the Tellers of the Exchequer and made him his executor to a fortune of £90,000'.[2] The Tellers of the Exchequer were government officials who received any money to be paid into the Exchequer, noted the amount in a book, and sent a copy of the entry, called a Teller's Bill, to the Tally Court to enable a tally to be made of it. At the close of the day, the money received by the Tellers, as established by the Bills, was taken from their chests to be deposited in the Treasury.[3]

In 1710, the clerk to the Third Teller was John Burton's uncle, Launcelot Burton.[4] The Leeds marriage register had, therefore, slightly exaggerated Launcelot's situation; he was never actually one of the Tellers, but he was a Teller's clerk, which was an important and lucrative position. It provided a salary of £100 per annum but, more importantly, granted Launcelot access to the financial operations of government allowing him to become, as Graham puts it, 'part of a community of overlapping personal and partisan interests' which allowed considerable opportunity for personal gain for officeholders and their friends, allies, and relatives. Launcelot and his brother, Bartholomew, filled key posts in the Pay Office of Guards and Garrisons and the Pay Office respectively. The brothers were private financiers with 'relatively close links to the Foxes and the Duke of Marlborough' and in 1701 had received the 'largest individual shares' of tallies

[1] Yorkshire, Archbishop of York Marriage Licences Index, 1613–1839 3/34, Marriage of Sarah Reveley and John Burton, 9 June 1735.
[2] Emily Hargrave, George Denison Lumb, and James Singleton, *The Registers of the Parish Church of Leeds: Volume 20* (1914), p. 330; also mentioned in *The Annals and History of Leeds, and Other Places in the County of York: From the Earliest Period to the Present Time* (J. Johnson, 1860), p. 125 and in Palmer, *Perlustration*, p. 393.
[3] M. R. Horowitz, 'An Early-Tudor Teller's Book', *The English Historical Review* (1989), pp. 103–116, at pp. 108–09.
[4] John Chamberlayne, *Magnae Britanniae Notitia* (London 1710), 'The Four Tellers', pp. 484–85.

of £54,000 and £24,913 respectively. Launcelot also provided credit to the government in 1703 and 1704 – including a £50,000 loan – at 5 per cent interest.[5] He continued in this role for many profitable years and was listed as Chief Clerk to the Teller, Lord Parker, in 1727 and 1731.[6] When Launcelot died in 1734, without any children, he left the considerable residue of his estate to his nephew, John Burton.[7] This was the bequest which allowed John Burton to pass his new wife's fortune to her sister.

Crucial to our story is the fact that in 1710 the Second Teller was The Right Honourable James Vernon Esquire, 'a functional man of government and business' who operated in various governmental roles in the late seventeenth and early eighteenth centuries.[8] The Burtons and the Vernons moved, therefore, in the same financial and government circles in the early part of the eighteenth century. How close the families were after James Vernon lost his post in 1710 is unclear, but Vernon's sons purchased property in Suffolk. The older son, James Vernon the Younger, was a British government official, courtier, diplomat, and Whig politician who owned an estate in Great Thurlow, Suffolk.[9] The younger, Edward Vernon, became an admiral and had an estate at Nacton, just outside the port of Ipswich.[10] It appears that while he was serving with the navy in Jamaica, Edward Vernon fathered a son with a woman named Anne Fuller, a 'gentlewoman' who had been born on Jamaica in 1721. This son was the man who owned Chiswick: John Vernon.[11]

Back in England, John Burton prospered and when he died in 1755 his sons – John, Leonard, Launcelot, and Thomas – inherited a substantial sum each.[12] Launcelot died young, John settled in Devon, Leonard in Northamptonshire, while Thomas Burton lived in Norwich, the county town of Norfolk, where there was another branch of

---

[5]   Aaron Graham, *Corruption, Party, and Government in Britain, 1702–1713* (Oxford: Oxford Historical Monographs, 2015), pp. 65–69.

[6]   *A True and exact List of the Lords and Commons of Great Britain* (London: E. Matthews, 1727), p. 44; Guy Miège, *The Present State of Great Britain, and Ireland. The Seventh Edition Corrected [of the Work Originally Compiled by G. Miege]* (London: A. Bettesworth, 1731), p. 172.

[7]   NA/PROB/11/666/379, Will of Launcelot Burton of Saint Anne Westminster, Middlesex, 27 August 1734.

[8]   Marshall, Alan, 'Vernon, James (bap. 1646, d. 1727), Government Official and Politician', *Oxford Dictionary of National Biography*, 23 September 2004, accessed 30 November 2022, www.oxforddnb.com/view/10.1093/ref:odnb/9780198614128.001.0001/odnb-9780198614128-e-28243. The number of tellers had been reduced from ten to four in the medieval period and the post was abolished in 1834, when the office's responsibilities were given to the new Comptroller General of the Exchequer.

[9]   Perry Gauci, 'Vernon, James II (1677–1756), of Westminster, Mdx', *The History of Parliament: The House of Commons 1690-1715*, ed. D. Hayton, E. Cruickshanks and S. Handley, 2002, accessed 1 December 2022, www.historyofparliamentonline.org/volume/1690-1715/member/vernon-james-ii-1677-1756.

[10] Harding, R., 'Vernon, Edward (1684–1757), Naval Officer', *Oxford Dictionary of National Biography*, accessed 1 December 2022, www.oxforddnb.com/view/10.1093/ref:odnb/9780198614128.001.0001/odnb-9780198614128-e-28237.

[11] The relationship is mentioned without attributing a source at All results for James Vernon (myheritage.com).

[12] City of Westminster Archives Centre, Westminster Burials, Burial of John Burton, St James, Piccadilly, 9 April 1755. They were rumoured to have inherited £20,000 each, see reports of the death of Launcelot Burton, Palmer, *Perlustration*, p. 393; *Gentleman's Magazine* (1764), p. 450.

the family.[13] In 1770 Thomas married Elizabeth Fisher, the daughter of William Fisher Esquire of Yarmouth, a banker.[14] This marriage and the wording of Burton's will suggests that he was most likely involved in finance and banking in the city.[15] Burton was a shrewd steward of his wealth, who was well thought of by his neighbours and was described by the diarist Sylas Neville as 'a very sensible good sort of man'.[16]

Meanwhile, in Jamaica John Vernon had also been successful, and by the 1770s was a merchant, who owned a wharf in Kingston as well as private and commercial property across the island and worked for both commercial and governmental interests.[17] Vernon's use of the appellation 'Esquire' indicates that he was firmly a member of the island's social elite.[18] The extent of Vernon's involvement in plantation ownership is unclear. There is some suggestion that he owned, or managed, Stonehenge sugar estate in Trelawney, and Mount Vernon in St Mary's, but this is not definite.[19] Vernon was first mentioned in relation to the Chiswick sugar estate in 1778, when he completed the estate's produce return. At this point Chiswick was 'the property of Matthew Wallen Esq.' who was also the owner of the eighty-five-acre Mount Pleasant estate in St Andrew.[20] It appears that Wallen owned various other properties on the island, since his daughter Mary Player Wallen was listed as owner of the Prospect Hill estate in St Andrew in 1836.[21] Comments by the botanist Anthony Robinson confirm that Wallen acquired Chiswick before 1763.[22]

[13] Edmund Farrer, *The Church Heraldry of Norfolk: pt. VIII. Part of the Norwich churches. pt. IX. Remainder of the Norwich churches, with those of Lynn, Thetford, and Great Yarmouth, and index, &c., to v. 3* (A. H. Goose and Company, 1893), p. 182, www.oxforddnb.com/view/10.1093/ref:odnb/9780198614128.001.0001/odnb-9780198614128-e-66570.

[14] *Norfolk Chronicle*, 5 June 1783.

[15] NA/PROB/11/1426/242, Will of Thomas Burton of Norwich, Norfolk, 12 June 1805. The estate contained only one named property, Chiswick plantation, and otherwise discussed financial instruments of varying kinds. There is no record of him being involved with the Barclay or Gurney family; see, for example, Margaret Ackrill and Leslie Hannah, *Barclays: The Business of Banking, 1690–1996* (Cambridge: Cambridge University Press, 2001).

[16] Basil Cozens-Hardy (ed.), *The Diary of Silas Neville, 1767–1788* (Oxford: Oxford University Press, 1950), p. 106.

[17] *Manchester Mercury*, 6 November 1781, p. 4 and *Oxford Journal*, 3 November 1781, p. 2, *The Scots Magazine*, 1 December 1781, p. 42; *Royal Gazette of Jamaica*, 18 August 1781, p. 11; *Royal Gazette of Jamaica*, 9 June 1781, p. 14 and 23 June 1781, p. 11; NA/PROB 11/1103/168, Will of Sir Simon Clarke of Hanover in the County of Cornwall, Island of Jamaica, May 1783; Deed Books for Jamaica, 1669-1797, Vol. 245; Folio 181, and Vol. 341, www.jamaican-familysearch.com/Members/j/James_deeds.htm.

[18] Christer Petley, 'Managing "Property" The Colonial Order of Things within Jamaican Probate Inventories', *Journal of Global Slavery* (2021), pp. 81–107.

[19] James Vernon – MyHeritage Family Trees – MyHeritage; Stonehenge, Trelawny, Jamaica (cockpitcountry.com); 'Jamaica Trelawney 127 (Stone Henge Estate)', *Legacies of British Slavery* database, accessed 20 October 2023, www.depts-live.ucl.ac.uk/lbs/claim/view/21942.

[20] Jamaica Archives and Record Department (hereafter JA)1B/11/4/8 fol.188, Chiswick, Accounts produce, 12 March 1778; NA/CO/137/28, Correspondence – Board of Trade, pp. 169–75.

[21] Parliamentary Papers p.297; NA/T71/865: claim from Mary Player Smith, as owner-in-fee; John Lunan.

[22] April G. Shelford, *A Caribbean Enlightenment. Intellectual Life in the British and French Colonial Worlds, 1750–1792* (Cambridge: Cambridge University Press, 202), p. 21.

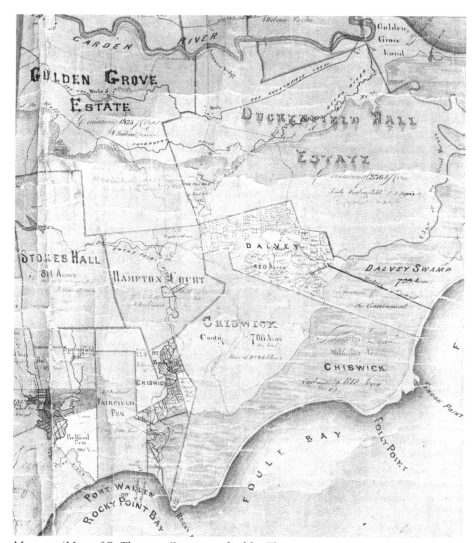

Map 1.   'Map of St Thomas, East, complied by Thomas Harrison, 1881', showing the boundaries of the Chiswick estate.

Although maps of Chiswick were made in the 1830s and sent to the Burton family, none survive, neither are there any at the National Library of Jamaica.[23] Chapter 3 reconstructs the internal layout of the estate, but its general outline when the Burtons inherited it can be identified with some accuracy from later letters and by reference to the 1881 map of St Thomas (Map 1).[24] Correspondence between their Jamaican managers and the Burtons indicate that from 1788 to 1833 the Chiswick estate was

---

[23]   BLO/MSS.W.Ind.s.18, fol. 111, Forsyth to Pitcairn & Amos, 15 August 1834.
[24]   JA/1B/21/24, 'Map of St Thomas, East, complied by Thomas Harrison, 1881'.

around 1,148 acres in size.[25] The 1881 map states the main area of Chiswick was 706 acres of 'dry land', which was separated from another section to the west stated to be 444 acres, and a small coastal enclave of 22½ acres to the south of these, making a total of 1,172½ acres, but this map includes land added after 1833. Originally, Chiswick and its neighbour Dalvey had been one estate, which was then divided between the original owner's two daughters and this meant that the exact boundaries of the estates had always been unclear.[26] The 1881 maps shows Chiswick as including 812 acres of 'swampy land' to the south known as 'the Great Morass' but this was purchased from Dalvey in 1833 along with some other land called the 'Dalvey square'.[27] The likelihood is that from 1788 to 1833 Chiswick was 1,148 acres in size and divided into three separate parcels of land by a 'J' shaped piece of land containing the Rocky Point Pen, part of the Fairfield Pen, and another area of Dalvey. On the southern boundary was the Great Morass, owned by Dalvey, and the rest of the Dalvey estate lay to the northeast and north. Hampton Court sugar estate ran along the northern boundary. The western parcel of Chiswick was sandwiched between the Stokes Hall and Hampton Court estates, along with the land of the Springfield, Fairfield, and Rocky Point Pens.

John Vernon seems to have been managing Chiswick in the 1770s and at least until 1779, when he last signed the produce return.[28] The returns from 1781 to 1786 continued to describe Wallen as the owner, but were signed by a variety of other men who were stated to be the estate's overseers.[29] An estate overseer was the senior white manager on a property and of similar social standing to a skilled white craftsman, such as a mason or cooper or a salaried official, like the supervisor of a workhouse. These men were probably reporting to Vernon. The sale of Chiswick to Vernon must have occurred between 1786 and 1788, since the crop return of 1789 described Chiswick as being 'The property of John Vernon Esquire deceased'.[30]

Although Vernon appears to have been survived by a wife and children in Jamaica, to whom he seems to have left other estates, for some reason he left Chiswick to the Burtons.[31] The long-standing family connection must have played a role in this decision and it may be that Vernon had met the Burtons on visits to England, since

.

[25] BLO/MSS.W.Ind.s.18, fol. 73, James Townson (hereafter Townson) to Pitcairn & Amos, 5 August 1833.

[26] 'Friendship Castle / Dalvey [Jamaica | St Thomas-in-the-East, Surrey]', *Legacies of British Slavery* database, accessed 7 November 2023, www.depts-live.ucl.ac.uk/lbs/estate/view/19527.

[27] BLO/MSS.W.Ind.s.17, fol. 163, James Bell to Mayhew, 8 April 1831; fol. 162, Forsyth to Mayhew, 11 April 1831.

[28] JA/B/11/4/9, fol. 50b and fol. 51, Chiswick, Accounts produce, 18 March 1779.

[29] JA/1B/11/4/9, fol. 219, Chiswick, Accounts produce, 1 September 1781; JA/1B/11/4/10 fol. 41b, Chiswick, Accounts produce, 21 August 1783; JA/1B/11/4/11, fol. 28 and fol. 29, Chiswick, Accounts produce, 22 March 1784; JA/1B/11/4/12, fol. 155, Chiswick, Accounts produce, 10 February 1785; JA/1B/11/4/12, fol. 156, Chiswick, Accounts produce, 17 February 1786.

[30] JA/1B/11/4/15, fol. 94b, Chiswick, Accounts produce, 12 March 1789.

[31] 'Dr James Vernon', *Legacies of British Slavery* database, accessed 20 October 2023, http://wwwdepts-live.ucl.ac.uk/lbs/person/view/2146649207. Dr James Vernon of Stonehenge Estate, surgeon Trelawny militia 1803 died, 21 January 1821 at Falmouth and was buried on the Estate, Stonehenge, Trelawny, Jamaica (cockpitcountry.com).

he might have owned property in London.[32] Such meetings would have made the Burtons aware of the operations of a sugar estate, and they may have expressed interest in it. Although there is no paperwork it seems likely that, since Burton was involved in finance, Vernon approached him to borrow the funds needed to purchase the estate from Wallen. If that was the case, then leaving it to the Burtons in his will may have been a debt repayment.

The trading and financial sectors of Norfolk were no strangers to involvement in the wider plantation economy and as a successful financier Thomas Burton would certainly have been aware of the lucrative potential of a sugar estate.[33] As Eric Williams put it, 'by 1750, there was hardly a trading or a manufacturing town which was not in some way connected with the triangular or direct colonial trade'.[34] Zahedieh has provided an excellent example of this in her recent study of the coppersmith William Forbes.[35] Bankers such as Burton provided the system's financial architecture, while the growing colonial market provided the industries of England and other nations with important markets for their goods.[36] By 1800 the colonies were providing nearly 20 per cent of England's imports, while the colonies purchased nearly 10 per cent of England's exports.[37]

Thomas Burton would have been cognisant of the fact that the entire edifice of Jamaican sugar production was built on slavery, and by 1788 the activity of the abolitionists was beginning to lay bare the brutality of the slave regime. Prior to the establishment of the Society for Effecting the Abolition of the African Slave Trade by William Wilberforce and his confederates in London in May 1787, there was very little discussion of the reality of slavery in Norfolk's public sphere. For example, local newspapers tended only to mention events in the Caribbean colonies that related to conflicts with France and Spain, the arrival of merchant ships in the ports, hurricanes, and very occasionally, slave rebellions.[38]

[32] 'John Vernon's Esq. sale', *Saunders's Newsletter*, 14 November 1786, p. 3.
[33] For detail of this involvement, see Richard C. Maguire, *Africans in East Anglia, 1467 to 1833* (Woodbridge: Boydell Press, 2021), esp. pp. 118–27 and 173–213.
[34] Williams, *Capitalism*, p. 52.
[35] Nuala Zahedieh, 'Eric Williams and William Forbes: Copper, Colonial Markets, and Commercial Capitalism', *Economic History Review* (2021), pp. 784–808.
[36] S. G. Checkland, 'Finance for the West Indies, 1780–1815', *The Economic History Review* New Series, Vol. 10 (1958), pp. 461–69; Ralph Davies, *The Rise of the Atlantic Economies* (London: Weidenfeld and Nicolson, 1973), chapter 14; Joseph E. Inikori, *Africans and the Industrial Revolution in England* (Cambridge: Cambridge University Press, 2002); Drescher, *Econocide*, pp. 21–23; Dunn, *Sugar*, pp. 97, 188, 201–12; Robin Blackburn, *The Making of New World Slavery: From the Baroque to the Modern, 1492–1800* (London: Verso, 1997), pp. 572–73.
[37] Stanley L. Engerman, 'Europe, the Lesser Antilles and Economic Expansion, 1600–1800', in *The Lesser Antilles in the Age of European Expansion*, ed. Robert L. Paquette, Stanley L. Engerman (Gainesville, FL: University Press of Florida, 1996), pp. 147–64 at p. 160; John J. McCusker and Russell R. Menard, *The Economy of British America, 1607-1789* (Chapel Hill, NC: University of North Carolina Press, 1985), p. 40.
[38] See, for example, reports of rebellion, *Norwich Mercury*, 19 July 1755; reports of conflict with the French, *Norwich Mercury*, 30 October 1756, 6 November 1756, 23 April 1757; a hurricane, *Norwich Mercury*, 19 March 1757; a description of Tobago, *Norwich Mercury*,

At the same moment the Burton brothers inherited Chiswick, however, the activity of the abolitionists changed all this. In Norwich, the first meeting against the slave trade to be organised was held in September 1787, only a few months after the establishment of the Society in London.[39] The years following 1787 saw the anti-slavery movement expand rapidly in Norfolk, with significant numbers of public meetings and subscriptions.[40] Suddenly, the region's papers were awash with articles and letters detailing the conditions suffered by enslaved people, both on their way from Africa and in the colonies themselves.[41] Support for the cause was geographically widespread and not limited to Norwich, with petitions against the slave trade being drawn up in the region's ports, including Yarmouth, and in market towns such as Harleston, Diss, East Dereham, Swaffham and Wymondham.[42] Debating societies such as Norwich's United Friars began discussing this 'most iniquitous traffick in human blood'.[43] The history of Norfolk's involvement in the anti-slavery campaign then mirrored that nationally, peaking in intensity in 1792 and then subsiding during the long grind through parliament that culminated in the abolition of the slave trade in British ships in 1807. The campaign, and the strong feelings it engendered among some, never disappeared, however.

Such abolitionist activity did not stop the Burton brothers from accepting ownership of Chiswick and its enslaved people in 1788. In the absence of any personal documents explaining why they followed this course of action; we must look elsewhere to explain the decision of the brothers to become slave owners. One place to begin is religious belief, or lack of it. As has been emphasised by Da Costa, Christianity was a pivotal element in the forces that undermined the system of slavery. In the colonies it provided enslaved people with a new way of thinking about their situation, and a means to express it.[44] In England, as Brown puts it, 'Christianity provided a framework for a moral critique of slavery in a language that metropolitan elites were obliged to regard.'[45] Many abolitionists were motivated by their strong

---

28 July 1781; and a shipwreck of a ship carrying 'plantation stores' off Yarmouth, *Norwich Mercury*, 15 February 1783.

[39] NRO/COL/9/59, 60, Thomas Ransome, 'On the Slave Trade and Subscription communicated by Bro. T Ransome', September 1787.

[40] See, for example, NRO/COL/9/1, The Friar's Society Minutes of Proceedings 1785 to 1794, Meeting of 11 September 1787; NRO/COL/9/59, 60, Thomas Ransome, 'A List of Local Subscribers to Anti-Slavery Cause, 1787'; *Norfolk Chronicle*, 27 December 1787; NRO/FEL/539/31, *Norwich Mercury*, 30 April 1791.

[41] See, for example, a sequence of letters against the slave trade, authored by 'Africanus', that appeared in the *Norwich Mercury* from 14 August 1787 to 24 November 1787.

[42] For examples, see C. B. Jewson, *The Jacobin City*, p. 28; *Norfolk Chronicle*, 11 February 1792; *Norfolk Chronicle*, 22 February 1792; *Norfolk Chronicle*, 18 February 1792, 3 March 1792; NRO/NNAS/G2/3-4, Tusculum Meetings, 13 February 1794; see Oldfield, *Popular*, p. 1; Anstey, *The Atlantic*, pp. 255–402.

[43] NRO/COL/9/7, Meeting of Society of United Friars, 5 February 1792.

[44] Emilia Viotti da Costa, *Crowns of Glory, Tears of Blood: The Demerara Slave Rebellion of 1823* (Oxford: Oxford University Press, 1997).

[45] Brown, *Reaper's*, p. 229.

religious faith.[46] Their campaign was founded on the understanding that slavery was wrong because all humans were created in the image of God, a fact that gives them 'the innate dignity of being a *person*, who is not just something, but someone'.[47] While more detailed research on this needs to be done, it is likely that that the majority of those involved in the East Anglian movement in the early period of abolitionism were spurred by such views. For example, Edward Harbord, Lord Suffield, joined the movement after a religious conversion, which saw him abandon his previous lip-service to Christianity and become a devout Christian.[48] Likewise, the baronet and the noted local Catholic Sir William Jerningham was one of the earliest subscribers to the abolitionist movement in Norwich.[49]

There is no evidence of such belief on the part of the Burtons. While it seems that the brothers were related to the puritan William Burton, they appear to have had no interest in religion. Later letters exhibit no attention to the topic and the lifestyles of the family members from 1788 to 1846 were, to all appearances, fixed on the pleasures of this world rather than the rewards of the next.[50] This made the Burtons possibly more representative of their social surroundings in the 1780s and 1790s than were the local abolitionists. Lack of religious enthusiasm, or even belief, was the more normative situation across urban England at this point, where a good proportion of urban men of all economic groups were drawn to hedonistic lifestyles, sexual licence, and religious indifference.[51] This moral vacuum left many people rather uninterested in the fact of slavery 4,000 miles away in the Caribbean and, in fact, the decadent and irreligious culture of the Jamaican planters was rather attractive to some. Before the abolitionist campaign gained traction, few commentators were concerned about the effect of slaveholding on general morality, and Caribbean planters were less disliked than, for example, East Indian nabobs.[52] As Burnard puts it in respect of Britain more widely, 'the values of abolitionists are not held to be characteristic of values generally in late Georgian Britain. West Indians had many attractive characteristics, by the lights of people who prided themselves on their modernity, liberalism and

---

[46] For approaches from this point, see William Hague, *William Wilberforce: The Life of the Great Anti-Slave Campaigner* (London: Harper Press, 2007); Russell Smandych, '"To Soften the Extreme Rigor of Their Bondage": James Stephen's Attempt to Reform the Criminal Slave Laws of the West Indies, 1813–1833', *Law and History Review* (2005), pp. 537–88.

[47] For a clear recent exposition of the theology underlying this doctrinal point, see *Catechism*, paragraphs 356–361, at paragraph 357.

[48] Richard Maguire, 'Harbord, Edward, third Baron Suffield (1781–1835)', *Oxford Dictionary of National Biography* (Oxford: Oxford University Press, 2021).

[49] NRO/COL/9/59, 60, Thomas Ransome, 'A list of local subscribers to anti-slavery cause, 1787'.

[50] G. E. Aylmer, 'Burton, William (c. 1608–1673), Merchant and Naval Administrator', *Oxford Dictionary of National Biography*, 23 September 2004, accessed 28 April 2023.

[51] Vic Gatrell, *City of Laughter: Sex and Satire in Eighteenth-Century London* (London: Atlantic, 2006).

[52] Sarah E. Yeh, '"A Sink of All Filthiness": Gender, Family, and Identity in the British Atlantic, 1688–1763', *The Historian* (2006), pp. 66–88; Linda Colley, *Britons: Forging the Nation, 1707–1837* (New Haven, CT: Yale University Press, 1992), pp. 105–17; Nechtman, *Nabobs*, pp. 156–57.

lack of religious zeal.'[53] Lacking as they were in any motivating religious belief, the Burtons do not appear to have any social connections with the region's anti-slavery grouping, not being mentioned in Suffield's papers, for example.[54] So, while they inherited Chiswick at a moment when the situation of enslaved workers in the colonies became far more visible to the British public, and when some of their contemporaries in Norwich were inflamed to campaign against the very operations that made Chiswick viable, the prospect of owning a sugar estate does not appear to have been a problem for them personally.

An important point when we try to understand the motivations of the Burtons in their acquisition of Chiswick is that the brothers did not have to keep hold of the estate in 1788. They could, for example, have sold Chiswick straight after inheriting it. In this context, the story of some banking contemporaries of Thomas Burton in Norwich – the Barclay brothers – is instructive in reflecting on the Burtons' decision. Around 1785 the Norwich Quakers and bankers David and John Barclay took possession of the Unity Valley Pen in Jamaica, in lieu of debts, from 'a respectable gentleman, now retired from business, and residing at Muiravon, near Edinburgh.'[55] The brothers decided that their Christian beliefs meant that they could not own slaves and determined to divest themselves of the property. The Barclays attempted to free the people on the estate but were prevented from doing so by their Jamaican agent, who refused to carry out their instructions, revealing the difficulties of absentee ownership quite clearly. He essentially told them that Jamaican society would not accept such an action. Concerned to ensure that the people would not continue in enslavement, it took around a decade for the Barclays to arrange an alternative plan. Eventually, they shipped Unity Valley's people to Philadelphia, where they were resettled as free people. They then sold the property for around £5,000, which was at least £2,500 below what they would have received for selling it with its enslaved workforce.[56] This was a major financial loss incurred purely because of religious beliefs.

There is much that can be said about the complexity of the Barclay brothers' story, but it is relevant to that of the Burtons because it reveals that genuine options existed for people who inherited property and enslaved people in Jamaica in the late eighteenth century. The fact was that the Burtons did not have to hold onto Chiswick and its people. The Barclay brothers showed that alternative paths could be chosen, if the will existed to follow them. Thomas Burton worked in the same industry as the Barclay brothers and in the same city, making it unlikely that he did not know of their story. Consequently, the decision taken by him and his brother to keep Chiswick, rather than sell it, reveals an active choice on their part to become slave-owners, and

53 Burnard 'Powerless', pp. 185–98, at p. 188.

54 Maguire, 'Harbord'.

55 NRO/RQG/539/493X1, 'Account of the emancipation of the Slaves of Unity Valley Pen in Jamaica by David Barclay 1801 2nd edn with appendix' (1811). For Barclay, see Jacob M. Price and Leslie Hannah, 'Barclay, David (1729–1809), Banker and Brewer', *Oxford Dictionary of National Biography*, 23 September 2004, accessed 20 October 2023, www.oxforddnb.com/view/10.1093/ref:odnb/9780198614128.001.0001/odnb-9780198614128-e-37150.

56 NRO/RQG/537/493x1, David Barclay's Letter Book 1788–1809, Letter to Alexander Macleod, 18 January 1797.

implies that they had no moral qualms about doing so. It has already been suggested that John and Thomas Burton inherited the Chiswick estate because of family business connections to John Vernon; indeed, it may be that they had loaned him the money to purchase it. As intelligent and educated men the Burtons understood the nature of the business that they had inherited and these circumstances suggest that the brothers chose to take control of the estate, rather than sell it. Burton and his brother would have known that ownership of a sugar estate and the enslaved people thereon offered the potential to provide them with a very substantial income. It seems that avarice provided the main motivation for their decision-making in the 1780s. Unlike Thomas' neighbours in Norwich, the Barclays, it seems that John and Thomas Burton were willing to choose the prospect of that considerable income and ignore the moral issue of their ownership of enslaved people at Chiswick. In a fundamental manner that decision set the framework for the Burton family's ownership of the estate until 1846. From the start, the Burton family's primary motivation in owning Chiswick and its people was to make money.

2

'JUDICIOUS MANAGEMENT': ABSENTEE OWNERSHIP IN THE LATE EIGHTEENTH CENTURY, 1788–1797

Having decided to keep Chiswick, Thomas and John Burton began operating as absentee proprietors. There were other absentee owners living in Norfolk and Suffolk in this period, for example, the Dallings lived at Earsham Hall in Norfolk, which was only fifteen miles from Thomas Burton's home in Norwich.[1] As a banker in the region, Thomas Burton would have been aware of families such as these, even if he was not friendly with the Dallings personally, and from enquiries he would have rapidly found out that it was quite feasible to continue to live in Norfolk and operate a sugar estate in Jamaica as absentee landlords. As has been said, this approach was not unusual. The end of the War of American Independence had seen the beginning of a significant restructuring of the plantation system in the British West Indies. As time progressed Jamaica was affected by a 'high incidence of absenteeism, resulting from remigration and the emergence of a new class of plantation owners who inherited their properties but never went to the West Indies'.[2] Contemporary estimates suggested that in 1775 around 234 of the island's 775 sugar estates were owned by absentees, minors, and incompetents. Over the next half-century 'Absenteeism increased both absolutely and relatively, for in 1832 the records show that as many as 540 out of a total of 646 sugar estates were Account Produce properties.'[3]

Absentee proprietors exerted control over their properties at an ocean's distance, usually working through a London-based factor. Thomas and John Burton worked through a firm of London merchants, who had probably been acting for Vernon previously, Maitlands.[4] The key figure here was Ebenezer Maitland, a London merchant whose business acumen would enable him to become a director of the Bank of England

[1] Maguire, *Africans*, pp. 138 and 142.
[2] Selwyn H. Carrington, 'Management of Sugar Estates in the British West Indies at the End of the Eighteenth Century', *The Journal of Caribbean History* (1999), pp. 22–53, at p. 27.
[3] Richard Sheridan, 'Simon Taylor, Sugar Tycoon of Jamaica, 1740–1813', *Agricultural History* (1971), pp. 285–96, at p. 287.
[4] For the Maitlands and their business, see NA/PROB/11/1005/225, Will of Alexander Maitland, merchant of Kings Arm Yard Coleman Street proved 27 February 1775; Phillips, 'An Antigua', p. 442; Fuller Maitland (formerly Maitland), Ebenezer (1780–1858), of Park Place; Shinfield Park, Berks.; Stansted Mountfitchet, Essex, and 11 Bryanston Square, Mdx.' FULLER MAITLAND (formerly MAITLAND), Ebenezer (1780–1858), of Park Place; Shinfield Park, Berks.; Stansted Mountfitchet, Essex and 11 Bryanston Square, Mdx. | History of Parliament Online, accessed 7 November 2023.

from 1798 to 1821.[5] Initially, Maitland worked in partnership with his father and brother and among their many business interests was a successful West India mercantile operation, in which they worked as factors and provided finance for plantation owners.[6]

Such London agents assisted the absentee owners in their dealings with Jamaican-based 'class of manager and/or attorneys' who increasingly were the key figures in the operation of British Caribbean estates.[7] The crop returns indicate that during the first two decades of Burton ownership a Scot named William Lumsden was running operations at Chiswick.[8] Lumsden was not a plantation owner in his own right and his will suggests he possessed one slave, named Lazard, and had a 'housekeeper' (a term often used to designate an enslaved mistress) named Elizabeth Christie.[9]

In theory, the role of the Jamaican attorney and manager was to act honestly and proactively for the absentee proprietors. In general terms, most attorneys had legal training, while managers tended to be planters, although some were merchants or professionals. Ideally, the manager/attorney would visit the estate at regular intervals, inspect it, discuss the situation there with the overseer – who lived on the estate – and ensure the crop was planted and cultivated effectively. In an ideal world, the attorney would liaise fully and honestly with the factors in London and with the proprietors, to keep them up to date with the myriad points of information about which they needed information throughout the process of sugar production. The letters sent to the Burton family from their managers during the 1830s provide examples of the basic work of managers on behalf of their clients, delivering weather reports, forecasts of the amount of sugar they expected the crop to yield, general detail about the condition of the estate, updates on the progress of the crop and the harvest, along with that of the subsequent preparation of the sugar and rum.[10] The attorney would ask the London factor to arrange for insurance when produce was shipped, provide the factor with bills of lading, the name of the captain and the departure date.[11] Most importantly, at the end of the process, the attorney would tell the owners the final amount the estate had yielded and provide detailed accounts of the expenses incurred in producing the crop.[12]

This mode of operation placed the absentee owner at a managerial disadvantage since, unless they had connections on the island who could check the work of the manager/attorney, the absentee had to trust in the attorney's good offices and honesty. Human nature meant that the service provided by such attorneys and managers was inconstant in quality, to say the least. Contemporary commentators such as Thomas Roughley argued that, in many cases, estate visits were 'seldom done oftener than once-

---

[5]   Bank of England, DS/UK/694, 'Ebenezer Maitland'; and M5/436-437, M5/440, Directors' Annual Lists, 1694–1935, Book 2, fols 105–127.

[6]   For example, see their loan to the owners of Amity Hall, NA/T/71/1200, Counterclaims: Jamaica: St Thomas in the East (1835–1841).

[7]   Carrington, 'Management', p. 27; Higman, *Plantation*.

[8]   See, for example, JA/1B/11/4/17 fol. 132, JA/1B/11/4/23, fol. 186.

[9]   NA/PROB/11/1467/206, Will of William Lumsden of Saint Thomas County of Surrey, Jamaica, 17 September 1807.

[10] BLO/MSS.W.Ind.s.17, fol. 126 Forsyth to Pitcairn and Amos, 20 December 1829.

[11] BLO/MSS.W.Ind.s.18, fol. 87, Forsyth to Pitcairn & Amos, 9 July 1832.

[12] BLO/MSS.W.Ind.s.17, fol. 16 Pitcairn & Amos to Farr, 28 January 1830.

a-year' and that, in consequence, many estates were 'governed without actually being inspected'. As we shall see, the incidence of visits by the various attorneys over the period of the Burton family's ownership appears to have been variable. Commentators such as Roughley also explained that, aside from the frequency of visits, the efficacy of such attorneys and managers was uneven. Since managers generally lacked any qualifications and were appointed largely through local connections, their operational effectiveness was dependent on chance, rather than planning. This meant that, too often, estate management was poor, meaning that 'happy results and promised returns yielded to the destructive consequences of ill-concerted schemes'.[13]

The same was true in respect of the actual day-to-day maintenance and operation of estates. Everyday operations were under the control of the overseer who, as one visitor to Chiswick put it, was 'responsible to the attorney for everything on the estate and, therefore, has the complete management of it'. In this role, the overseer was required to 'cultivate the canes properly' as well as to 'make good sugar and rum', run the rest of the estate and livestock, and manage the enslaved workforce.[14] Once more, the effectiveness of an individual overseer was a matter of chance. Because appointments to such positions were made through local Jamaican social connections, not all overseers were up to the task, making it quite possible that poor overseers could be appointed, and the operations of the estate could suffer in consequence. Of course, the attorney was meant to ensure that the overseer was effective but, again, this was difficult for the absentee to assess.

This management structure created a layer of charges for the proprietors on top of the actual costs of production. In the early years of the system an attorney or manager might receive a commission of 5 to 6 per cent of the gross value of the annual production, although over time many owners changed this remuneration package to an annual salary of, perhaps, £300. An overseer might receive over one hundred pounds sterling.[15] Such additional costs were significant enough, but there were also 'extensive opportunities for peculation and fraud' consequent on this structure. With no owners to check on them physically, attorneys could abuse their position in many ways. Examples abounded of situations where merchants, attorneys, and overseers were said to have colluded to overcharge absentee proprietors for livestock and estate supplies or have used the enslaved labourers owned by their clients to work on their own estates to the detriment of the absentee's property.[16] So great were the problems of these managerial arrangements that, as early as 1740, the 'Account Produce' law required attorneys to submit, under oath, annual accounts relating to the estates under their management.[17]

Of course, not all attorneys and managers were incompetent, nor were they all untrustworthy. Some experienced attorneys in Jamaica, such as Simon Taylor, William Miller, and Joseph Gordon made fortunes as they managed numerous estates

[13] Thomas Roughley, *The Jamaica Planter's Guide* (1823), p. 5.
[14] NRO/MC1519/1/813X9, William Wright to Susanna Wright, 10 April 1825, fol. 8.
[15] BLO/MSS.W.Ind.s.17, 1816-1832, fol. 164, Pitcairn & Amos, to Mayhew, 4 April 1831.
[16] Sheridan, 'Simon', p. 288.
[17] *The Laws of Jamaica: Comprehending all the Acts in Force* (St Jago de la Vega, Jamaica: Printed by Alexander Aikman, 1790), 1, pp. 278–79.

and thousands of enslaved people and made significant sums for their clients.[18] The majority of attorneys were not, however, engaged in such large-scale operations and generally ran only a few estates, often alongside other mercantile operations. This was the case at Chiswick throughout the period of Burton ownership, where the attorneys were almost all small-scale operators like William Lumsden.

On inheriting the property Thomas and John Burton found that the commercial situation at Chiswick was problematic and that the estate was 'encumbered with heavy debts' that were later said to have been in the region of forty thousand pounds.[19] Although the details have been lost, it is likely that a sizeable proportion of this was owed to the London agents Maitlands. This level of indebtedness was common. In 1774 Edward Long suggested that an estate making £6,000 per year would be burdened with contingent expenses of around £2,000, or one-third of its income.[20] As Table 3 shows, it appears that in the 1790s Chiswick was returning a net income of around £6,000 per year. The interest rate for loans against Chiswick in later years were normally around 5 per cent, and if this rate is taken as indicative, then a debt of £40,000 would have required interest payments of £2,000 per year, or one-third of its income, which is consistent with Long's suggestion.[21] As well as this debt, the new owners of Chiswick also had to pay 'legacies to different individuals' specified in Vernon's will. Only one of these legacies is recorded – an annuity of twenty pounds per annum created by Vernon in his will for Mrs Elizabeth Henckell, which was to be paid from the produce of the estate.[22] Henckell's legacy was paid until her death in 1830, but there is no record of any others, so they cannot be quantified exactly.[23]

Table 1.   The produce of the Chiswick estate, 1777–1788. *

Crop year	Return made	Hogsheads of sugar	Puncheons of rum
1777	12 March 1778	185	99
1778	March 1779	242	114
1781	September 1781	209	110
1782	21 August 1783	228	182
1783	22 March 1784	186	167
1784	February 1785	222	195
1785	February 1786	219	170
1788	12 March 1789	298	166

*   Sources: JA/1B/11/4/8, fol. 188; JA/1B/11/4/9, fol. 50 and fol. 219; JA/1B/11/4/10, fol. 155; JA/1B/11/4/11, fol. 28; JA/1B/11/4/12, fol.41 and fol. 94; JA/1B/11/4/15, fol. 172; JA/1B/11/4/16, fol. 142; JA/1B/11/4/20, fol. 60; JA/1B/11/4/31, fol. 118b; JA/1B/11/4/17, fol. 132; JA/11/4/18, fol. 112; JA/11/4/19, fol. 40b; JA/1B/11/4/20, fol. 179; JA/1B/11/4/22, fol. 171; JA/1B/11/4/23, fol. 186.

[18]   Butler, *The Economics*, p. 59.
[19]   BLO/MSS.W.Ind.s.17, fols 151–152, Thomas Burton to Mayhew, 11 October 1830.
[20]   Edward Long, *The History of Jamaica*, 3 vols (London, 1774), Vol. 1, p. 462.
[21]   BLO/MSS.W.Ind.s.17, fol. 125, Pitcairn & Amos to Mayhew, 6 March 1830.
[22]   BLO/MSS.W.Ind.s.17, fols 151–152, Thomas Burton to Mayhew, 11 October 1830.
[23]   BLO/MSS.W.Ind.s.17, fol. 155, Pitcairn & Amos to Mayhew, 2 October 1830.

The Burton brothers also discovered that 'the estate itself was in a low state of cultivation'.[24] As Table 1 shows, in 1777 only 185 hogsheads of sugar were produced, and during the 1780s production at Chiswick struggled, with the average annual crop having been about 223 hogsheads of sugar. These production levels reflected the wider economic situation in Jamaica rather than any issues specific to Chiswick, and similar lower production levels can be seen at estates such as Mesopotamia.[25] The key cause of this was the interruption to trade resulting from the American Revolution which produced short-term economic difficulties across Jamaica, as American privateers and French warships preyed on British shipping including slave traders. This activity disrupted the supply of enslaved people to the island and between 1776 and 1778 slave imports into the British West Indies declined by one-quarter. In 1780 only 3,763 slaves were landed in Jamaica, in contrast to the 60,480 that had landed in the three years before the conflict.[26] Since the Jamaican enslaved population was never self-supporting the falling numbers of new arrivals meant that there were fewer enslaved workers available to cultivate the land, which reduced production levels. The disruption to trade caused by the conflict also triggered famine among Jamaica's enslaved population, which reduced production levels further and produced terrible suffering.[27]

This fall in workforce numbers exacerbated existing issues of declining soil fertility on the island caused by decades of heavy sugar cultivation, which Jamaican planters had addressed by increasing the numbers of enslaved people cultivating the land. Comparisons between Jamaica and Saint Domingue suggest that Jamaican sugar estates 'often had roughly 75 per cent more slaves per hectare of sugarcane as their Saint-Domingue counterparts', reflecting the use of intensive farming methods intended to compensate for declining soil conditions. The drop in slave imports in the late 1770s and early 1780s curtailed this response to reduced soil fertility and contributed to a deterioration in production levels. Jamaica's sugar production fell from 51,218 casks shipped to Britain in 1775 to 30,2982 in 1783, while increased insurance costs cut into profit margins.[28]

Furthermore, the 1780s saw a series of hurricanes that caused significant property damage in Jamaica, with the worst of these being those of 1780, 1781, and 1786. The 1780 storm was localised to the west, but the others affected the east, where Chiswick was located. Such storms could be devastating for planters meaning that, as the planter William Beckford put it, 'in the space of a few days the independent were reduced to penury'.[29] These hurricanes reduced Jamaica's economic activity,

---

[24] BLO/MSS.W.Ind.s.17, fols 151–152, Thomas Burton to Mayhew, 11 October 1830.
[25] Dunn, *A Tale*, p. 36.
[26] Keith P. Herzog, 'Naval Operations in West Africa and the Disruption of the Slave Trade During the American Revolution', *American Neptune* (1995), pp. 42–48.
[27] Richard B. Sheridan, 'The Crisis of Slave Subsistence in the British West Indies During and After the American Revolution', *William and Mary Quarterly* (1976), pp. 615–41.
[28] Burnard and Garrigus, *The Plantation*, pp. 245 and 221.
[29] William Beckford, *A descriptive account of the Island of Jamaica* (London, 1788), 1, pp. 129–36, at p. 134.

affecting production especially badly in 1780 and 1781.[30] Chiswick's coastal situation made it especially vulnerable to such extreme weather events and, over the years, the injury from storms there could be extensive, damaging buildings, uprooting trees, and destroying crops.[31]

It may be that Vernon had been able to take advantage of the difficult financial conditions of this period to purchase the estate. Certainly, many proprietors had been forced to sell – a survey of the Jamaican House of Assembly in 1792 found that of 775 sugar estates on the island in 1772, 177 had since been sold for debt.[32] It seems that Vernon had intended turning operations around, but his plans came to naught because he was called to meet his Maker. Nonetheless, his instinct was correct; these problems were not terminal. Jamaica's total wealth continued to increase between 1778 to 1787 – probably by around 5 per cent. This was a lower level of growth than previously, but it was still in a positive direction. The colony was not in any state of economic collapse, merely a temporary lull.[33] Indeed, as fate would have it, the Burtons inherited Chiswick just as that the economic situation began to improve. The Jamaican sugar crop of spring 1788 exceeded that of any other year for the previous fifty years.[34] At Chiswick the crop of 1788 was the largest for a decade, being 62 per cent larger than that of 1777.

Although the Burton brothers had no direct experience of plantation ownership, they knew how to run estates and businesses in England. The approach that they decided upon in relation to Chiswick was later termed 'judicious management' and seems to have been focused on targeted capital investment, the control of costs, improvement in cane cultivation, and the repayment of debt.[35] This last area was rather unusual, and meant that rather than merely spending the profits from Chiswick, the brothers appear to have decided to use a proportion of their income to remove the debt attached to the property and so maximise the family's returns in the longer term.

The Burtons faced a volatile market situation, especially in relation to sugar prices in the 1790s. The initial effect of the American conflict had been to cause sugar prices on the London market to fall to an average of £38 per hundredweight in 1776. From that low point prices had steadily increased, and from 1788 to 1798 the average price swung between a low of £49 per hundredweight in 1794 and £71 per hundredweight in 1798. The slave revolt on Saint Domingue in 1792 had destroyed the production and trade of the French colony and this supported sugar prices, although the

---

[30] Michael Chenoweth, 'The 18th Century Climate of Jamaica: Derived from the Journals of Thomas Thistlewood, 1750–1786', *Transactions of the American Philosophical Society* New Series, Vol. 93, No. 2 (2003), pp. i, iii–ix, 1–49, 51–101, 103–43, 145–53; Michael Chenoweth, 'A Reassessment of Historical Atlantic Basin Tropical Cyclone Activity, 1700–1855', *Climatic Change* (2006), pp. 169–240.

[31] For discussion of hurricanes at Chiswick, see NRO/MC1519/1,813X9, William Wright to Susanna Wright, 15 May 1825; BLO/MSS.W.Ind.s.17, fol. 147 Pitcairn & Amos to Mayhew, 28 September 1830.

[32] Craton and Walvin, *A Jamaican*, p. 168.

[33] Trevor Burnard, 'Et in Arcadia Ego: West Indian Planters in Glory, 1674–1784', *Atlantic Studies* (2012), pp. 19–40.

[34] *London Times*, 30 April 1788, quoted in Chenoweth, 'The 18th Century', p. 6.

[35] BLO/MSS.W.Ind.s.17, fols 151–152, Thomas Burton to Mayhew, 11 October 1830.

increases in prices caused by this reduction in global supply were curtailed since the government deliberately intervened to lower sugar prices at home.[36]

How did this global situation affect Chiswick? As Table 2 shows, the first decade of ownership saw respectable results for the Burtons and their managers. The crop records show that from 1789 to 1798 Chiswick saw consistently higher levels of production than in the previous decade, with most crops exceeding 300 hogsheads of sugar, and the average being 309 hogsheads. The smaller crops of 1792 and 1797 probably reflected the effects of hurricanes in October of 1791 and 1796.[37] Chiswick's levels compare favourably with Worthy Park sugar estate, which was a larger size than Chiswick, but produced only 181 hogsheads in 1786, 172 in 1787, 248 in 1790, peaked at 371 in 1794, and then fell to 269 in 1796. After this date, however, Worthy Park increased production markedly, but this was due to significant investment and innovative management by its new owner, Rose Price, which led to production rising to 468 hogsheads in 1797.[38] In contrast, from 1797 Chiswick's production began to plateau.

Table 2.   The produce of the Chiswick estate, 1789–1798. *

Crop year	Return made	Hogsheads of sugar	Puncheons of rum
1789	11 March 1790	338	193
1790	18 March 1791	310	176
1791	13 March 1792	348	212
1792	18 March 1793	281	154
1793	29 March 1794	300	178
1794	9 March 1795	343	163
1795	21 March 1796	320	150
1797	17 March 1798	270	122
1798	25 March 1799	270	122

* Sources: JA/1B/11/4/17, fol. 132; JA/11/4/18, fol. 112; JA/11/4/19, fol. 40b; JA/1B/11/4/20, fol. 179; JA/1B/11/4/22, fol. 171; JA/1B/11/4/23, fol. 186; 1799; JA/1B/11/4/26, fol. 22; JA/1B/11/4/27, fol. 186; JA/11/4/29, fol. 203.The return for 1796 has not been located.

This improved production appears to have been the consequence of two factors, which have been highlighted in other research. The first reason for the increase in production was a change in cane type. Later letters confirm that Chiswick was replanted with 'Bourbon' cane in the 1790s.[39] Bourbon cane had been introduced onto Jamaica at the end of the eighteenth century because it had a much heavier cane body than the 'Creole' cane and so yielded much more sugar per acre, especially

---

[36]   Carrington, 'Management', pp. 35–36; Sheridan, 'Simon', p. 285.
[37]   Chenoweth, 'A Reassessment', table IV.
[38]   Craton and Walvin, *A Jamaican*, p. 175.
[39]   William and Mary Libraries: SC 01621 (hereafter WM) WM/SC/01621, Townson to Mayhew, 24 February 1838.

when combined with improved production methods.[40] The introduction of Bourbon cane was a common response in Jamaica to the declining fertility of the soil, and by the turn of the century most plantations on Jamaica were planted with it, with creole cane only to be found in a few places in the parishes of Trelawney and St James.[41]

The second reason for the improvement in productivity appears to have been that the Burtons adopted the policy followed by other planters in Jamaica, that of 'improving their human property so as to sustain plantation profits'; in other words, they purchased more slaves. Between 1789 and 1795 Jamaican planters imported an average of 16,224 enslaved Africans a year.[42] The year 1793 saw the largest number of enslaved people arriving on the island in its entire history, 28,344.[43] As has been stated, Jamaican planters had increased the numbers of slaves on their plantations to compensate for declining soil fertility and the return of slave imports to normal levels improved productivity generally.

Unfortunately, in contrast to the records of estate such as Mesopotamia, there are no detailed records of the workforce at Chiswick before 1817.[44] Nonetheless, by analysing the ages of the enslaved people recorded at Chiswick in the 1817 census, it is possible to conclude that the Burtons did purchase slaves in the 1790s. The average age of Africans when they arrived in the island was between ten and thirty years and an examination of the ages of Chiswick's people recorded in 1817 allows an estimate to be made of how many of those would have been within that age band in the first decade and a half of the Burton family's ownership. The records show that sixty of the enslaved workers, or slightly less than one-third of the total population in 1817, had been aged between ten and thirty between 1788 and 1807, and so were likely to have been brought onto the estate in that period.[45] This would have been around five per year.

It is not possible to know how low the numbers of people at Chiswick had fallen in the 1770s. At the Mesopotamia estate, the population was increased by imports from around 260 in the 1770s to 383 in in 1792.[46] Barrett's analysis of the records of Worthy Park has found that there were around 3.58 such workers per hectare of planted cane in Jamaica in this period.[47] Higman's survey of estate maps found that, on average 24 per cent of the total area of an estate was in cane, which suggests that in the 1790s perhaps 276 acres (112

[40] Carrington, *Sugar Industry*, pp. 157–64; McCusker, *Essays*, pp. 324–26; Roberts, *Slavery*, pp. 39–40; Ryden, *West Indian Slavery*, pp. 223–34.

[41] Gilbert Farquhar Mathison, *Notices Respecting Jamaica, in 1808-1809-1810* (London: J. Stockdale, 1811), pp. 58–60.

[42] Burnard and Garrigus, *The Plantation Machine*, pp. 233 and 248.

[43] Slave Voyages, 'Estimated annual number of slaves who embarked on ships in Africa and disembarked in Jamaica from 1607 to 1840', chart, 11 January 2021, Statista, accessed 3 February 2023, www.statista.com/statistics/1101390/slaves-brought-africa-to-jamaica-1607-1840/.

[44] See, for example, Dunn, *A Tale*, pp. 132–38.

[45] NA/T/71/145, Office of Registry of Colonial Slaves and Slave Compensation Commission, Slave Registers 1817 (hereafter Slave Registers), fols 849–55.

[46] Dunn, *A Tale*, pp. 25, 37, 40.

[47] Ward J. Barrett, *The Efficient Plantation, and the Inefficient Hacienda* (Minneapolis, MN: Associates of the James Ford Bell Library, University of Minnesota, 1979), p. 22.

hectares) were in plant at Chiswick.[48] If Barrett's findings were transferred to Chiswick this would suggest a population of around 400 people there, however, the earliest record of the estate's enslaved population, in 1810, records only 245 people.[49] Mortality rates among the enslaved population in Jamaica were around 1 or 2 per cent in the late eighteenth and early nineteenth centuries.[50] Using that statistic and working back from the number of 245 in 1810 would suggest the population of Chiswick before the abolition of the slave trade in 1807 to have been around 283 people, well below the numbers suggested by Worthy Park and Mesopotamia. However, an 1873 article on the industry suggests that an estate of 900 to 1,000 acres, so 20 per cent smaller than Chiswick, was expected to have around 250 enslaved workers.[51] Using this as a guide would suggest around 280 workers at Chiswick, which is more in line with the numbers that are available.

It may be that the Burtons made large purchases of enslaved people in the early years of their ownership, to bring the levels back up to this number. Overall, however, this analysis suggests that the Burtons were careful purchasers of enslaved Africans, who did not follow the moves of some on the island and expand their workforces substantially in the 1790s. By this date the more astute planters were concerned about the replacement rate among the enslaved population, and a pro-natalist policy was endorsed by the assembly as early as 1788. As the campaign against the slave trade waxed ever stronger such planters became aware of the need to develop a self-sustaining population. Simon Taylor, for example, attempted to improve the birth-rate on his properties.[52] At Worthy Park, Rose Price made substantial investment to increase the numbers of enslaved workers from 338 in 1791 to 528 in 1794, 'a level that was approximately maintained until Emancipation' and allowed the estate to mitigate the impact of the abolition of the slave trade.[53] Many owners did not, however, made the purchases of enslaved Africans prior to 1807 necessary to maintain their workforces thereafter, either through lack of foresight or lack of capital. It seems likely that the Burtons, living far away in Norfolk, were part of this group. Instead, it appears probable that they maintained the level of workforce inherited from Vernon and chose only to purchase perhaps five people per year to replace losses in Chiswick's workforce, rather than raising the numbers of workers on the estate to higher levels. This decision may have been, in part, because of their absentee status, which meant that they were not able to keep abreast of the views of the more forward-thinking planters on the island.

Improved productivity on any given plantation did not necessarily result in increased profitability, however. The next question to be considered is the degree

[48] B. W. Higman, 'The Spatial Economy of Jamaican Sugar Plantations: Cartographic Evidence from the Eighteenth and Nineteenth Centuries', *Journal of Historical Geography* (1987), pp. 17–39, at p. 31.
[49] BLO/MSS.W.Ind.s.17, fol. 96, Pitcairn & Amos to Farr, 2 September 1829; BLO/MSS.W.Ind.s.18, fol. 73, Townson to Pitcairn & Amos, 5 August 1833; 1811 Jamaica Almanac – St Thomas in the East Slave-owners (jamaicanfamilysearch.com).
[50] Robert William Fogel, *Without Consent or Contract: The Rise and Fall of American Slavery* (New York and London: W. W. Norton, 1989), p. 124.
[51] 'Sugar Farm in Jamaica', *The Penny Magazine*, 3 September 1873, pp. 348–49, at p. 349.
[52] Sir William Young, *The West Indian Common Place Book* (1807), p. 13; Higman, *Plantation*, pp. 166–226.
[53] Craton and Walvin, *A Jamaican*, p. 172.

to which these improving production figures were translated into actual profits. Although the accounting records for Chiswick in this period have been lost, crop records make it possible to estimate the profitability of Chiswick in the 1790s. These records show the amounts of sugar and rum exported, exclusive of that retained for estate use, and have been used for calculations that are presented in Table 3. This focuses on sugar and rum sales since – while plantation receipts could also come from the sale of livestock, provisions, and the hiring out of enslaved workers – there is no evidence that Chiswick hired its workers out to other estates or ever sold provisions, which tended to be in short supply there. A few livestock sales were recorded in the 1810s, as were the sales of some mahogany logs, but the proceeds were too low to be material to the overall income figures.[54]

There has been extensive discussion among historians about the price of sugar in this period. As there are no records giving the price obtained for Chiswick's sugar at this time, the price used here is based on Carrington's estimated average prices for hogsheads of sugar from Jamaica. Carrington was unable to estimate prices for 1796 and 1797, but detailed analysis of crop accounts from Jamaica by historians such as Ryden has shown that, while the long-run price of sugar, net of shipping costs and inflation, was in decline between 1750 and 1807, the 1790s saw sugar prices rise and then peak around 1797.[55] Ryden's figures concur with the estimates of Eltis, Lewis and Richardson's suggesting an average sugar price of 64 shillings per hundredweight in the period 1795 to 1799 (roughly £54 per hogshead).[56] Although later figures from Chiswick suggest rum prices were as low as £9 per puncheon in the 1830s, for this earlier period Higman estimates a median of £14, while Craton and Walvin suggest £15 11s per puncheon after all costs have been deducted.[57] The assumption here is £15 per puncheon.

Any time series attempting to calculate income based on hogshead numbers is only approximate since, as Higman has shown, the weight of a hogsheads was not standard and could vary from 1,500 lbs to 2,000 lbs.[58] In 1807, Sir William Young estimated a hogshead of sugar as thirteen hundredweight.[59] Examination of the records from Worthy Park for the years 1776 to 1796 led Craton and Walvin to provide an average weight of 16.88 hundredweight per hogshead.[60] The decision has been made here to follow Craton and Walvin's lead, and assume each hogshead to have been 16.88 hundredweight. Although Ward suggested the loss of weight of sugar in shipment through leakage might average 14 per cent, in the absence of any data to

---

[54] See, for example, JA/1B/11/4/45, fol. 117, Crop return 1812, which shows the sale of mahogany logs and an 'old heifer' for £96.

[55] David Beck Ryden, 'Does Decline Make Sense? The West Indian Economy and the Abolition of the British Slave Trade', *Journal of Interdisciplinary History* (2001), pp. 347–74, at p. 365.

[56] Ryden, 'Sugar, Spirits, and Fodder', p. 52; Eltis et al., 'Slave Prices', p. 679.

[57] BLO/MSS.W.Ind.s.17, fol. 16 Pitcairn & Amos to Farr 28 January 1830, lists rum puncheons selling at nine pounds per puncheon. The prices of puncheons in the 1790s found by Philips was similar; Ulrich B. Phillips, 'A Jamaica Slave Plantation', *The American Historical Review* (1914), pp. 543–58, at p. 557; Craton and Walvin, *A Jamaican*, p. 172; Higman, *Slave*, p. 236.

[58] Higman, *Slave*, p. 238.

[59] Sir William Young, *The West Indian Common Place Book* (London, 1807), p. 48.

[60] Craton and Walvin, *A Jamaican*, p. 117.

confirm that in respect of Chiswick, and because later shipments from Chiswick do not mention such losses, no adjustment has been made for this.[61]

These estimated income figures have then been adjusted to allow for a plethora of production costs, charges, and duties. A credible estimate of the costs in the 1790s can be made using data gathered in relation to other estates in the period, and by reference to costs at Chiswick from the early 1830s. There were three main categories of expenditure that affected sugar estates. The first were termed by Chiswick's managers the 'Island' or 'Jamaican' Expenses, and were expenses incurred locally in the colony on taxes, salaries, and the purchase of food, lumber, and livestock.[62] The second were called at Chiswick the 'London supplies' and were the price of the shipments from London of estate stores.[63]

In 1830 the Jamaican expenses of Chiswick were suggested to average around £1,435 and the supplies from London around £650, making a total of £2,085.[64] While inflation will have affected prices in the period from 1788 to 1830, this increase will have been counterbalanced by the fact that the numbers of enslaved workers on Chiswick declined by at least one-quarter. It seems reasonable to suggest, therefore, that the deduction for Jamaican Expenses and London Supplies in the earlier periods was like that in the 1830s and in Table 3 it is assumed to have been £2,000 per annum. Although the 1830s expenses included salaries, for this earlier period they have been added to the figure. Based on data from the 1820s, salary costs have been estimated at £40 per year for each of two bookkeepers, £150 for the overseer and of £300 per annum for the attorney, making a total of £530 to be added.[65] The overall estate expenses are, therefore, estimated to have been £2,530 per annum. Letters written in the 1820s indicate that improvements were also made to the mills and machinery in the 1790s, suggesting that the Burton brothers made capital investments, such as buying new stills.[66] There would also have been costs for general repairs and the replacement of livestock on an annual basis. Without any paperwork these are difficult to determine, however, and so no reduction has been made for these.

These costings from the 1830s also included the duty required to be paid on the estate's produce. The American Revolution had seen the duty on British-Caribbean produce entering Britain increased from a little under 6/4 per hundredweight in 1776 to over 11/8 in 1781. This increase was designed to pay for the costs of the conflict and duties were raised further in subsequent years to 27 shillings per hundredweight in 1805. They peaked at 30 shillings in 1818 before being permanently fixed at 27 shillings in 1826.[67] That being the case, the duty allowed for in the later estate expenses figures was significantly greater than that in the 1780 and 1790s, and so no further adjustment for duty has been made to the estimates presented here.

---

[61] Ward, 'The Profitability', p. 199.

[62] BLO/MSS.W.Ind.s.17, fol. 16, Stevens Wood & Wilkinson to Mayhew, 19 January 1829.

[63] BLO/MSS.W.Ind.s.17, fol. 53, Pitcairn & Amos to Mayhew, 6 April 1829.

[64] BLO/MSS.W.Ind.s.17, fol. 125, Pitcairn & Amos to Mayhew, 6 March 1830.

[65] NRO/MC1519/1/813X9, William Wright to Susanna Wright, Chiswick, 10 April 1825, fols 8–9.

[66] NRO/MC1519/1/813X9, William Wright to Susanna Wright, 10 April 1825, fols 2–11.

[67] Ragatz, *Fall*, p. 165; 'Account of Rates of Duty on British Plantation Sugar Imported into Great Britain, 1776–1826', *Parliamentary Papers, House of Commons*, 1826, XXII (328).

The next area of expenses were the variable costs of marketing the sugar and rum, including freight costs, insurance costs, dock dues, brokerage, commission, and charge on stores. In 1807 Young estimated that these amounted to between 23 shillings per hundredweight in wartime and 16 shillings per hundredweight in peacetime.[68] Ward suggested a framework to estimate costs across the eighteenth and nineteenth century based on his findings that the factor's commission was standardised throughout the period at 2½ per cent, and that rates for freight and insurance were quite uniform. From 1793 to 1798 the freight rates for sugar from Jamaica to London were 9 shillings per hundredweight. Insurance rates were running at 11 per cent, reflecting the wartime situation.[69] Applying Ward's suggestions to Chiswick's levels of production produces a set of estimated costs of sugar production in the 1790s.

Finally, there was the cost of purchasing new slaves. If we are correct and at least fifty new enslaved workers might have been purchased during the decade between 1788 and 1798 then assuming an average price in the period of £48, this would suggest that, in any year, the Burtons might have spent around £250 on new slaves.[70] These have been added to the expenses and salaries to produce a total fixed cost deduction of £2,780, which is very similar to the £3,100 per annum estimated for, the slightly larger, Worthy Park in the same period.

The results are detailed in Table 3 and suggest that the gross income per year for Chiswick in this period was around £9,041, which is analogous to the £8,960 estimated for Worthy Park. Net profits, before deduction of annuities and loans, totalled around £52,012, or around £5,779 per annum, in line with the estimated annual net profit at Worthy Park of £5,000 per year. These estimated profit figures would have been reduced by the, largely unknown, annuities that were attached to the property, as well as by the repayments required to service the 'heavy debts'. After allowing £2,000 for interest, these estimates suggest that the income from the estate might have averaged £3,779 per annum, divided between Thomas and John Burton, with Thomas receiving around £2,494 each year.

This was a very large sum indeed. By means of a comparison, in 1814 Patrick Colquhoun estimated the average family income of different classes and occupational groups in England. He suggested that eminent merchants and bankers made around £2,600 annually, that gentry incomes ranged from £800 to £3,510, and those of the nobility from £5,010 to £10,000.[71] Receiving two-thirds of the average profits of Chiswick, which was then added to his other income, ensured that Thomas Burton was among the wealthiest people in Norfolk. While tentative in nature, these figures suggest that Thomas and John Burton had moved into the realm of plantation ownership with some success and skill. Viewed purely from a financial perspective, their decision to keep Chiswick in 1788 had been vindicated.

---

[68]   Source is Sir William Young, *The West Indian Common Place Book* (London, 1807), p. 42.
[69]   Ward, 'The Profitability', pp. 198–99.
[70]   This average figure is taken from Eltis et al, 'Slave', p. 679.
[71]   Patrick Colquhoun, *A Treatise on the Wealth, Power, and Resources of the British Empire* (London, 1814), p. 124. On English gentry incomes, see G. E. Mingay, *English Landed Society in the Eighteenth Century*, new edn (1963; London: Routledge, 2007), pp. 20–23.

Table 3. *Estimated net profit of the Chiswick estate, 1788–1798.**

Crop year	Hogsheads of sugar sold in London	Estimated price per hogsheads of sugar (£ sterling)	Estimated gross income (£ sterling)	Insurance costs at 11% (£ sterling)	Factor costs at 2½ % (£ sterling)	Freight (9s per cwt) (£ sterling)	Estimated net profit on sugar (after fixed expenses)	Net profit (with rum at £15 per puncheon)
1789	338	35	£11,830	(£1,301)	(£296)	(£2,567)	£4,886	£7,271
1790	310	15	£4,650	(£512)	(£116)	(£2,354)	(£1,112)	£1,063
1791	348	36	£12,528	(£1,378)	(£313)	(£2,643)	£5,414	£8,039
1792	281	25	£7,025	(£773)	(£176)	(£2,134)	£1,162	£3,067
1793	300	33	£9,900	(£1,089)	(£248)	(£2,279)	£3,504	£5,694
1794	343	30	£10,290	(£1,132)	(£257)	(£2,605)	£3,516	£5,541
1795	320	33	£10,560	(£1,162)	(£264)	(£2,431)	£3,923	£5,783
1797	270	41	£11,070	(£1,218)	(£277)	(£2,051)	£4,744	£6,259
1798	270	54	£14,580	(£1,604)	(£365)	(£2,051)	£7,780	£9,295

* Sources: JA/1B/11/4/8, fol. 188; JA/1B/11/4/9, fol. 50 and fol. 219; JA/1B/11/4/10, fol. 155; JA/1B/11/4/11, fol. 28; JA/1B/11/4/12, fol. 41 and fol. 94; JA/1B/11/4/15, fol. 172; JA/1B/11/4/16, fol. 142; JA/1B/11/4/20, fol. 60; JA/1B/11/4/31, fol. 118b; JA/11/4/18, fol. 112; JA/11/4/19, fol. 40b; JA/1B/11/4/20, fol. 179; JA/1B/11/4/22, fol.171; JA/1B/11/4/23, fol. 186.

Nevertheless, the crucial element in this success had been their active decision to own and purchase slaves. What Thomas and John Burton thought about the enslaved workers they purchased and owned is difficult to establish, since no correspondence from this period remains. The only hint of their thinking can be found in Thomas Burton's will, which was drafted in the 1790s. From this document one might surmise – very tentatively – two things. First, that he did not view the enslaved workers at Chiswick in the same fashion as did resident planters or those planters that had returned to England. Second, that Thomas Burton did not dwell on the shared humanity of his enslaved workforce to any great degree and may have unconsciously sought to distance himself from them.

The will makes it clear that Thomas did not share the culture of planters who had lived on the island. In their wills, such planters often referred to specific enslaved people, who had been favourites, or mistresses, or were their children. For example, John Scott, who owned the Retreat and Clarendon estates in Saint Thomas-in-the-East and had retired to Garboldisham in Norfolk in 1803, mentioned numerous enslaved people on the two estates by name in his will, such as 'Jane Anderson, my late housekeeper in Jamaica', along with her five children, Favel, Eleanor, George, Henry, and Jerry Scott. He left annuities to all indicating that they were his children. He also left a money to another woman named Mary Sharp and her two daughters, as well as freeing a woman named Nanny and her two daughters, 'of who I am the reputed father'.[72] Scott's will revealed, therefore, a great deal about his lifestyle, sexual activity, and his cultural milieu in Jamaica. Read 'against the grain' like this, the document shows Scott to have been fully immersed in the hedonistic lifestyle of the colonial planter class and enmeshed in the racialised attitudes of the colony.

In sharp contrast, the will of Thomas Burton was that of a man completely separated from the behaviours of Jamaican planter society and the reality of his ownership of enslaved people. Burton's document was that of a provincial English family man whose lifestyle had been lived according to the norms of Norfolk's society. Geographic distance meant that he had never encountered the enslaved people at Chiswick personally and, consequently, he had never formed any type of personal relationship with them. There were no mistresses or illegitimate children to free, in fact there were no enslaved people at Chiswick of which he had any true individual awareness. Reading the will, one might suggest that physical distance allowed the creation of emotional distance. To Thomas Burton, Chiswick and its people were purely part of a list of assets, which he knew only in terms of business, ledgers and produce, simply being mentioned as 'slaves' before he moved onto another asset.

The will suggests, therefore, that the people of Chiswick were not imagined by Burton as real. Rather, they were notes on a balance sheet. The very format of the will, and the fact that the law allowed enslaved people in Jamaica to be listed as assets in such a document, facilitated a process of emotional distancing that enabled his ownership of them. Burton's description of Chiswick's people was not personal or empathetic. It was generic and legalistic, designed to cover all eventualities in respect of a type of property he had never seen. He went on to describe the rest

[72] NA/PROD/11/1551, Will of John Scott of Garboldisham, 7 January 1814. For more on Scott, see Maguire, *Africans*, p. 140.

of his English estates, including his money, investments, buildings, real estate, and any other possessions in Great Britain in similar generic terms.[73] The emotional and intellectual distancing from Jamaica and its culture, and the enslaved people of Chiswick, was even more clear in the will of his brother, John, which did not even mention Chiswick or its enslaved people specifically.[74]

We do not know whether Thomas or John Burton lost sleep thinking about the issue of slavery as the campaign against the slave trade gathered pace in the 1790s. It seems possible, however, that such book-keeping techniques enabled them to limit the degree to which they might have begun to conceive of a shared humanity with the enslaved workers on their property. To the brothers, unlike the Barclays elsewhere in Norwich, the Jamaican sugar estate and its 'slaves' were recorded and perceived as business assets, nothing more. It was this type of emotional separation that the abolitionists sought to remove during the 1790s and 1800s through their leaflets, speeches, and campaign ideas, epitomised by the famous slogan 'Am I not a man and a brother?' In the interim, such an approach allowed John and Thomas Burton to detach themselves from the enslaved people already on Chiswick and authorise the purchase of new people to add to its workforce.

Curiously, this approach also probably separated the Burtons from the 'planter class' more generally. If the brothers' detached approach meant that Chiswick and its people were reduced to numbers and names on a balance sheet, then any connection with the planters of Jamaica was also delimited. As has been said, the Burton brothers' wills shared no cultural characteristics with those of the returning planter class and, while there were other absentee planters in the region, such as Crisp Molineux from St Kitts, at Garboldisham, the Dalling family, the Blake family, and William Colhoun, there is little evidence of any social or business connection between these absentees and the Burton family during the 1790s.[75]

As the campaign against the slave trade grew, the brothers did not write any letters to the local Norfolk newspapers to defend it or appear at any local meetings. In the years from 1788 to 1807, and indeed to 1846, the family was not mentioned as slave-owners in any local newspaper, for example. Neither did they engage with the, sometimes raucous, activities of other members of the planter lobby. There was no East Anglian equivalent of the West Indian committees that can be found in other locations around the country in this period and the nearest such organisation was the London Society of West India Planters and Merchants. Despite that fact that roughly two-thirds of the Society's most active members were related to Jamaica, the Burtons do not appear to have attended any meetings, and there is no record of them engaging with the London West India Committee.[76] Neither is there any intimation in their papers that the Burton family were affected by the planter 'tropes' identified by Draper; for example, an idea of a 'special relationship' between enslaved

---

[73] NA/PROB/11/1426/242, Will of Thomas Burton of Norwich, Norfolk, 12 June 1805.

[74] NA/PROB11/1411/154, Will of John Burton of Jacobstowe, Devon, 13 July 1804.

[75] For details, see Maguire, *Africans*, pp. 138–44 and Chapter 6.

[76] For example, there is no record of them in Angelina Osborne, 'Power and Persuasion: The London West India Committee, 1783–1833', unpublished PhD thesis, University of Hull, 2014.

and absentee master, or of 'bonds of obligation'.[77] Instead, the family letters explored the topic of absenteeism only in a commercial fashion and looked at the situation in Jamaica and events relating to it from a recognisably English vantage point. While Ryden has argued that the statistics show that the Society was built around a 'network of Jamaica planters', the Burton brother's apparent lack of involvement in such a network suggests that a proportion of the absentee owners of Jamaican estates were not part of it.[78]

Of course, the lack of any evidence of engagement by the Burtons with planters' opposition to abolition in the 1790s and early 1800s may be purely a consequence of the lack of surviving records. It also might be a result of judgement and timing. The abolition campaign stalled in the early 1790s as Parliament worried over the impact of such a move on colonial stability and as the enslaved people of Saint Domingue successfully overthrew the French regime.[79] Therefore, the family were only in the early years of ownership as the campaign waxed and then waned and so the brothers may not have had chance to build any relationships with other absentees. Nonetheless, the Burton brothers' lack of involvement in the discussions about slavery and abolition throughout the years of their ownership points toward an idea the family were not coupled, culturally or politically, to the Jamaican planter class in any meaningful manner.

A key reason for this was, probably, that the Burtons were not Jamaican, or 'Creole' in identity. Trevor Burnard has argued that Jamaica was a 'failed' society in terms of having created a 'settler identity' and, as such, 'increasingly diverged from Anglophone social, cultural, and economic norms' over this period.[80] He has shown that over the decades after 1788 there was a general rejection of the claim of white West Indians to be 'British', and traces this to the abolitionist attacks in the 1780s.[81] The Burtons, as long-standing residents of Norfolk and Suffolk, were not seen as part of such a group, nor thought of themselves in such a manner. Neither were they returning colonial planters who, having made a fortune in the colonies, came back to Britain and established communities in London, Bath, and Bristol, while purchasing estates across the country. Even before abolitionism these returnees were ruthlessly ridiculed in plays, novels, broadsides, newspapers, and cartoons, while their lack

[77] Nicholas Anthony Draper, 'Possessing Slaves: Ownership, Compensation and Metropolitan British Society at the Time of Emancipation', PhD thesis, University College London, 2008, chapter 2.
[78] Ryden, 'Sugar, Spirits, and Fodder', pp. 42–43.
[79] Michael Duffy, 'The French Revolution and British Attitudes to the West Indian Colonies', in *A Turbulent Time: The French Revolution and the Greater Caribbean*, ed. David Barry Gaspar and David Patrick (Bloomington, IN: Indiana University Press, 1997), pp. 78–101; Anstey, *Atlantic*, pp. 275–78; J. R. Oldfield, *Transatlantic Abolitionism in the Age of Revolution: An International History of Anti-Slavery, c.1787–1820* (Cambridge: Cambridge University Press, 2013), pp. 104–09.
[80] Trevor Burnard, 'A Failed Settle Society: Marriage and Demographic Failure in Early Jamaica', *Journal of Social History* (1994), pp. 63–82 and 77.
[81] Burnard, 'Powerless', p. 188.

of a local lineage could prove problematic at times.[82] In the 1771 elections for a parliamentary seat in Monmouthshire, Valentine Morris, the owner of the Piercefield estate overlooking the River Wye near Chepstow, was attacked by his opponents because of the slavery-based foundation of his fortune and his lack of local landed pedigree.[83] In Norwich, Thomas Burton had a local pedigree and, moreover, did not enter local politics or raise his profile in such a fashion as to allow such attacks. Rather, he lived a quiet life as an established member of the local urban business class. He did not think of himself as 'a planter', but as an inhabitant of Norfolk. The same was true of his brother in Devon. Moreover, since neither brother had been to Jamaica and they did not have the accents, habits, views, nor customs of returned planters, it appears that they were not perceived by their peers as 'planters' and their ownership of Chiswick was viewed as a business issue, not a social or moral one.

The lack of cultural connection is, perhaps, one reason for a crucial factor in the long-term story of the Burton family and Chiswick – the estate's lack of debt. The 1780s and 1790s saw the debt-driven collapses of many plantation owners, such as Sir Charles Price and his son at Worthy Park.[84] During the sugar boom years of the 1790s high sugar prices had 'lured Jamaican planters, more than any other British colonial group, to expand their operations and build new sugar estates on property previously thought of as non-viable' meaning that the number of sugar estates on the island increased from 710 in 1789 to 859 in 1804.[85] When prices fell there was a slew of insolvencies, with some 212 sugar plantations in insolvent situations by 1807.[86] The Burtons had no such problems and instead, using the profits from the estate, they paid off the large debts they had inherited with Chiswick 'in the course of a few years'.[87] In this instance, it seems likely that their choice to remain in Norfolk, and their distance from Jamaican planter society culturally, prevented them being drawn into the feverish atmosphere of the period that caused many other estate-owners to overstretch themselves financially.

Looking at the period from 1788 to 1797 from a purely business perspective, it is apparent that, although the Burtons were newcomers to the business of sugar planting and began their management during a frantic period in the sugar markets, their first decade of ownership was financially successful. They oversaw a substan-

---

[82] Srinivas Aravamudan, *Tropicopolitans: Colonialism and Agency, 1688–1804* (Durham, NC: Duke University Press, 1999), chap. 1; O'Shaughnessy, *An Empire*, chap. 1, esp. pp. 2–18.

[83] Susanne Seymour, Stephen Daniels, and Charles Watkis, 'Estate and Empire: Sir George Cornewall's Management of Moccas, Herefordshire and La Taste Grenada', *Journal of Historical Geography* (1998), pp. 313–51, p. 318.

[84] Craton and Walvin, *A Jamaican*, pp. 155–64.

[85] Ahmed Reid and David B. Ryden, 'Sugar, Land Markets and the Williams Thesis: Evidence from Jamaica's Property Sales, 1750–1810', *Slavery & Abolition* (2013), pp. 401–24, at p. 418; Craton and Greenland, *Searching*, pp. 39 and 48.

[86] *Journals of the Assembly of Jamaica*, 11 (Scholarly Resources Microfilm, Reel No. 6), pp. 618–20. This report stated that there were sixty-five sugar estates that were 'thrown up' since 1799. In addition, there were thirty-two sugar estates had been sold by order (or threat of order) by the court of chancery since 1802, and 115 sugar estates that were to be sold by order of the court of chancery.

[87] BLO/MSS.W.Ind.s.17, fols 151–152, Thomas Burton to Mayhew, 11 October 1830.

tial increase in estate productivity, and this resulted in high profit levels, which provided the brothers with a joint income that exceeded £3,000 per year. Moreover, the profits from the estate were so large that the brothers had been able to clear Chiswick's substantial debts, which meant that the estate was well-set to withstand varied economic conditions. Moving away from purely financial considerations, however, the Burton brothers had achieved these high levels of productivity and profits by deciding to engage fully with the requirements of Jamaican sugar estate ownership and had accepted the ownership of enslaved people. Indeed, they had been willing to purchase extra slaves to rejuvenate their business. There is no evidence of moral qualms on their part either in respect of slave ownership or making these new purchases.

Bearing in mind the Burton brothers' drive to maximise profits and their willingness to own and purchase enslaved people then, if the suggestions about the clues from the brothers' wills are accepted and placed in the context of the activity in their region in respect of abolitionism in this period, it seems reasonable to make some estimates about the views and ideas of the Burton brothers. The growth in absentee ownership in this period has been presented by Higman in a largely negative light and Dunn has described it as 'Increasingly ... nakedly exploitative profit making', where ownership was largely divorced from residency and involvement.[88] The Burton brothers' situation conforms to this characterisation. From the beginning of their ownership, the brothers focused purely on profit-making to the exclusion of other considerations, such as the morality of owning people. There is no direct evidence that allows us to investigate whether they ever considered the moral issue of slave ownership, and it may never have occurred to them to think about it.

Nonetheless, during the period that the brothers acquired and began to run Chiswick the social and cultural context in which they lived, Norwich and Norfolk, was one in which the question of the morality of slave ownership was being openly considered and discussed. There was extensive coverage of the topic in the region's newspapers, debating societies, and public sphere about the issue and this atmosphere of debate makes it unlikely that the Burton brothers were unaware of the issues involved. In that context, their decision to take up the ownership of Chiswick and its people was an active choice. Moreover, the details of the actions of the Barclays in respect of Unity Valley Pen demonstrate that this was not the only option available for a person who inherited a plantation at this time. Seeing as Thomas Burton worked in the same city and industry as the Barclay brothers the Burtons are very likely to have been aware of the Barclays' story. In consequence, it is reasonable to infer that the Burton brothers made an informed decision about the path they would follow and opted to become slave-owners because of the potential financial rewards that situation offered to them. The financial consequence of this choice had been great wealth for both brothers and owning Chiswick's enslaved people had made them some of the richest people in Norfolk and Devon. The wider consequences of their choice would become clearer over time.

[88] Higman, *Plantation*, pp. 22–29; Dunn, *A Tale*, p. 4.

3

'DELIGHTFULLY SITUATED':
A BURTON IN JAMAICA, 1798–1801

Among the Burton brothers only Thomas was blessed with children, eight in total. There were his four daughters – Caroline, Charlotte, Harriet, and Maria – and four sons. The eldest son was Thomas Burton II, who was born in 1773, attended Norwich School and then Rugby School, before graduating from Trinity Hall, Cambridge, in 1790.[1] The next was Launcelot, who was born in Yarmouth in 1775 and also attended Rugby.[2] The third son was Charles Fisher, born in 1778.[3] The youngest son was Frederick, who was baptised in Norwich in 1787.[4] Both Charles and Frederick followed military careers, and Thomas was preparing to run the family's affairs in England. Launcelot was destined, however, to follow a very different path.

In the spring of 1798 Launcelot Burton was twenty-three years old, unmarried and without responsibilities. At some point in that year Launcelot and his father agreed that he would travel to Jamaica to run the Chiswick estate on behalf of the Burton family. This was a radical change in management approach since, in a decade of ownership, none of the family had travelled to the island to look the estate over. They had no maps of Chiswick, no description of it, and no first-hand knowledge of life on their sugar estate, how it operated, or how its enslaved people were treated. This lack of knowledge may have been one reason for Launcelot's mission, along with a desire on his part for adventure. Another potential reason can be discerned from clues in the crop records, which had reported that the production figures for 1797 and 1798 were identical. This may have been the product of chance and a completely innocent coincidence, but they may have raised doubts over the accuracy of Lumsden's reporting. For men as astute as the Burton brothers, coincidences such as this needed investigation, especially in the context of the well-known opportunities for fraud that existed in the absentee/attorney relationship.

[1] NRO/PD/28/14, Great Yarmouth, St Nicholas, Baptism of Thomas Burton, 8 March 1773; F. Temple (ed.), *Rugby School Register. From 1675 to 1867 inclusive* (1867), p. 41; John Venn and John Archibald Venn, *Alumni Cantabrigienses: A Biographical List of All Known Students, Graduates and Holders of Office at the University of Cambridge, from the Earliest Times to 1900* (Cambridge: Cambridge University Press, 2011), p. 469.
[2] NRO/PD/28/14, Great Yarmouth, St Nicholas, Baptism of Launcelot Burton, 3 April 1775.
[3] NRO/PD/90/5, Norwich, St John de Sepulchre, Baptism of Charles Fisher Burton, 1 October 1778.
[4] NRO/PD/90/5, Norwich, St John de Sepulchre, Baptism of Frederick Burton, 15 February 1787.

It seems the Burton brothers chose, therefore, to follow an approach used by many absentee owners – the employment of two estate managers in the island, or a manager and an attorney, to run an estate. Often the work of such teams was delineated, with one being focused on planting and the other on mercantile matters, but the core idea of such dual management was to institute a system whereby there was joint responsibility for the bills and accounts of an estate, with the aim of controlling costs on the estate and reducing any chance of misappropriation. Part of Launcelot's mission would seem to have been aimed at providing a trusted second manager.

Even if the figures were correct, the Burtons would also have been concerned to have seen the fall in production for 1797 and 1798. Chiswick had produced only 270 hogsheads of sugar in each year, a fall of 13 per cent below the average of the previous years, and the lowest production figure since 1785. Since there had been no unusual weather events to disrupt production, this was a matter which required investigation. This was especially important because sugar prices, which were still high in 1798, were vulnerable to changes in the military and political situation. Prices had been elevated by a speculative 'bubble' in West India commodities resulting from the French occupation of Holland in 1795, which caused Hamburg to become the primary entrepot for the import of sugar into Europe. In a rising market, the merchant houses in the city borrowed heavily to speculate, driving commodity priced upwards. The 'bubble' eventually collapsed in the winter of 1799, when unusually harsh weather clogged the port with sea ice and 152 commercial houses collapsed.[5] Given the close connections between the merchant communities of Yarmouth and Hamburg, it may have been that Thomas Burton was aware of the speculation in the market and was anticipating the eventual collapse of prices. Rising sugar prices had compensated for the fall in production to date, but if they suddenly fell, then this would result in a marked change in the profit margin of Chiswick.

This combination of factors: the family's lack of knowledge about the estate itself, aberrations in the crop returns, a fall in production, and the volatility of sugar prices, seem to have finalised the idea that a member of the family needed to travel to Jamaica. With one of their number on the estate the Burtons would have far greater control of operations and an improved ability to respond to any challenges. Moreover, if this was done, they would be able to reduce the management costs substantially. Of course, Lumsden would remain involved in the running of the estate, working alongside Launcelot. As a novice planter, Launcelot needed to draw on Lumsden's extensive experience of working in sugar cultivation while he acquired his own knowledge of the complex processes of sugar cultivation.

Launcelot arrived in Jamaica at some point during 1798/9. There was a house at Chiswick, and so he headed the forty or so miles from Kingston to the estate to begin his new role.[6] With his arrival the family now gained, for the first time, a first-hand view of the estate, its layout, and its operations. Launcelot was greeted with a panorama described by a family friend, Captain George Bent, when he visited the estate in 1801. 'The Estate', Bent wrote, 'is delightfully situated on an eminence

[5] See Thomas Tooke, *Details on High and Low Prices of the Thirty Past Years, from 1793 to 1822* (London: John Murray, 1824), pp. 124–25; Ryden, 'Sugar', p. 60.

[6] JA/1B/11/4/26 23, Chiswick Estate,1799 and 1B/11/4/27 187, Chiswick Estate, 1800.

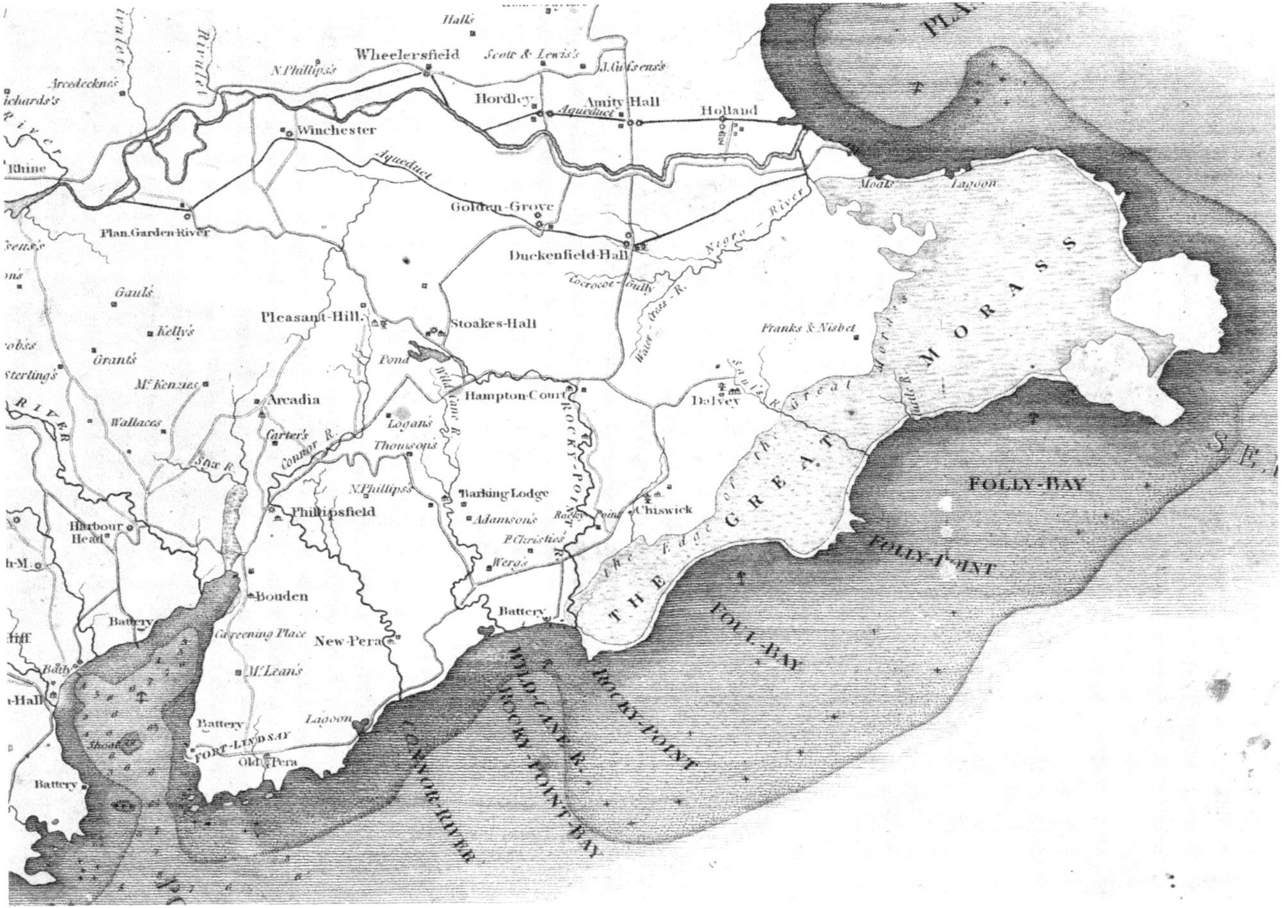

Map 2. Excerpt from James Robertson's map of the county of Surrey in Jamaica (1804) showing the internal layout of the Chiswick estate.

commanding a very near and wide view of the sea.'[7] James Robertson's 1804 map of the county of Surrey (Map 2) shows the location and distribution of 830 sugar estates, including Chiswick, along with selected topographic details, including windmills, cattle mills, and the great houses on many plantations. While such map details tend to be generic, and so must be treated cautiously, Robertson's map suggests that Chiswick's manufacturing buildings were situated in the centre of the estate, forming a ribbon development running from east to west, parallel to the road running from Fort Lindsey in the west to Dalvey in the east.

This layout seems to be confirmed by Bent's 1801 letter. Looking northwards from the main house, Bent noted that to the west was a ribbon development wherein 'Buildings, store houses, and offices succeed each other, connecting the whole of the extensive property with the planter's mansion.'[8] This succession of buildings began with 'a dwelling house and an overseer's house' as Robertson's map indicates.[9] The former provided Launcelot with his new home and was set away from the main complex to provide some degree of privacy. The overseer's house was between the main house and the manufactory complex, reasonably close to the manufactory to enable him to exert control over the operating hub of the estate, but at sufficient distance to provide a reasonably rewarding lifestyle. Beckford commented that 'The overseer's house is commonly, if the situation will permit it, upon an eminence, and overlooks his offices, the stock-house, the hospital, [...], the cooper's, wheelwright's, carpenter's, and blacksmith's shops; and last of all the works...' This was the case at Chiswick, where the overseer's house had a view of these buildings and the works spreading away from it to the west. Beckford described overseer's houses as generally comprising 'a front and back piazza, of a hall in the centre, and of a bed chamber at one end, and of two other smaller apartments that are taken from the pent-house of the gallery behind'.[10]

Moving west along the ribbon development was the accommodation and office for the small team of two or three 'bookkeepers', planters who assisted the overseer in running the estate.[11] The bookkeepers' office was close to, but detached from, their accommodation. The latter was a one-storey high wooden house, which was 'raised from the ground several feet for the benefit of coolness' on stone foundations, with its windows covered with 'sashes'. It was fronted by a 'piazza' that ran its length and

---

7   Morris Bent, 'A "Royal American"', *Journal of the Society for Army Historical Research* Vol. 1, No. 3 (1922), pp. 98–104, at p. 99. This article would appear to have been written by a later member of the Bent family and seems to have used a family heirloom, now lost, described as 'the clearly written pages of the vellum-bound volume before me, where are entered in the father's hand, his son's letters from the date of his joining in 1800 to that of his untimely death three years later'. See Morris Bent, 'A "Royal American"', *Journal of the Society for Army Historical Research* Vol. 1, No. 1 (1921), pp. 15–20, at p. 15. This source was not specifically identified in the article and has not been located at any public archive.
8   Bent, 'A "Royal American"', p. 99.
9   BLO/MSS.W.Ind.s.18, fol. 105, Townson to Pitcairn & Amos, 27 June 1834; *Morning Herald (London)*, 18 December 1839, p. 8.
10   Beckford, *A descriptive*, pp. 14–15.
11   NRO/MC1519/1/813X9, William Wright to Susanna Wright, Chiswick, 10 April 1825, fol. 8.

contained two parlours and five bedrooms.[12] As one bookkeeper noted pithily in the 1820s when he arrived and saw his accommodation, 'I will not be hurt by very luxurious living.'[13]

The basic role of bookkeepers was 'to see the negroes do their work properly'. Operating as supervisors, their roles varied across the year. In the period while the cane was growing, 'out of crop' as it was termed, the bookkeepers had to 'attend to the stock or the negroes working in the field'. This role was delineated by the strict racial hierarchy, since 'of course, in this country a white is not expected to work with his hand (at least not on Estates)'. In this supervisory role the bookkeeper 'has to walk behind them and if he sees any of them slow, or doing their work bad, he points it out to the driver', this latter person being an enslaved worker responsible for direct control of the gang. Overall, the bookkeeper's life 'out of crop' at Chiswick was judged to be 'not too harassing'. During crop, however, life was more rigorous. Alongside overseeing the harvest, the bookkeepers had to supervise the labourers who toiled in the boiling and distilling houses and any bookkeeper was expected 'to make good sugar & rum before they get any increase in salary'. Where larger estates might have five or six bookkeepers, Chiswick had a small team of two or three. This meant that they were required to work night shifts in the boiling and distilling houses several days per week.[14]

Along the higher ground to the west were the two mills, 'not unpleasingly breaking a most romantic prospect'.[15] Bent's description suggests that the sugar works were located centrally in the estate and as closely as the landscape allowed to the cane fields. This was normal since such proximity minimised the costs and time expended in transporting cane from the fields to the mill. In the 1790s, and indeed for the next fifty years, cane transportation at Chiswick was by cattle-drawn wains, which limited the cane supply area.[16] Decisions regarding the size of the cane supply area and the positioning of the sugar works were also affected by the capacity of the sugar factory, and the factory position was, in turn, affected by the availability of power. In many places across Jamaica, animal-powered mills were replaced or augmented by water-mills through the eighteenth century, and a few estates used windmills. There were two rivulets running through the Chiswick estate, but they were not of adequate size to provide power.[17] This meant that unlike like some surrounding estates in St Thomas-in-the-East, such as the neighbouring Dalvey and the Holland estate, there was no watermill. Nor was there any use of aqueducts to improve water supply at Chiswick, as there was at Belvedere.[18] Chiswick's manufacturing processes were powered by a cattle mill and the 'breeze mill', which was built of stone and resembled

---

[12] NRO/MC1519/1/813X9, William Wright to Susanna Wright, Chiswick, 13 January 1825, fol. 6; William Wright to Susanna Wright, Chiswick, 10 April 1825, fol. 1.

[13] NRO/MC1519/1/813X9, William Wright to Susanna Wright, 15 May 1825, fol. 2.

[14] NRO/MC1519/1/813X9, William Wright to Susanna Wright, 10 April 1825, fol. 8.

[15] Bent, 'A "Royal American"', p. 99.

[16] BLO/MSS.W.Ind.s.18, fol.41, Forsyth, and Townson to Pitcairn & Amos, 16 and 24 August 1832.

[17] *Morning Herald (London)*, 18 December 1839, p. 8.

[18] James Hakewill, *A picturesque tour of the island of Jamaica* (London, 1825); Frank Cundall, *Historic Jamaica: With Fifty-two Illustrations* (London: Institute of Jamaica, 1915), p. 249.

a 'small English tower mill'.[19] Wind power was an option both because at the location most suitable for the central manufactory the 'elevation is good', and the land to the south sloped gently downwards from the centre of the estate to the sea, providing a reasonably reliable breeze.[20]

The other essential buildings for manufacturing sugar and rum were then placed close to these sources of power. Alongside the mills, there was a boiling house and a curing house, which contained the 'boiling and curing still' along with all 'the necessary utensils for the manufacture of sugar'.[21] There were also multiple 'trash houses', where the rubbish left over from sugar production was placed.[22] Trash houses were used to store and dry the crushed canes for use as fuel in the boiling house furnaces. Because trash houses were a great fire risk, they were generally placed on the extremity of the works, if possible, separated from it by a stream. Alongside these workspaces, and running towards the east, Chiswick also had other necessary elements to allow its population to operate. As the planter William Beckford suggested in 1790, in general, the central complex would have 'a stable and a corn-house, a kitchen, a waste-house, a buttery, and a store, with pig-sties [*sic*], a poultry-yard, a pigeon house' and these could all be found at Chiswick.[23]

The final element in the layout was the workers' village. Jamaican workers usually lived in detached houses or huts rather than in barracks, in contrast to enslaved communities elsewhere in the Americas.[24] Since the enslaved workers spent long hours in the factories, the location of the sugar works was the crucial criterion in any decision about the situation of the workers' village. The workers needed to be close to the sugar works to maximise efficiency at the busiest time of the year – because the field workers staffed the mills at night after working in the fields during the day. Likewise, the estate's tradesmen lived and worked near the factory to ensure repairs and maintenance could be carried through swiftly.[25]

In his 1801 letter George Bent stated that 'the little negro town' was 'on a hillock to the left' and noted that the worker village was well ordered and organised, with the houses 'neatly arranged, and shaded from the heat of a vertical sun by a pillared row of cocoa-nut trees'. He went on to observe that 'Below it in the same direction, are the sugar works; and beyond, on higher ground again, is the mill'.[26] Since the two mills at Chiswick were in a straight line running south-west from the overseer's house, and as Bent was describing the estate with his back to the sea, this suggests that the 'town' was to the west of the main house and the overseer's house. This conforms with Higman's analysis of estate maps which has shown that between 1760 and 1860 there was an average distance between works and village of 384 yards, as

---

[19] NRO/MC1519/1/813X9, William Wright to Susanna Wright, Chiswick, 10 April 1825, fol. 2.
[20] BLO/MSS.W.Ind.s.19, fol. 130, Townson to Steward & Westmoreland, 18 January 1839; *Morning Herald (London)*, 18 December 1839, p. 8.
[21] Morning Herald (London), 18 December 1839, p. 8.
[22] BLO/MSS.W.Ind.s.17, 1816–1832, fol. 148, Forsyth to Pitcairn & Amos, 13 August 1830.
[23] Beckford, *A descriptive*, p. 15; NRO/MC1519/1/813X9, William Wright to Susanna Wright, Chiswick, 10 April 1825, fol. 1.
[24] Higman, *Jamaica Surveyed*, pp. 257 and 260.
[25] BLO/MSS.W.Ind.s.18, fol. 43; Forsyth to Pitcairn & Amos, 10 October 1832.
[26] Bent, 'A "Royal American"', p. 99.

opposed to a distance between great house and village of 418 yards. On average, the works covered seven acres, the great house three acres, and the village eleven acres. The exact layout varied according to local conditions, but Higman suggests that the works, village, and great house 'were typically located at the points of a triangle very nearly equilateral in shape and fell within a circle with a radius of only 250 yards'.[27] Bent's letter suggests that the sugar works sat south of the village and to the west of the houses – with each of these locations forming the approximate 'points of a triangle' that Higman identifies.

The extensive writings and advice on sugar cultivation that Launcelot would have read in England before departure suggested that the greatest efficiency for an estate was achieved when the sugar works were located centrally, and when there was a degree of overall symmetry in the layout of estate buildings and crops. As Thomas Roughley explained in 1823, 'Whether on a level or a hilly estate, the great utility of a central situation to place the manufacturing houses upon, must be apparent to every[one] interested in such an undertaking.'[28] The works–village–great house complex provided the central business point of the estate, and the rest of the estate was then organised to attempt to maximise profits in relation to that business core. Of course, estate shape, topography, and soil type made each location unique, but owners aspired to situate the primary crop cane fields closest to the main complex, with the fields for the food crops slightly further out.[29] Higman's analysis of plantation maps showed that the average distance from the works to the furthest cane field was 1,320 yards, to the furthest pasture was 1,610 yards, and to the furthest provision ground was 1,727 yards.[30]

Looking north from the main house's balconies Bent recorded that 'The rising grounds opposite are clothed, from the valley upwards, with sugar canes, now flourishing in verdant beauty, the crop season being just completed.'[31] In addition, there was also cane land to the south of the central complex where the fields were 'flat along the seashore.'[32] Exact areas of land in cane are not recorded until the 1830s but in 1786 there were around 254 acres in plant canes and ratoon at Worthy Park and, as been stated earlier, Higman's findings suggest that in the 1790s perhaps 276 acres were in plant at Chiswick.[33]

---

[27] Higman, *Jamaica Surveyed*, pp. 81–82. For more on villages, see Douglas V. Armstrong, *The Old Village and the Great House: An Archaeological and Historical Examination of Drax Hall Plantation, St Ann's Bay, Jamaica* (Urbana, IL: University of Illinois Press, 1990), and B. W. Higman, *Montpelier, Jamaica: A Plantation Community in Slavery and Freedom, 1739–1912* (Kingston, Jamaica: University of the West Indies Press, 1998).

[28] Roughley, *Jamaica*, p. 82.

[29] For provision crops, see John H. Parry, 'Plantation and Provision Ground: An Historical Sketch of the Introduction of Food Crops into Jamaica', *Revista de Historia de América* (1955), pp. 1–20.

[30] Higman, *Jamaica Surveyed*, p. 82.

[31] Bent, 'A "Royal American"', p. 99.

[32] NRO/MC1519/1/813X9, William Wright to Susanna Wright, Chiswick, 10 April 1825, fols 6–7.

[33] Craton and Walvin, *A Jamaican*, p. 171; Higman, 'The Spatial', pp. 17–39, at p. 31.

As time progressed and he gained experience, Launcelot would come to understand the difference between the planted and ratoon cane. The former was newly
planted in the current season and raised from seeds or seedlings. Ratoon cane was
the result of a method of propagation in which subterranean buds on the stubble (the
part of the cane left underground after harvesting) were left to regrow and produce
a succeeding crop, called the 'ratoon' or the 'stubble crop'. The first crop was called
'the plant', the second was called the 'first ratoon', the third was called the 'second
ratoon', and so on. Ratooning had the advantage of reducing the cost of cultivation
because the ratoon did not need new seed, nor extensive preparation of the land.
It also resulted in the cane ripening early, a month or so before the planted cane,
which increased the effective manufacturing period for the estate, again enhancing
production. Ratooning had limitations, however, with a decline in cane yield occurring as time progressed, especially with poor ratoon management. At Chiswick the
ratooning period varied between three to five years.[34]

Aside from the cane lands there were also provision grounds, where the enslaved
workers were allowed to grow their own produce. A letter from 1833 confirms that
there were provision grounds used to provide 'for people' but does not provide exact
details of their location or size. However, it stated that in 1833 this land together with
'ruinate & woods' covered 348 acres.[35] Ruinate was land previously cultivated that
had been abandoned and reverted to bush. With no details for earlier periods, we
must estimate their extent in the 1790s. Higman has argued that the area of provision
grounds in Jamaica increased from a mean of 50 acres in the 1760s to a peak of 366
acres around 1800. His work suggests that between 1790 and 1799, on average, about
12 per cent of a Jamaican sugar estate was woodland, 4 per cent was ruinate, and
29 per cent was provision grounds.[36] Applying these percentages to Chiswick's 1,148
acres would suggest that there was 138 acres of woodland, 46 acres of ruinate, and 333
acres of provision grounds, totalling 517 acres. This estimated figure of 333 acres for
Chiswick's provision grounds is close to the average provided by Higman's research
and, therefore, seems a reasonable assessment.

Higman found that these provision grounds tended to be 'pressed to the limits
of the plantation' and so they may have lain to the north of the works–village–great
house complex, where the ground became more rugged.[37] Wherever they were
located, the presence of these provision grounds suggests that the Burtons, or John
Vernon, had followed the precepts of the Consolidated Slave Act in 1781. This was
passed in response to abolitionist pressure and had recommended improvements in
the quality and quantity of food given to slaves, along with their clothing, as well as
lessening of punishments and attempts to improve the birth rate. Clauses two and
three of the Act required planters to provide their workers with provision acres,
along with sufficient time to tend them.[38]

[34]   NRO/MC1519/1/813X9, William Wright to Susanna Wright, Chiswick, 10 April 1825, fol. 2.
[35]   BLO/MSS.W.Ind.s.18, fol.73, Townson to Pitcairn & Amos, 5 August 1833.
[36]   Higman, 'The Spatial', pp. 26 and 31.
[37]   Higman, 'The Spatial', pp. 30–32.
[38]   Stephen Fuller (agent for the island of Jamaica), *The New Act of Assembly of the Island of
      Jamaica* (London: R. White, 1789).

Around 250 acres was used for pasture for the cattle and other animals, this was probably around the separated parcel to the west of the main complex, where the presence of other pens suggest the land was more suitable for such uses. To the south there was the 'swamp between the sea beach and the cane field', the Great Morass, where the people of Chiswick supplemented their diet by foraging for 'crabs, oyster, fish & etc.'; although this area technically belonged to Dalvey.[39] There were about three hundred acres to the north of the cane fields, nearly one-third of the estate, which was 'rude wild wasteland and very mountainous' and unusable for cultivation.[40] There was also some 'mountain land', which was unsuitable for cane, but which 'abounds in food', which lay seven miles to the north-east of the main estate and was occupied by a group of Maroons who paid a small rent.[41]

Having acquainted himself with the layout, Launcelot's next task was to learn how to cultivate sugar. The soil on the Chiswick estate was 'a poor dry soil', light and gravelly in consistency, which was susceptible to drought and periods of low rainfall and did not produce sugar and rum with the 'finer qualities'.[42] Over the next few decades the Burtons would be continually reminded, to their chagrin, that 'Chiswick sugars are of an inferior quality and colour' and so could not be expected to obtain the higher market prices that some other producers received.[43] Indeed, at times when the market was slow, the London agents would receive sugar from Chiswick and tell the Burtons that because of 'the difficulty of selling such ordinary dark sugar as comes from Chiswick' their produce was remaining unsold at even low prices.[44]

The soil preferred a steady level of rainfall. Too little rain made the land increasingly unproductive, and drought would often delay the crop. Experience taught men like Lumsden the level and timings of the 'usual rains', and so enabled them to manage the timing of cultivation and harvest, but Launcelot needed to acquire this understanding.[45] Chiswick was also prone, however, to sudden, prolonged downpours, which were a boon and a problem.[46] Such rains 'set the sap of the canes in motion' and so were beneficial to production.[47] Indeed, during periods of drought, the hope of the managers was that 'Should we get some heavy rain, which we have a right to expect, it will make a great difference in their [the canes] appearance

---

[39] BLO/MSS.W.Ind.s.17, fol. 162, Forsyth to Mayhew, 11 April 1831; BLO/MSS.W.Ind.s.18, fol. 36, Pitcairn & Amos to Mayhew, 9 August 1832; BLO/MSS.W.Ind.s.17, fol. 163, J. Bell to Mayhew, 8 April 1831.

[40] NRO/MC1519/1/813X9, William Wright to Susanna Wright, Chiswick, 14 February 1825, fol. 5; BLO/MSS.W.Ind.s.18, fol. 73, Townson to Pitcairn & Amos, 5 August 1833.

[41] WM/SC/01621, Townson to Mayhew, 7 August 1842, and 24 June 1842.

[42] BLO/MSS.W.Ind.s.17, fol. 98 and fol. 117, Forsyth to Pitcairn & Amos, August 1829, and 15 November 1829; BLO/MSS.W.Ind.s.18, fol. 3, Forsyth to Pitcairn & Amos, 20 November 1831.

[43] BLO/MSS.W.Ind.s.17, fol. 116, Pitcairn & Amos to Farr, 28 January 1830.

[44] BLO/MSS.W.Ind.s.17, fol. 174, Pitcairn &Amos to Mayhew, 1 July 1831.

[45] For example, BLO/MSS.W.Ind.s.17, fol. 162, Forsyth to Pitcairn & Amos, 14 March 1831.

[46] BLO/MSS.W.Ind.s.17, fol. 98 and fol. 117, Letters from Forsyth to Pitcairn & Amos, August 1829 and 15 November 1829.

[47] BLO/MSS.W.Ind.s.18, fol. 29, Townson to Pitcairn & Amos, 13 October 1833.

before crop.'[48] Nonetheless, 'late rain' was undesirable as it made 'the produce so dark' because it 'retarded the ripening of the cane'.[49] Likewise, too much rain affected the production of sugars adversely and 'operated against their manufacture'.[50]

William Wright, a Norfolk farmer who worked on the estate in the mid-1820s, described the cultivation of the sugar cane at Chiswick in marvellous detail, and it would have been little different twenty-five years earlier under Launcelot. The field labourers were organised into the two 'gangs' that carried out the hard labour in the fields. The first gang of the most able men and women were required to carry out the most difficult and hazardous work in the fields, six days per week, from sunrise to sunset. There were two planting seasons: 'Spring', which was from March to May, and 'Fall' which was from August to December. The cane, Wright told his mother, was planted in rows, the land having been 'prepared in trenches similar to the Northumberland mode of growing turnips, but the trenches are wider'. Manure was placed in the trenches at the minimum rate of fifty pounds per acre, before the 'soft top of the old cane', specifically the 'first few joints' was planted in it, this was called 'holing'. The soil was then drawn up until the land was flat and irrigation channels were placed at right angles to the planted ridges to deal with heavy rain. Cane planted in the spring took thirteen months to get to maturity, that planted in fall took an extra two months. The rainy season generally lasted from June to September, and during this period there was a constant need to clear the land of weeds, a labour-intensive task.[51]

This work was carried out by a workforce that was probably around 280 in number. Within the workforce there was a leadership group including a senior man, called the 'head driver', along with other 'drivers', and around fifteen skilled workers or 'tradesmen' such as carpenters and coopers. There were a small number of domestic staff, and twenty to thirty children under the age of six, who were deemed too young to work in the fields. In the normal course of events around 7 to 8 per cent of the workforce on the estate would be too old or too unwell to work.[52] Some of the people had been at Chiswick for decades, like the sixty-year-old Lucy, and others in their fifties, such as Monimia, Mary, Esther, Scotland, Sandy, and Hereford. There were, of course, younger women and men such as the thirty-year-old Quasheba, alongside Mary Ann, Electra, Sally, Vernon, Homer, and Mandrake.[53] In 1817 44 per cent of the estate's population was African, imported via the slave trade, rather than native-born 'Creoles', which suggests that when Launcelot arrived at least 60 per cent of the enslaved population would have been

---

[48] BLO/MSS.W.Ind.s.18, fol. 87, Forsyth to Pitcairn & Amos, 9 July 1832.

[49] BLO/MSS.W.Ind.s.18, fol. 93, Townson to Pitcairn & Amos, 13 December 1833.

[50] BLO/MSS.W.Ind.s.18, fol. 29, Forsyth to Pitcairn & Amos, 9 July 1832.

[51] NRO/MC1519/1/813X9, William Wright to Susanna Wright, Chiswick, 10 April 1825, fols 6–7.

[52] These estimates have been calculated by simple extrapolation from a later breakdown of the workforce (1834). The proportions of workers were calculated as a percentage of the 1834 workforce and then that percentage applied to the estimated workforce figure to reflect the much greater number of workers on the estate in the 1790s; for the 1834 list, see BLO/MSS.W.Ind.s.18, fol. 111; Townson to Pitcairn & Amos, 10 August 1834. See also NRO/MC1519/1/813X9, William Wright to Susanna Wright, 10 April 1825, fols 6–7.

[53] NA/T/71/145, Slave Registers 1817, fols 850–854.

African. There is no record of where they might have originated or of their physical appearance, meaning their tribal background cannot be determined.[54] Nonetheless, since most of the enslaved people imported into Jamaica in the period 1792 to 1807 were from the Bight of Biafra or Central Africa, this would have been the likely origin of most of the Africans on the estate.[55]

Wright recorded the gruelling work regimen in place on the estate in the 1820s. This was likely to have been even harder during Launcelot's time at Chiswick, as by the later date it may have been made less arduous by the impact of policies of amelioration. Wright recorded that the gangs 'turn out at daybreak' and then worked until ten o'clock, when they 'are allowed half an hour to breakfast'. The people were then required to work until half past twelve 'when a conch shell which sounds like a harvest horn is blown from the house and heard all over the estate' and the people broke from work for two hours. The conch shell sounded the return to work until nightfall. The undercurrent of his description was clearly that of coercion. The people at Chiswick worked if they were required and not a moment longer. Wright noted that at the sound of the conch shell for lunch 'they instantly leave working' and returned only at the sound of it after the break. The regime was supported by the threat and reality of the whip, or as Wright put it euphemistically to his mother, any late arrival to 'turn out' was met with 'a pretty severe argument'.[56] In the face of this, any illusions that Launcelot Burton might have held about the reality and brutality of the business of slavery will have disappeared very soon after he had arrived.

Harvest took place in the early months of the year, running from January to June, although the aim at Chiswick was to clear the canes before 'the May rains' arrived and 'cut up' the ground. If the crop was not in by this point, the labourers had to work 'through wet and dirt' to finish the harvest.[57] The first gang would cut the row by row, using a 'bill'. The work gang 'cut it at the top of the root (or slub as it may be called), trim off the trash and top and throw it behind them, others follow and tie them up in small bundles with part of the top'.[58] Throughout the harvest, the labourers were in the fields cutting the canes from dawn to dusk, and when the light failed some were sent to the mill to work through the night.[59] The work was organised in such a fashion that it was 'chiefly women who cut canes in crop time, while the men boiled the sugar and attended wains & stock'.[60] The cut canes from the fields were carried in ox-drawn wains from the fields, staffed by 'wainmen' who usually had 'boys to assist'. The work-rate was ferocious and left the enslaved workers deprived of sleep and vulnerable to accidents.

The cut canes were then placed in a stack near the mills and processed. Sugar cane deteriorates within days of harvest meaning that it needed to be at least semi-refined

[54] Hall, *In Miserable*, p. 135.
[55] For African backgrounds, see John Thornton, *Africa and Africans in the Making of the Atlantic World, 1400–1800*, 2nd edn (Cambridge: Cambridge University Press, 1998), chaps 2–4.
[56] NRO/MC1519/1/813X9, William Wright to Susanna Wright, Chiswick, 15 May 1825, fol. 5.
[57] BLO/MSS.W.Ind.s.18, fol. 131, Townson to Pitcairn & Amos, 10 February 1835.
[58] NRO/MC1519/1/813X9, William Wright to Susanna Wright, 10 April 1825, fol. 2.
[59] BLO/MSS.W.Ind.s.18, fol. 129, Townson to Pitcairn & Amos, 22 January 1835.
[60] BLO/MSS.W.Ind.s.18, fol. 119, Townson to Pitcairn & Amos, 25 August 1838.

on site. At the cattle mill four pairs of oxen were required to provide the power for the processes, which was a constant drain on livestock health. The windmill required no animals, but production was dependent on the weather. Inside each mill the layout was the same. An axletree turned a large wooden post, encased in iron, in the centre of the mill. Some eight feet from the bottom there was a wheel, which turned large iron-covered rollers on each side. Canes were placed between one roller and the post and drawn out between the other roller and the post. The juice extracted by this crushing fell into a 'receiver', which was covered by a grate to prevent trash falling into it and was transferred to the boiling house by lead gutters.[61] Since the mills were on land above the boiling house, this transfer was done by gravity, an advantage since some estates – where the mill was below the level of the boiling house – needed a pump to do this. Experts recommended that the mill was close to the boiling house to reduce the gutter length.[62] Operations in Chiswick's mill were run by an experienced man called the 'Boatswain', who was assisted by two 'mill feeders' and two 'cane carriers' who moved the cane through the process. Around five 'cattle boys' looked after the cattle and another cleaned.[63]

The boiling house was a large stone building 'open like an English brew house'. Once in the boiling house the juice was stored initially in lead-covered wooden receivers known as clarifiers or cold receivers. It was then tempered with lime, which was imported from Britain, to remove dirt. The juice was then boiled in two 'large copper pans' before being drawn into a series of four coppers, of decreasing size, which were set in brickwork and heated by furnaces situated outside the boiling house. The sugar granulated in the final, smallest copper or 'tache' and was then placed in wooden boxes called coolers.[64] This process was under the control of four skilled workers – called the 'head boiler' and the 'under boilers' – who ensured it was carried through effectively. The fuel for the boilers was brought from the trash houses by 'trash carriers' and loaded by the 'stoker'. The pace of work was relentless. The coppers were started at six o'clock on Sunday night and worked non-stop until daybreak the following Sunday. The boilermen worked all day and every third night, in harsh conditions, 'for six months in the year near large fires amidst the steam of sugar and rum'. Workers taken straight from a day's labour in the fields covered the other nights in the cycle.[65]

The cooled sugar was placed next into hogsheads, and these were placed on wooden beams which spanned the curing house, another 'long stone building'. It was here that the molasses and treacle was drained off via holes in the bottom of the hogsheads. This process increased the drying time by five weeks or so. The molasses fell into a receiver and was moved via a pipe to the distilling house, which was

[61] NRO/MC1519/1/813X9, William Wright to Susanna Wright, 10 April 1825, fol. 2.

[62] Roughley, *The Jamaican*, pp. 189–204.

[63] BLO/MSS.W.Ind.s.18, fol. 129, Townson to Pitcairn & Amos, 22 January 1835.

[64] Zahedieh suggests that a typical seventeenth-century sugar factory housed five coppers, with the largest containing 150 gallons, and two small stills, embodying around 10 hundred-weight (0.5 tons) of copper; Nuala Zahedieh, 'Colonies, Copper, and the Market for Inventive Activity in England and Wales, 1680–1730', *Economic History Review* Vol. 66 (2013), pp. 805–25, p. 811.

[65] NRO/MC1519/1/813X9, William Wright to Susanna Wright, 10 April 1825, fol. 3 and fol. 11.

operated by the 'stillermen'. Likewise, the 'skimmings' taken off in the boiling house were taken by pipe to the distilling house. Both were placed in a large vat, were 'well stirred up' and then left to ferment in stone or wooden cisterns. After a few days standing, the contents were distilled and run off to produce 'low wine' and then distilled again to produce rum. The consensus in Jamaica was that an excellent crop was 2 hogsheads of sugar per acre, but this was only achieved with the first two crops on the best land. At Chiswick the third crop often required three acres for a hogshead. A crop usually took five to seven months to be taken in, and in that time required 'all your hands'.[66]

When the sugar was fully cured, the hogsheads were carted to a wharf and shipped. One quirk of Chiswick's location as a coastal estate was its possession of its own wharf, which was located on the coast to the south, in the small twenty-two-acre piece of land separated from the main parcel by Rocky Point and Fairfield Pens.[67] Shipping the sugar and rum was the responsibility of the attorney, and for men like Lumsden, who had lived many years on the island a network of connections existed to enable them to facilitate this process. Launcelot, again, needed time to create such networks, although he was able to work with Lumsden in the interim. The tendency was for the estate to ship its produce with the same captains and vessels year after year. Examples of such long-standing partners in the included Captain Henry Wood of the *Nisbet*, Captain John Paules of the *Queen*, and Captain John Picke of the *Martin*.[68] Such partnerships were based on trust and a record of reliability built up over time.

Aside from the actual physical arrangements for shipping, Launcelot also had to learn how to provide the paperwork required to support the process. 'Bills of lading' listing the number of hogsheads of sugar and puncheons of rum on each ship had to be made out prior to each shipment and then were sent ahead of the ship by the packet, this enabled the agents in London to arrange for insurance before sailing and also allowed them to advise the proprietors of the situation.[69] The dependable ships' captains were also entrusted with valuable private correspondence and packages that were felt to be too important to send via the packet.[70] Nonetheless, Launcelot had to learn to use the faster packets in an agile fashion to communicate swiftly with London and his family when required.[71] Moreover, he had to learn how to obtain money to enable him to pay for goods and services on the island, using Bills of Exchange drawn against his father and uncle, via Maitlands in London.[72]

---

[66] NRO/MC1519/1/813X9, William Wright to Susanna Wright, 10 April 1825, fol. 3. For other mention of these buildings and procedures, see BLO/MSS.W.Ind.s.17, fol. 162, Forsyth to Mayhew, 11 April 1831; BLO/MSS.W.Ind.s.18, fol.12, Forsyth to Pitcairn & Amos, 15 January 1832; fol. 46, Pitcairn & Amos to Mayhew, 11 March 1833; fol. 105, Townson to Pitcairn & Amos, 27 June 1834; fol. 129, Townson to Pitcairn & Amos, 22 January 1835.

[67] BLO/MSS.W.Ind.s.18, fol. 111, Forsyth to Pitcairn & Amos, 29 June 1834.

[68] JA/1B/11/4/38, fol. 204, Crop Return.

[69] BLO/MSS.W.Ind.s.17, 1816–1832, fol. 7, Pitcairn & Amos to Farr, 5 January 1829; fol. 45, Pitcairn & Amos, 31 March 1829.

[70] BLO/MSS.W.Ind.s.18, fol. 33, Pitcairn & Amos to Mayhew, 5 October 1836.

[71] BLO/MSS.W.Ind.s.17, 1816–1832, fol. 127 Pitcairn & Amos to Mayhew, 22 March 1830.

[72] BLO/MSS.W.Ind.s.17, 1816–1832, fol. 166, Forsyth to Pitcairn & Amos, 13 March 1831.

Related to this was the matter of supplies for the estate. No Jamaican estate was self-sufficient, even a proportion of the food for the workforce needed to be imported from Britain, and Chiswick was no exception. The attorney had to ensure that the order for the year's supplies was made out and sent to London in good time, to guarantee that the supplies were shipped back before essentials ran out. The list for any year was usually sent to Britain in the preceding autumn, and the supplies were purchased by the London agents before being shipped back to Jamaica over the next few months. The costs for these purchases were placed to the account of the Burtons by Maitlands and this debt was then cleared in the new financial year, normally around April.[73] The supplies required were many and various. They included food items such as barrels of herring, pork, olive oil, salt, and oatmeal. There was also equipment needed for sugar production and the maintenance of the estate, such as replacement barrels for sugar, cooper's nails, rivets, puncheon hoops, axles, blacksmith's coal, glue, temper lime, paint, lead, and paintbrushes. There were also personal items for the workforce, such as hats, coats, needles, thread, candles, soap, hairbrushes, and even quills.[74]

The estate also required animals to help with all its operations. Horses, mules, and oxen were needed to pull wagons, supply fertiliser, and power the cattle mill. Chiswick had pasture and woodland that allowed it to meet some of these livestock requirements but was not self-sufficient in this respect. Consequently, Launcelot had to learn how to purchase extra livestock, foodstuffs, and fuel from the owners of the nearby ranches or pens that had been developed in areas unsuitable for sugar cane cultivation, such as the Fairfield Pen to the west.

Table 4 summarises the results of Launcelot's first few years of activity. Carrington has calculated the average price for sugar from Jamaica per hogshead in 1800 was £24 but does not provide a figure for 1799 or 1801. Comparison with produce from elsewhere can fill the gap. The price per hogshead from St Vincent was the same in 1799 and 1800, while the price from Tobago was 10 per cent higher in 1800. Both prices dropped in 1801.[75] The assumption made here, therefore, is that the price for sugar from Jamaica remained the same for these three years, at £24 per hogshead, which seems reasonable since it only rose to £25 in 1802. The costs have been assumed to be unchanged from those levels used in previous calculations.

Launcelot's first full year at the estate, 1799, saw an excellent crop produced, of 364 hogsheads of sugar and 146 puncheons of rum. His second year, 1800, saw a substantial fall in production, to 240 hogsheads of sugar and 106 puncheons of rum. This appears to have been a result of a hurricane in October 1800.[76] This fall in production coincided with a fall in sugar prices stemming from the collapse of the Hamburg speculative bubble. The consequence of this was a marked reduction in

---

[73]   BLO/MSS.W.Ind.s.17, 1816-1832, fol. 53, Pitcairn & Amos to Mayhew, 6 April 1829; fol. 102 Pitcairn & Amos to Mayhew, 9 November 1829; BLO/MSS.W.Ind.s.18, fol. 33, Forsyth to Pitcairn & Amos, 12 November 1832.

[74]   BLO/MSS.W.Ind.s.18, fol. 78, Pitcairn to Mayhew 12 October 1833; BLO/MSS.W.Ind.s.19, fol. 32, Pitcairn & Amos to Mayhew, 23 September 1836.

[75]   Carrington, 'Management', p. 50.

[76]   Chenoweth, 'A Reassessment', table IV.

Table 4. Estimated net profit for Chiswick estate, 1799–1801.*

Crop year	Hogsheads of sugar sold in London	Estimated price per hogsheads of sugar (£ sterling)	Estimated gross income (£ sterling)	Insurance costs at 11% (£ sterling)	Factor costs at 2½% (£ sterling)	Freight (9s per cwt) (£ sterling)	Estimated net profit on sugar (after fixed expenses)	Net profit (with rum at £15 per puncheon)
1799	364	24	£8,736	(£961)	(£218)	(£2,765)	£2,012	£3,902
1800	240	24	£5,760	(£634)	(£144)	(£1,823)	£379	£1,365
1801	228	24	£5,472	(£602)	(£137)	(£1,732)	£221	£1,305
								£6,572

* Sources: JA/1B/11/4/26, fol. 22; 1B/11/4/27, fol. 186; 1B/11/4/29, fol. 203.

profits. The results for the 1801 crop were also poor, with only 228 hogsheads of sugar being made, meaning that the eventual profit for 1801 would be only £1,305. The average profit for these three years was £2,191, around 38 per cent of the average for the preceding decade.

Launcelot was facing real problems in Jamaica. What he might have done in response cannot be known, since Jamaica was an unforgiving and harsh mistress. As the sun rose over Chiswick estate in the last week of August 1801, Launcelot set off from his house to Kingston, where he met with William Lumsden and other friends such as George Bent. On Wednesday 26 August, while in the port, Launcelot 'fell a victim to that relentless fever from which even the most temperate is not exempt'. His condition deteriorated rapidly and by Saturday it was clear to his friends that he was not going to recover. The people who knew him came to visit him as his life ebbed away. Bent recorded that 'I bade him good-bye on Saturday night!' The fever reached its deadly apogee on Sunday, and in the Jamaican darkness, during the early hours of Monday 30 August, Launcelot Burton passed away. He was twenty-six years old.[77]

---

[77] Bent, 'A 'Royal American'', p. 99; *Morning Post*, 'Deaths at Jamaica in August', 26 October 1801, p. 4; *Gentleman's Magazine*, Volume 71, Part 2 (1801), p. 1212.

4

'A MOST UNEXPECTED AND SEVERE STROKE OF FATE': A NEW GENERATION AND ABOLITION, 1802–1815

The news of Launcelot's death, described as a 'most unexpected and severe stroke of fate to his kinsfolk and friends', took a month or so to reach Thomas and Elizabeth Burton in Norfolk via the packet. By that time Launcelot had been buried in Kingston parish churchyard, with his tombstone describing him as 'Launcelot Burton, Esq. – Attorney to Chiswick'.[1] The deadly possibilities that could befall those travelling to Jamaica were not a secret from those who remained in Norfolk, since the deaths in the colony were related with efficiency in the newspapers in both London and Norfolk for their readers to contemplate.[2] The reality was that such sudden deaths among young and otherwise healthy people in Jamaica were common. Tropical diseases such as yellow fever ravaged those who arrived on the island from elsewhere in the world, and little could be done in the face of their depredations. George Bent recorded the devastating toll of disease upon his regiment while it was stationed in Jamaica, noting that 'We buried five officers in one week recently.'[3] Bent would die from the fever only two years after Launcelot.[4]

With Launcelot's sudden death looming over their thoughts, the family reverted to absentee ownership and no Burton visited Chiswick, or Jamaica, again. Lumsden resumed full control of Jamaican operations as attorney.[5] As Table 5 shows, after the poor years of 1800 and 1801, production levels recovered and rose to 286 hogsheads in 1803. There was a fall to 186 hogsheads the following year, which seems most likely to have been the consequence of a hurricane that struck Jamaica on 18–19 August 1804.[6] The harvest of 1805 was a mammoth 338 hogsheads, the largest crop since 1794, reflecting a bumper harvest across the island whose size was not exceeded until 1937.[7]

---

[1] James Henry Lawrence-Archer, *Monumental Inscriptions of the British West* (London: Chatto & Windus, 1875), p. 139.

[2] See, for example, the reports of the deaths of James Sharpe, *Norfolk Chronicle*, Saturday 29 July 1826, p. 2; Samuel Beck of Lynn, *Norfolk Chronicle*, Saturday 11 July 1829, p. 2.

[3] Bent, 'A 'Royal American'', p. 100.

[4] Bent, 'A 'Royal American'', p. 15.

[5] JA/1B/11/4/37, fol. 118b; JA/1B/11/4/100, Crop Return, 25 March 1805.

[6] Chenoweth, 'A Reassessment', table IV.

[7] Craton and Walvin, *A Jamaican*, p. 179.

Table 5.   The produce of the Chiswick estate, 1803–1815.[*]

Crop year	Date of return	Hogsheads sugar	Puncheons of rum
1803	2 March 1804	286	120
1804	25 March 1805	186	80
1805	24 March 1806	338	158
1806	21 March 1807	300	147
1807	26 February 1808	272	145
1808	March 1809	274	112
1809	21 February 1810	243	110
1810	22 March 1811	195	90
1811	19 March 1812	179	80
1812	24 March 1813	181	88
1814	23 March 1815	194	97
1815	23 March 1816	180	77

[*]   Sources: JA/1B/11/4/31, fol. 118b; 1B/4/33, fol. 100; 1B/11/4/34, fol. 188; 1B/11/4/36, fol. 100; 1B/11/4/37, fol. 60; 1B/11/4/38, fol. 204; 1B/11/4/40, fol. 93; 1b/11/4/42, fol. 120; 1B/11/4/43, fol. 201; 1B/11/4/45, fol. 117; 1B/11/4/48, fol. 53; 1B/11/4/49, fol. 138; 1B/11/4/51, fol. 34. The returns for 1802 and 1813 have not been located. Tierces appear in the documents from 1809 and have been converted at the ratio of 1½ tierce to 1 hogshead.

Research on other estates has suggested that sugar production was 'robust' across the island in the first decade of the 1800s and this was the case at Chiswick, which averaged 254 hogsheads per year in this time.[8] This average was, nonetheless, 19 per cent under the previous decade's average of 313 hogsheads per annum. By 1815 output had fallen to 180 hogsheads, a decrease of 47 per cent in only ten years. This fall would seem to have been the consequence of several factors. Some were specific to Chiswick and related to the fact that from 1805 onwards the entire management structure of the plantation was altered, first in England and then in Jamaica. The others were more general and applied to most Jamaican plantations in this period: the type of sugar being grown and the abolition of the slave trade in 1807.[9]

The first change was the loss of the oversight of John and Thomas Burton, who died in 1804 and 1805 respectively. With no children or wife, John Burton's short will, only one-page in length, left his brother Thomas £10,000 in cash, while his estates in Devon and his one-third share of Chiswick went to their other brother, Leonard, who lived in Ringstead, Northamptonshire.[10] Leonard had, heretofore, been uncon-

[8]   Dunn, *A Tale*, p. 40.
[9]   For extensive discussion of the problems faced in this period, see Ryden, 'Sugar, Spirits, and Fodder', pp. 41–64.
[10]   NA/PROB11/1411/154, Will of John Burton of Jacobstowe, Devon, 13 July 1804.

nected with the estate and had no other plantation property himself, and so had no experience of running a sugar estate in Jamaica.[11]

This fact became very important after the death of Thomas Burton in 1805, since the division of the estate among Thomas' children meant that the inexperienced Leonard became largest single shareholder in Chiswick. Thomas' will, originally written in 1795, divided his two-thirds of Chiswick amongst his seven surviving children. Having left all his household goods to 'my dear wife Elizabeth' the first and only major asset that Burton described specifically was 'all my part share and interest of and in the plantation or estate called Chiswick in the island of Jamaica'. In this description he included all the land, buildings, cattle, utensils and the 'slaves' in any way connected to his two-thirds share of the estate, anywhere on the island. While the will mentioned other potential assets, mainly different types of financial investments, it did so generically, rather than listing any specifically. Likewise, it did not specifically name any other land or property, not even his residences in Yarmouth and Norwich.[12]

Burton's assets were then placed in a trust and their father's two-thirds of the sugar estate was divided equally among the seven remaining Burton children in equal shares, as tenants-in-common, with the eldest two sons Thomas and Charles as trustees. Henceforth, each of the siblings owned one-seventh of two-thirds of Chiswick, or if Leonard's share was included, each Burton child owned 2/21 of the plantation, while Leonard owned 7/21. The will stipulated that the two-thirds interest in Chiswick could not be sold before the sons had attained the age of twenty-one and, even then, directed that any sale required the 'consent and approbation' in writing of at least two of the sons, excluding Frederick, who was only eight when the will was drafted.[13]

From the proceeds of the trust, including the income from Chiswick, Burton's widow received a substantial annuity of £500 per annum for the rest of her life. The trust was to provide annuities for the children as tenants in common once they had reached the age of twenty-one or, in the case of his daughters, were younger but had married. The eldest son, Thomas Burton, was to receive £200 per year, and the other children £100 per year each. The will specified that the daughters' shares in the trust were to be held 'independent of any husband' and not subject to any marriage settlement. Furthermore, the daughters or their husbands were not allowed to dispose of any of their shares without the consent of all the other siblings.[14]

These events had significant managerial consequences. From the end of 1805 Chiswick had lost the two men who had run it successfully from 1788 and was now in the hands of three untested trustees, Charles, Thomas, and Leonard Burton. Going forward, however, their inexperience in plantation affairs was not as important as their disinterest. Leonard Burton owned one-third of Chiswick outright, and so was

[11] NRO/PD/28/136, Great Yarmouth, St Nicholas, Burial of Thomas Burton, 29 April 1805; *Norfolk Chronicle*, Saturday 27 April 1805, p. 2.

[12] NA/PROB/11/1426/242, Will of Thomas Burton of Norwich, Norfolk, 12 June 1805.

[13] NA/PROB/11/1426/242, Will of Thomas Burton of Norwich, Norfolk, 12 June 1805; Palmer, *Perlustration*, pp. 393–94.

[14] NA/PROB/11/1426/242, Will of Thomas Burton of Norwich, Norfolk, 12 June 1805.

the person who really decided what happened there, but he was far more concerned with running his extensive estates in Northamptonshire and Devon.[15] These large landholdings provided him with a good income and many responsibilities, leaving him with little time to consider affairs in Jamaica.[16]

Likewise, Charles and Thomas – who as trustees made the final decisions with Leonard – were also uninterested in the running of the sugar estate. Thomas had married Mary Watson in 1802 and was busy raising a family.[17] Fond of outdoor activities and sports and, by his own admission, 'not being a man of business', Thomas felt that he lacked the financial skills and shrewdness of his father and shied away from Chiswick's management.[18] Similarly, Charles Fisher Burton preferred other activity to managing the estate's affairs. A captain in the Inniskilling Dragoons, his military duties meant that Charles did not treat Chiswick as a high priority.[19] Finally, Frederick, also an army officer – who was not a trustee in any case – showed no interest in the family sugar estate.[20]

There is no evidence that the Burton sisters were involved in any meaningful managerial decisions regarding Chiswick, and when Harriet married Jarrett Dashwood in 1802, her new husband displayed no interest in the sugar estate.[21] The Dashwood family were wealthy merchants in Norwich, and so had extensive commercial experience. Although Jarrett had been ordained and took over one of the family's livings, he vacated it on his marriage, apparently because he and Harriet had received an income for life.[22] Chiswick was not mentioned in the couple's marriage settlement.[23] Harriet retained the income from Jamaica for her own use during her natural life and, while under property law Jarrett Dashwood had obtained a life interest in his wife's share, he always argued that he took no interest in it. As he explained many years later, 'Mrs Dashwood under her late father's will is sole proprietor of 1/7 of the 2/3rds share of the said Chiswick Estate & it is therein expressly declared that no husband of any of his daughters shall interfere with the said estate.'[24]

[15] 'Parishes: Ringstead', in *A History of the County of Northampton: Volume 4*, ed. L. F Salzman (London: Victoria County History, 1937), pp. 39–44. *British History Online*, accessed 7 February 2023, www.british-history.ac.uk/vch/northants/vol4/pp39-44.

[16] *The Universal British Directory of Trade, Commerce, and Manufacture* (London, 1790), p. 609; 'A Petition of Leonard Burton Esquire, Lord of the Manor of Denford', *Journals of the House of Commons* (London: Order of the House of Commons, 1803).

[17] *Norfolk Chronicle*, 9 October 1802, p. 2.

[18] BLO/MSS.W.Ind.s.17, fols 151–152, Thomas Burton to Mayhew, 11 October 1830.

[19] *Norfolk Chronicle*, 22 March 1806, p. 2.

[20] NRO/Bishop's transcripts, Film number 1278920, Burial of Frederick Burton, 14 October 1818; *Norfolk Chronicle*, 10 October 1818, p. 2.

[21] NRO/ANF/12/43/212, Marriage licence bond: Revd. Jarrett Dashwood and Harriet Burton, Caistor St Edmund, 7 September 1802; NRO/PD/589/5, Marriage of Harriet Burton and Jarret Dashwood, 17 July 1807.

[22] CCEd Person ID: 112456, CCED: Search (theclergydatabase.org.uk), accessed 19 December 2022; NRO/AG/115/233X4, Attested Copy Declaration of Trust as to certain stock in 3% consuls for securing an annuity of £80 to Jarrett Dashwood, 13 October 1802.

[23] BLO/MSS.W.Ind.s.17, fol. 33 Stevens, Wood & Wilkinson to Mayhew, 4 February 1829.

[24] NRO/AG/114/233X4, Attested copy marriage settlement of Revd. Jarrett Dashwood with Harriet Burton of Bracondale, 6 September 1802; BLO/MSS.W.Ind.s.19, fol. 167, Jarrett

Five years after Harriet's nuptials, in 1807, Charlotte Burton married the Reverend James Willins.[25] Unlike Jarrett Dashwood, Willins was not a man of significant means, but was a long-serving clergyman who had been ordained in 1789. At the time of their marriage, he was the rector at St Michael Coslany, Norwich, and later he gained the stipend of nearby Bawburgh, which brought him £40 a year.[26] Willins had gained a life interest in Charlotte's share in Chiswick, and these funds were a significant addition to their income. Like Dashwood, Willins was uninterested in managing the estate and looked only for the annual income payment to arrive. From 1806 onwards, therefore, none of the Burtons, by blood or marriage, were overly attentive to the operation of Chiswick. This was a significant alteration from the tight control maintained over it from 1788 to 1805 by Thomas and John Burton.

At the same time as these changes within the family, there was also gradual alteration in the people employed to run the estate. The experienced Lumsden died around 1807 and appears to have ceased running the plantation before this, since the crop returns of 1805 and 1806 were signed by Robert Anderson, who signed as the 'overseer'.[27] The new attorney was a man named William Holgate.[28] He owned the Windsor Forest sugar estate, which was a similar sized sugar estate to Chiswick and lay fifteen miles to the north.[29] The journey between the estates was difficult, however, requiring a traveller to follow the coast road around the east end of the island. Consequently, it seems that Holgate did not spend significant amounts of time at Chiswick, leaving it largely to Robert Anderson to operate the plantation.

These generational shifts occurred at a tricky moment for planters in general. One problem they faced resulted from the introduction of Bourbon sugar cane in the late eighteenth century. As has already been said, along with many other planters, the Burtons had introduced Bourbon cane to the estate to improve the yield per acre, a common response to the declining soil fertility. During the 1790s this had allowed planters to increase production and so take advantage of the high prices. Over time, however, planters came to realise that Bourbon cane had its drawbacks and as the absentee owner of the Castle Wemyss estate, Gilbert Mathison, put it, 'the Bourbon cane, from which great wealth has been flowing for a long course of years into their pockets, is now degenerated in its character'. Mathison argued that Bourbon cane need active cultivation and regular manuring to yield well.[30] It took time for this issue to be understood by planters and even then, the availability of manure was a logistical problem, requiring active management of the sort that Chiswick now lacked. Chiswick gradually shifted from Bourbon cane to 'violet' cane, but Holgate and his overseers do not seem to have addressed the issue of depleted soil fertility and it was noted in the 1820s that the cane land on Chiswick was not still receiving

---

Dashwood to Mayhew, 27 December 1843.

[25] NRO/PD/28/71, Marriage of Charlotte Burton and James Willins, Great Yarmouth, 3 March 1807.

[26] *Ipswich Journal*, 4 August 1792, p. 4; CCED. Person: Willins, James (1789–1827) CCEd Person ID: 116207; CCED: Persons Index (theclergydatabase.org.uk), accessed 19 December 2022.

[27] JA/1B/11/4/37, fol. 33; JA/1B/11/4/37, fol. 119.

[28] NA/T71/145, Slave Registers 1817, fol. 849.

[29] NA/T/71/145, Slave Registers 1817, fol. 369.

[30] Mathison, *Notices*, pp. 61–65.

sufficient manure because insufficient was available from the livestock on the estate and none was being purchased elsewhere.[31]

Aside from the problems of Bourbon cane, the new generation of Chiswick's owners also faced volatility in the sugar markets. West Indian estates, such as Chiswick, produced a raw brown sugar called muscovado, which was shipped to Britain where sugar bakers refined it further into table sugar. This was a result of mercantilist policies designed to protect British sugar refiners, that enforced a prohibitive duty on all forms of refined colonial sugar, penalising any efforts by planters to improve the quality of their product above the level of muscovado.[32] This had not been a problem during the 1790s, where a general shortage of sugar meant that the 'inferior' muscovado could still command high prices. Problems arose after 1800 when the poorer quality muscovado was pushed out of European markets in the face of strong competition from foreign producers, such as Spanish Cuba, Brazil, and the remaining French West Indian colonies.

The war made things worse since, while the Peace of Amiens eased the situation temporarily, when conflict resumed export markets for Caribbean sugar were lost by actions such as the blockade placed by the British government on the Elbe that lasted from 1803 to 1805.[33] This combination of circumstances meant that muscovado prices peaked at the turn of the century, before dropping well below their half-century linear trend.[34] In home markets that were now awash with sugar, British sugar bakers preferred other types to muscovado, driving its price further downwards. In this already difficult situation Chiswick was trying to sell poorer quality muscovado, meaning that the estate's diminishing amounts of produce were being sold at the lower end of, already depressed, prices.[35]

To make the overall situation even worse, in 1807 Parliament abolished the slave trade in British ships, an event that the abolitionist Thomas Clarkson described as Christianity's greatest triumph.[36] Abolition was not unexpected, and the final passage of the bill had been preceded by twenty-five years of debate on the subject, so the Burtons cannot have been surprised by it. The campaign against the slave trade that had peaked in Norfolk in 1792 was rekindled in the early 1800s. Evidence of renewed support for it can be seen in the years running up to 1807, with the county's newspapers reporting in detail upon the speeches of Wilberforce, parliamentary debates on the subject, and the voting records of MPs and Lords in the Houses of Parliament.[37]

---

[31] WM/SC/01621, Townson to Mayhew, 24 February 1838; NRO/MC1519/1/813X9, William Wright to Susanna Wright, 10 April 1825, fol. 6; 15 May 1825, fol. 3.

[32] W. A. Green, 'The Planter Class and British West Indian Sugar Production, Before and After Emancipation', *The Economic History Review* (1973), pp. 448–63, at p. 463.

[33] Ryden, 'Sugar', p. 52.

[34] Ahmed Reid and David B. Ryden, 'Sugar, Land Markets and the Williams Thesis: Evidence from Jamaica's Property Sales, 1750–1810', *Slavery & Abolition* (2013), pp. 401–24, at p. 418.

[35] BLO/MSS.W.Ind.s.18, fol. 3, Forsyth to Pitcairn & Amos, 20 November 1831.

[36] Thomas Clarkson, *The History of the Abolition of the African Slave-Trade*, 2 vols (1808).

[37] See, for example, *Bury and Norwich Post*, 24 June 1801, p. 2; *Norfolk Chronicle*, 16 June 1804, p. 4; *Norfolk Chronicle*, 9 February 1805, p. 2; *Norfolk Chronicle*, 23 February 1805, p. 1; *Norfolk Chronicle*, 28 June 1806, p. 2; *Norfolk Chronicle*, 14 February 1807, p. 4; *Norfolk Chronicle*, 7 March 1807, p. 4; *Bury and Norwich Post*, 4 February 1807, p. 4.

The quarterly meetings of the Norwich Corporation invariably saw a toast made for the abolition of the trade.[38] Whether the Burtons attended such events is unclear, although they were regularly seen at Yarmouth's social gatherings, but they could not have been unaware of the gathering momentum for abolition.

Once again, there is no evidence that the family spoke publicly against this renewed movement for abolition in any of their documents, local newspapers, or in the records of the opponents of the movement. It may be that the Burtons were part of the group of absentee owners that some historians have suggested were convinced by the abolitionist arguments that ending the slave trade would enhance colonial security and maintain profits.[39] Debates in Parliament suggested that the abolition of the slave trade would not result in a fall in the slave population of the island and so would be economically beneficial. Lord Grenville argued, for example, that in many places in Jamaica, 'the list of births is equal to the catalogue of mortality'.[40] Given their detachment from the discussion of such matters in Jamaica, it may be that the Burton siblings and their uncle simply accepted such abolitionist statements, especially since there was no alternative thread of argument to be found in the region's newspapers.

Whatever their views, the family do not seem to have planned to protect Chiswick's operations in the event of abolition and it may be that the lack of interest of Leonard, Charles, and Thomas Burton in Chiswick's operations meant that they simply did not grasp the full impact that the abolitionist triumph would have. The reality was that, although enslaved people could still be transported between colonies and sold internally in Jamaica, the ban on the slave trade prevented Jamaican planters from replenishing their population by imports. Since the Jamaican population of enslaved workers had never been self-supporting and planters relied on imported Africans to maintain their workforces, this decision challenged the operational basis of plantation agriculture in Jamaica at its most basic level. From 1700 to 1808 the number of enslaved people in Jamaica had increased from 45,000 to 354,000. This increase was ended by the abolition of 1807 and the years thereafter saw a gradual decline.[41]

The inaction of the Burtons in the run-up to 1807 is probably representative of many absentee owners and suggests that many absentees were hampered in their ability to make such strategic decisions because of their relative disconnection from day-to-day operations. Although the Burtons were only one family and one estate, they were substantial members of the planter class in Jamaica. Higman has analysed the 1817 census data as a whole and found that only 5.1 per cent of slave owners owned 150 or more enslaved people. The Burtons were, therefore, members of a small and economically important group in the Jamaican economy and their response to abolition is suggestive of a lack of foresight, planning, and understanding of the event

[38] *Norfolk Chronicle*, 23 June 1804, p. 2.
[39] Petley, 'Slaveholders', p. 69; Philip Morgan, 'Ending the Slave Trade: A Caribbean and Atlantic Context', in *Abolition and Imperialism in Britain, Africa, and the Atlantic*, ed. Derek R. Peterson (Athens, OH: Ohio University Press, 2010), pp. 101–28.
[40] *Substance of the Debates on the Bill for Abolishing the Slave Trade* (London: W. Phillips, 1808), p. 7.
[41] Drescher, *Econocide*, p. 64; Higman, *Slave*, p. 61, 94–95.

and its consequences among some absentees.[42] Moreover, in the decade following abolition, the new generation of Burtons made no effort to increase the number of enslaved workers by internal purchase from other plantations. This meant that the abolitionists' success in 1807 inaugurated a gradual decline in the number of enslaved workers at Chiswick that was never arrested. In 1812 the number was recorded as 240.[43] By 1817 there were 201, a fall of 18 per cent in seven years, and probably one hundred under the number there had been during the estate's heyday in the 1790s.[44]

Understanding the impact of these various factors requires careful thought. The production and estimated profit figures for Chiswick from 1803 to 1815 are presented in Table 6, which uses the same parameters as those used in Table 3, except no allowance is made for the purchase of enslaved people, since none were purchased in this period. Sugar prices have been taken from Tooke's estimates, which are used by Ryden, and are exclusive of duty.[45] These calculations suggest that the estimated average net annual income for Chiswick from 1803 to 1815 was £6,138, showing that, at the most obvious level of analysis, Chiswick remained a very profitable operation, especially as the debts had now been paid. The Burton siblings and their uncle were receiving a good level of income, of around £585 per year each, with their uncle receiving an average of £2,046 per year. Nevertheless, digging slightly more deeply into the figures provides hints of subtle indicators of the negative change that had begun. While profits were good, production was on a downward trend and by 1815 had fallen below 180 hogsheads per year. After 1810 Chiswick would never produce over 200 hogsheads again. These consistently declining levels of production meant that continued high profits were reliant on sugar prices remaining firm going forward. If prices fell, the family would find their income curtailed dramatically.

Responding to this complex of factors – a declining workforce, falling production levels, and greater vulnerability to changes in sugar prices – required foresight and planning by the family, along with a reconsideration of approach in the new economic environment, but this was lacking. Not only were Thomas, Charles, and Leonard Burton uninterested in close management, but the new division of ownership acted as a block to the family's ability to respond to the changing situation. To understand this effect, it is necessary to examine the new distribution of profits. One-third of the profit was going to Leonard Burton, meaning that he was receiving an excellent return. Since he was already extremely wealthy from his estates in Lincolnshire and Devon, moreover, there was no real pressure on Leonard to explore the gradual downturn of productivity. The same was true for the Burton siblings, who were receiving a handsome annual bonus from Chiswick to augment their income from the rest of the family trust.

No figures survive for the 'non-Chiswick' part of the family income from their father's trust, but an idea of the Burton sibling's supplemental income can be gleaned from his will. Since this was made in 1795 when the income from Chiswick was higher but was being used to pay off the estate's debts, it provides a sense of the levels

---

[42] Higman, *Slave*, pp. 68–70, 274–75.
[43] 1812 Jamaica Almanac Portland, St. David and STIE (jamaicanfamilysearch.com).
[44] NA/T/71/145, Slave Registers 1817, fol. 854.
[45] Ryden, 'Sugar', p. 52; Tooke, *High and low Prices*, appendix to part 4, pp. 46–49.

Table 6. Estimated net profit of the Chiswick estate, 1803–1815. *

Crop year	Hogsheads of sugar sold in London	Estimated price per hogsheads of sugar (£ sterling)	Estimated gross income (£ sterling)	Insurance costs at 1½% (£ sterling)	Factor costs at 2½% (£ sterling)	Freight (9s per cwt) (£ sterling)	Estimated net profit on sugar (after fixed expenses)	Net profit (with rum at £15 per puncheon)
1803	286	40	£11,440	(£1,258)	(£286)	(£2,172)	£5,194	£6,994
1804	186	48	£8,928	(£982)	(£223)	(£1,412)	£3,781	£4,981
1805	338	46	£15,548	(£1,710)	(£389)	(£2,567)	£8,352	£10,722
1806	300	40	£12,000	(£1,320)	(£300)	(£2,279)	£5,571	£7,506
1807	272	35	£9,520	(£1,047)	(£238)	(£2,066)	£3,639	£5,814
1808	274	38	£10,412	(£1,145)	(£260)	(£2,081)	£4,396	£6,076
1809	243	42	£10,206	(£1,122)	(£255)	(£1,845)	£4,454	£6,104
1810	195	41	£7,995	(£879)	(£200)	(£1,481)	£2,905	£4,255
1811	179	39	£6,981	(£768)	(£175)	(£1,360)	£2,148	£3,348
1812	181	43	£7,783	(£856)	(£195)	(£1,375)	£2,827	£4,027
1814	194	62	£12,028	(£1,323)	(£301)	(£1,474)	£6,400	£7,855
1815	180	56	£10,080	(£1,109)	(£252)	(£1,367)	£4,822	£5,977

* Sources: JA/1B/11/4/31, fol. 118b; 1B/4/33, fol. 100; 1B/11/4/34, fol. 188; 1B/11/4/36, fol. 100; 1B/11/4/37, fol. 60; 1B/11/4/38, fol. 204; 1B/11/4/40, fol. 93; 1b/11/4/42, fol. 120; 1B/11/4/43, fol. 201; 1B/11/4/45, fol. 117; 1B/11/4/48, fol. 53; 1B/11/4/49, fol. 138; 1B/11/4/51, fol. 34. The returns for 1802 and 1813 have not been located.

of income Burton was expecting from other areas of the trust. As has already been said, he envisaged his other assets providing £500 per annum for his wife, £200 for his eldest son, and £100 each for the seven other children, with Launcelot being still alive at this point. This was a total of £1,400 per year. Assuming a relatively 'safe' set of investments, in government stock for example, and an annual return of 5 per cent, the trust would have needed to be something of the level of £29,000 in value to achieve such a return on investment. Burton was wealthy, but it is unlikely that his estate excluding Chiswick would have exceeded such levels. Given this, it seems reasonable to assume that these were the sums he expected the rest of his assets to provide and that he envisaged the income from Chiswick would supplement this. Taken together with their income from Jamaica, therefore, this suggests that the Burton siblings were probably receiving annual incomes of around £700 to £800 pounds per year from all sources between 1805 and 1815.

This made the individual Burton siblings very wealthy in comparison to most of the British population, with incomes on par with those of minor gentry, and meant that there was no obvious need for them to consider the underlying trends at Chiswick. The problem was that, in contrast to their uncle Leonard, the lion's share of each Burton sibling's income – 85 per cent – was being provided by the Chiswick estate. This meant that, after their father's death, the drawings from the sugar estate constituted the central part of the income for each of the Burton siblings in any given year. The annual success of operations in Jamaica thus became far more important to the individual family members than they had been to Thomas Burton prior to 1805.

This meant that, since each member of the family was proportionality more reliant on the income from Chiswick than their father had been, it became more difficult for them to forego income in any one year for the benefit of the estate. In the 1790s, under Thomas and John Burton, who had other sources of income, capital expenditure could be provided relatively easily by reducing estate drawings. This had allowed the brothers to pay off the estate's debts, replace equipment, and to purchase more enslaved workers. After 1805 such capital investment was far more difficult because, rather than two very wealthy brothers making such decisions, it was the seven siblings who were well-off but highly dependent on maximising the income they received from Chiswick who had to agree on reductions in drawings to allow capital expenditure. Leonard Burton also had to concur. Obtaining agreement for change had become far more difficult.

This mixture of continuing good income levels and an inability to forego income from the estate appears to have combined with the disinterest in Chiswick exhibited by Thomas, Charles, and Leonard to cause inaction. Capital investment appears to have stopped in at Chiswick during this period and letters from the 1820s make it clear that the estate was falling into a considerable state of disrepair.[46] Moreover, nothing was done in relation to worker numbers. For example, no enslaved people were purchased for Chiswick between 1803 and 1815, although such things were possible even after 1807 using Jamaica's internal market. At Mesopotamia the Barhams responded to a fall in population from 332 in 1803 to 298 in 1813 by

[46] NRO/MC1519/1/813X9, William Wright to Susanna Wright, 10 April 1825, fol. 6.

purchasing a coffee plantation and moving fifty-five enslaved people across to their sugar estate.[47] Such actions were difficult for absentee owners to push forward and required an engagement with commercial operations that was lacking from the Burtons. It seems likely that this commercial failure was a consequence, at least in part, of the family's emotional disengagement from the enslaved people of Chiswick. Because the Burtons, consciously or unconsciously, chose not to think about the enslaved people on their property they were prevented from even thinking about such matters.

By 1815, therefore, Chiswick was in a delicate condition. The estate was still very profitable, but the consequences of the decline of workforce numbers, along with the problems with Bourbon cane, were being manifested in falling production levels. The Burtons' profits depended on continuing firm sugar prices, but these might fall in the future and the history of the sugar industry was one marked by price volatility. The only way to provide a cushion against any potential fall in sugar prices was increased production, which might have been achieved by purchasing more enslaved workers in the internal market, buying a steam engine, or even thinking about the diversification of crops, but such strategic changes required decisive and strong leadership, along with capital investment. Prudent management would have seen planning undertaken to mitigate such price falls. This was not forthcoming.

As the economic and political environment changed between 1803 and 1815 the Burtons did not respond. Instead, the estate was beset by a lack of vision and poor commercial understanding which was, in all likelihood, a function of the Burton family's absentee status and, counterintuitively, the continuing high levels of return and its lack of debt. The Burtons were doing very well in the early years of the nineteenth century and the potential negative consequences of the changes that had begun to affect sugar estate owners do not seem to have occurred to the family. For planters who remained in Jamaica it was difficult enough to respond, even when they were living on their estate and could recognise the challenges. In contrast, the view from Norfolk was somewhat benign. Living four thousand miles away, the second generation of Burtons to own Chiswick – who were physically and intellectually disengaged from the estate, its people, and its commercial environment – did not perceive it as a business needing active management and commercial engagement, nor did they see the storm clouds gathering. The intellectual and emotional disconnection from the reality of Chiswick, its operations, and its enslaved workers that had characterised the family's ownership from 1788 meant that to Thomas Burton, his brothers, sisters, and his uncle, Chiswick was a name that was attached to a large cheque once per year and very little else. Tightly focused as they always had been on amassing wealth, so long as sugar prices held their levels and despite the passage of the Abolition Act, for the Burton family the times seemed good.

---

[47] Dunn, *A Tale*, p. 41.

5

LUCY WALLEN AND THE PEOPLE OF CHISWICK: AMELIORATION AND DECLINE, 1816–1822

The good times ended with the cessation of the Napoleonic Wars. Sugar prices peaked in 1815, offering hope of a resurgence, but fell back to depressed levels thereafter. Prices in London dropped from an average of 61 shillings per hundredweight in 1815 to around 36 shillings in 1821. From 1816 onwards, there was just too much sugar available for higher prices to be maintained. Jamaican sugar production fell gradually thereafter and stabilised at around 70,000 tons per year from 1821, but this fall made no difference to overall levels of sugar available as the newly opened colonies of Trinidad, the Guianas, and Mauritius, along with Cuba and Brazil, provided new sources of supply. Prices would remain low throughout the 1820s, posting an average of around 30 shillings per hundredweight.[1] From 1816, therefore, the Burtons lost the higher levels of sugar prices that had been camouflaging the consequences of declining production levels at Chiswick.

Over the next few years there was a rapid turnover of overseers on the estate. Robert Anderson was replaced in 1815 by Charles Carter who was replaced by Alexander Cummings in 1816.[2] He only lasted until 1819 when Robert Hamilton was appointed, he remained in post until 1824.[3] The attorney, Holgate, died around 1820 and was replaced by a man named John Mackenzie, who was an active attorney and managed around ten estates and pens in St Thomas-in-the-East.[4] These managers presided over a rapid downturn of the estate's fortunes, which is shown in Table 7. In 1816 Chiswick saw a calamitous collapse in production to 110 hogsheads, nearly 40 per cent under that of the previous year, and around 67 per cent below that of 1805. Once again, the culprit appears to have been bad weather. From 18 to 22 October 1815 a significant hurricane ranged from Jamaica to the Caicos Islands, a direction making it very likely that Chiswick fell into its path.[5] While production levels recov-

---

[1]   Craton and Walvin, *A Jamaica*, pp. 188–89.
[2]   JA/1B/11/4/49, fol. 138, Crop Return, 23 March 1816; JA/1B/11/4/51, fol. 34, Crop Return, 25 March 1817.
[3]   JA/1B/11/4/54, Crop Return, 23 March 1820.
[4]   NA/T71/146, Register of Chiswick Estate, 1820; 'John Mackenzie or McKenzie', *Legacies of British Slavery* database, http://wwwdepts-live.ucl.ac.uk/lbs/person/view/2146653167, accessed 15 March 2023.
[5]   Chenoweth, 'A Reassessment', table IV.

ered somewhat in the following years the average production from 1816 to 1822 was only 147 hogsheads per year, a marked reduction from the previous decade.

The combined effect of lower sugar prices and declining production on the Burton family's profits is revealed in Table 7. The parameters and methodology remain the same as those prior to 1815, however, shipping costs had been trimmed, since insurance costs fell in the period after 1815, averaging around 7 per cent. This helped margins, while freight rates and factor costs remained around the same.[6] Despite this, the estimated average profit per year in this period was now only £2,131 – around 35 per cent of that during the previous decade.

Although a hurricane affected production in 1816, the root of the problem was the decline in worker numbers. This was the case across Jamaica following the abolition of the slave trade, the effects of which were now beginning to bite. In Jamaica the planters understood this problem and attempts were made to address the issue. For example, in 1816 the Slave Code had proposed to reward mothers of six live children with exemptions from field work, and some owners had begun incentive schemes to encourage women to have children. Others, including some absentees such as Henry Goulburn, turned to the internal slave trade for additional numbers.[7] Even for those who attempted such measures the results were meagre, but the Burtons did not follow either path, leaving the estate to decline. The numbers of enslaved people on Chiswick continued to fall, from 201 in 1817, to 184 in 1820, and to 179 in 1823, meaning that the plantation was operating with something like 60 per cent of the population of enslaved workers than had existed in the 1790s.

The full nature of this decline can be understood by analysing the 1817 return, which provides the first full listing of the enslaved population at Chiswick. There were ninety-five men and boys, and 106 women and girls, a sex ratio which was below the average for St Thomas-in-the-East generally, where there was an average of 103.4 males to 100 females.[8] Before 1807 there was a marked imbalance among Jamaica's enslaved population with men outnumbering women, which was the direct result of the fact that men were preferred by buyers. From 1807, with imports ended, the gender-ratio gradually normalised as natural population patterns took hold.[9] At Chiswick this had already happened.

By 1817 there were eighty-eight Africans living at Chiswick, comprising around 44 per cent of the estate's population, this was above the average for Jamaica of 37 per cent.[10] At Worthy Park, for example, the figure was 37 per cent.[11] This preponderance of Africans, who had arrived before 1807, meant that Chiswick's working population was aging faster than the average on the island. Ideally, owners wanted the population to be concentrated in the major working age-groups of 15–44 years.

[6]   Ward, 'The Profitability', pp. 198–99.
[7]   Turner, Mary, 'Slave Workers', in *West Indies Accounts: Essays on the History of the British Caribbean and the Atlantic Economy in Honour of Richard Sheridan*, ed. Roderick A. McDonald (Kingston: University of the West Indies Press, 1996), pp. 92–106, at p. 235.
[8]   General statistics from Higman, *Slave*, p. 72; NA/T/71/145, Slave Registers 1817, fols 849–855.
[9]   Craton and Walvin, *A Jamaican*, pp. 127–28.
[10] General statistics from Higman, *Slave*, pp. 76–81; NA/T/71/145, Slave Registers 1817, fols 849–855.
[11] Craton and Walvin, *A Jamaican*, p. 196.

Table 7. *Estimated net profit of the Chiswick estate, 1816–1821.* *

Crop year	Hogsheads of sugar sold in London (puncheons of rum in brackets)	Estimated price per hogsheads of sugar (£ sterling)	Estimated gross income (£ sterling)	Insurance costs at 7% (£ sterling)	Factor osts at 2½% (£ sterling)	Freight (9s per cwt) (£ sterling)	Estimated net profit on sugar (after fixed expenses)	Net profit (with rum at £15 per puncheon)
1816	110 (32)	47	£5,123	(£564)	(£128)	(£827)	£1,074	£1,554
1819	142 (55)	39	£5,538	(£388)	(£138)	(£1,079)	£1,403	£2,228
1820	167 (62)	36	£6,012	(£421)	(£150)	(£1,269)	£1,642	£2,572
1821	168 (74)	32	£5,376	(£376)	(£134)	(£1,276)	£1,060	£2,170

* Sources: JA/1B/11/4/51, fol. 34; JA/1B/11/4/49, fol. 138, JA/1B/11/4/51, fol. 34; JA/1B/11/4/54. The returns for 1817, 1818, and 1822 have been converted at the ratio of 1½ tierce to 1 hogshead.

In 1807, this was the situation across the island but in 1817, while the average age of the enslaved population at Chiswick was thirty-five only, eighty people (40 per cent) of Chiswick's workforce – men such as Nat Burton and women like Cecilia Vernon – were in the prime age range.

Examination of the estate's population at the extremes of the age range reveals more. In 1834 the assistant commissioners for returns included a category of 'aged, diseased, or otherwise non-effective' where the term 'aged' included all those over seventy. In 1817, the oldest person at Chiswick was Lucy Wallen, an African, who was eighty years old.[12] There were then seventeen people in their seventies: Sandy, Ned Wallen, James Burton, William Brown, Hector, James Jackson, Tacitus, Peter, Charles, Monimia, Mary Clair, Sally Burton, Hannah, Sarah, Patience, Betty, and Mary McKenzie. All but two were Africans. This meant 9 per cent of the population was 'aged', which was well above the mean for Jamaica of 5 per cent, and around that of Westmoreland, which had the highest percentage of aged on the island.[13]

At the other end of the age scale, there were too few children on the estate. The youngest people at Chiswick in 1817 were Lucia, Juliet, and Andrew Wallen, all of whom were aged two. Overall, there were fourteen children under six years, or 7 per cent of the population. This was far below that of the average for even the parish with the lowest percentage of children under six, St Mary, with around 11 per cent. Worthy Park's population of children under six comprised around 17 per cent at this point.[14] Expanding the range slightly, at Chiswick there were fifty-two people under eighteen, or 26 per cent of the population, which was well under that at other plantations in St Thomas-in-the-East. For example, at Lysson's and Hector's River there were around 32 per cent in this age group.[15]

Nor was the estate's population showing any sign of ending these trends. Dunn's analysis of the demographic situation at Mesopotamia between 1762 and 1833 found that there were 331 more recorded deaths among the enslaved people than births.[16] Unfortunately, the records of Chiswick do not provide such a long time series, but the data conform with Dunn's findings. Between 1817 and 1820 there were four births and twenty deaths at Chiswick. These deaths were largely of aged Africans, although one four-year-old girl named Juliet had also died.[17] From 1820 to 1823 there were six births and eleven deaths. Once again, the deaths included several elderly Africans, such as James Jackson, aged seventy-four, and a seventy-five-year-old woman named Hannah. Three people in their twenties had also died, including two of people of mixed heritage – Amelia and William Lumsden – along with a twenty-seven-year-old woman named Katy Wallen.[18] Thus, Chiswick's death rate continuously exceeded its birth rate, and showed no sign of alteration.

---

[12] NA/T/71/145, Slave Registers 1817, fols 849–855.
[13] NA/T/71/145, Slave Registers 1817; fols 849–855.
[14] Craton and Walvin, *A Jamaican*, p. 196.
[15] NA/T/71/145, Slave Registers 1817, fols 849–55; Higman, *Slave*, pp. 80–81 and p. 95.
[16] Dunn, *A Tale*, pp. 24–25.
[17] NA/T/71/146, Slave Registers 1820, fols 64–65.
[18] NA/T/71/145, Slave Registers 1817, fols 849–855.

The major commercial consequence of this fall in overall numbers and an aging population was that Chiswick was increasingly reliant upon hired labour to dig the cane holes, in the form of jobbing gangs. Indeed by 1825 'almost all the cane lands' at Chiswick were being prepared by hired labour.[19] In general, during the preparation of the crop two jobbing gangs were hired to dig cane holes, one of sixty workers and the other of forty-eight.[20] Once the hired gangs had prepared the land, Chiswick's labourers were barely able to provide the essentials of planting, manuring, and cleaning the canes for the next crop, as well as trying to deal with weeds, and maintain the property generally. This hire was, furthermore, expensive and increasing in cost. As an example, the digging of cane holes was generally charged at a minimum of six pounds an acre, so digging out the fifty acres that were generally planted in any season was costing £300 per year.[21] This enabled the estate to continue to produce sugar, but added large sums to the costs of production, which cut into the profits being made. The owners of jobbing gangs were in a good bargaining position and had 'raised themselves to opulence' by providing labour to hard-pressed estates like Chiswick.[22] The estimates in Table 7 do not make an adjustment for these costs, but if they were added to the calculations, then the average profit at Chiswick in this period would have been even lower, at £1,831 per year.

One way this problem of productivity might have been addressed was through amelioration. The period 1788 to the early 1830s was marked by heated debate in Britian and the colonies on 'how imperial labour should be organized' a debate that ran alongside discussions about the future of the empire more generally. After 1807, with the end of the slave trade assured, criticism of the West Indian slave system itself increased and campaigners moved their attention to the 'amelioration' of the conditions in which enslaved people were held. Pressure mounted on owners to improve the conditions of their enslaved workers, and peaked in the 1820s. Burnard and Candlin identify three general positions among historians about the amelioration of slavery in the British West Indies.[23] Some historians, such as J. R. Ward, have suggested that amelioration was largely a success, at least judged on its own terms, in that productivity rates increased from the 1780s and finding that many planters demonstrated a concern for innovations that resulted improvements in nutrition and health.[24] Ward has recently produced powerful evidence suggesting an increase in the average height of enslaved people in Jamaica's workhouses in the early nineteenth century and has argued that these data show that 'the British West Indies slave

[19] NRO/MC1519/1/813X9, William Wright to Susanna Wright, 10 April 1825, fol. 6.

[20] NRO/MC1519/1/813X9, William Wright to Susanna Wright, 9 September 1825, fol. 3.

[21] NRO/MC1519/1/813X9, William Wright to Susanna Wright, 12 July 1825, fols 3–4.

[22] NRO/MC1519/1/813X9, William Wright to Susanna Wright, 9 September 1825, fol. 4.

[23] Trevor Burnard, and Kit Candlin, 'Sir John Gladstone and the Debate over the Amelioration of Slavery in the British West Indies in the 1820s', *Journal of British Studies* Vol. 57 (2018), pp. 760–82, at p. 763.

[24] J. R. Ward, *British West Indian Slavery, 1750–1834: The Process of Amelioration* (Oxford: Oxford University Press, 1988), pp. 7, 144, 208, 235. See also Sheridan, *Sugar*, pp. 481–85; O. P. Starkey, *The Economic Geography of Barbados* (New York: Columbia University Press, 1939), pp. 94–115.

regime improved substantially during its later years' and amelioration had, in this regard, succeeded.[25]

In contrast, Christa Dierksheide has suggested that most slave-owners resisted the implementation of amelioration schemes, and that this eventually led to emancipation rather than reform. In this view amelioration was a failure.[26] A third approach has been offered by Caroline Quarrier Spence, who suggests that amelioration can be understood in two phases – the first from the 1790s to 1823, which was led by planters. The second phase, from 1823 to 1833, was controlled by abolitionists who used amelioration to achieve abolition.[27] Burnard and Candlin have argued that the process of amelioration needs to be understood in the wider context of imperial protection and have used the activity of Sir John Gladstone to explore this issue. They conclude that amelioration was a failure economically but delayed the final date of emancipation.[28]

Can the evidence from Chiswick shed any light on these debates? Unlike the papers of Gilbert Mathison, who proactively engaged with amelioration, the Burtons' papers contain no overt discussion of the movement, or any instructions issued to the managers at Chiswick to improve the conditions of the workforce.[29] Nonetheless, careful examination of the correspondence provides data with which to work. For example, the presence of a hospital on an estate has been suggested as an indicator of amelioration efforts.[30] There is a record of a hospital for the workforce at Chiswick existing in the 1820s. This was often full in times of epidemics, such as that of dysentery in 1833, and measles in 1837, with the Burtons paying for medical care.[31] When the hospital was constructed is unclear, but its existence is certainly a hint that the Burtons were looking at matters of amelioration. Of course, as Craton has pointed out, the limitations of contemporary medicine meant that in many case its presence in places such as hospitals was counterproductive.[32] This is borne out at Chiswick, where the medical attendant employed in the 1830s was 'Mr Pine', who also supplied coffee to the estate, and appears to have had no medical qualifications.[33]

One can also glean information about potential changes to diet and provisions at Chiswick from the paperwork that are suggestive of some degree of engagement with amelioration. Pares and Ward have pointed to efforts to improve the diet of

[25] J. R. Ward, 'The Amelioration of British West Indian Slavery: Anthropometric Evidence', *Economic Historical Review* (2018), pp. 1199–226.

[26] Christa Dierksheide, *Amelioration and Empire: Progress and Slavery in the Plantation Americas* (Charlottesville, VA: University of Virginia Press, 2014), chapter 6.

[27] Caroline Quarrier Spence, 'Ameliorating Empire: Slavery and Protection in the British Colonies, 1783–1865', PhD thesis, Harvard University, 2014, pp. 304–10.

[28] Burnard and Candlin, 'Sir John', pp. 779–82.

[29] Ursula Halliday, 'The Slave Owner as Reformer: Theory and Practice at Castle Wemyss Estate, Jamaica, 1800–1823', *Journal of Caribbean History* (1996), pp. 65–82.

[30] Sheridan, *Doctors*, p. 73.

[31] NRO/MC1519/1/813X9, William Wright to Susanna Wright, Chiswick, 10 April 1825, fol. 1. BLO/MSS.W.Ind.s.18, fol. 73, Townson to Pitcairn & Amos, 5 August 1833; BLO/MSS.W.Ind.s.19, fol. 53, Pitcairn & Amos to Mayhew, 10 March 1837.

[32] Craton and Greenland, *Searching*, p. 131.

[33] BLO/MSS.W.Ind.s.19, fol. 59 Pitcairn & Amos to Mayhew, 24 April 1837.

enslaved workers as indicative of the positive effects of amelioration.[34] Turner reports the views of George Richards at the Bog estate in Vere, who argued that reductions in workload and increases in food would help improve slave fertility and sugar production.[35] Likewise, others have argued that settler concern over the provision ground system resulted in an improved supply of provisions on the island and so changes in this might be evidence of amelioration efforts.[36] The records of Chiswick provide circumstantial evidence in these areas. It seems that after 1807 the workers were encouraged to reduce their dependence on plantains, which were vulnerable to storms, and replace them with other produce. Reports from the 1820s noted that the people grew a variety of crops, including pineapples, oranges, guava, bananas, yams, and plantains. They also made use of calabash trees on the estate to provide wood for 'jars, dishes and mugs'.[37] These changes would appear, potentially, to be part of some form of amelioration activity on the estate.

The names of the workforce hint, perhaps, at some efforts at amelioration. By 1817 only two of the enslaved workers retained African names – a fifty-year-old named Quasheba and the forty-eight-year-old Juba. The rest had common European names, or ones taken from literature (Romeo and Juliet), from classical mythology or history (Tacitus), from British locations (Scotland), or others that reflected, perhaps, their special status (Favourite). One hundred and twenty had, however, both Christian names and surnames, providing evidence of a process of baptism that had occurred gradually in Jamaica during the period of amelioration. When and how this took place at Chiswick is unclear. Some owners had allowed missionaries to operate on their estates as a means of improving worker behaviour, but such instruction was expensive, in the region of £200 per year.[38] There is no mention of any such expenditure in the accounts of Chiswick, and letters from the 1820s indicate that there was no missionary activity on the estate or religious instruction.[39] Although St Thomas-in-the-East was home to a branch of the Incorporated Society for the Instruction and Religious Conversion of the Negroes, there is no direct evidence of them being active on Chiswick.[40] The baptismal record does suggest, nonetheless, that some form of missionary activity had been going on.

[34] Richard Pares, *A West India Fortune* (London: Longmans, 1950), p. 126; Ward, *British*, pp. 65–74.

[35] Turner, 'Planter', p. 235.

[36] I. Berlin and P. D. Morgan (eds), *Cultivation and Culture: Labour and the Shaping of Slave Life in the Americas* (Charlottesville, VA: University of Virginia Press, 1993), p. 28; Higman, *Slave*, p. 204; M. Mullin, *Africa in America: Slave Acculturation and Resistance in the American South and the British Caribbean* (Urbana, IL: University of Illinois Press, 1992), pp. 143–45; J. M. Pilcher, 'The Caribbean from 1492 to the Present', in *The Cambridge world history of food*, vol. 1, ed. K. F. Kiple and K. C. Ornelas (Cambridge: Cambridge University Press, 2000), pp. 1278–88, at pp. 1281–82; Parry, *Plantation*, pp. 17–19.

[37] NRO/MC1519/1,813X9, William Wright to Susanna Wright, 15 May 1825.

[38] Turner, 'Planter', p. 236.

[39] NRO/MC1519/1/813X9, William Wright to Susanna Wright, 9 September 1825, fols 4–5.

[40] Mary Turner, 'The Bishop of Jamaica and Slave Instruction', *The Journal of Ecclesiastical History* (1975), pp. 363–78, pp. 368–69, 371; *Report of the Incorporated Society for the Conver-*

This indirect evidence can be supplemented by consideration of work routines. Higman has argued that there is evidence for a long-term reduction in working time on the island, from more than 5,000 hours annually per enslaved person in the 1770s, to 4,000 hours by the early nineteenth century.[41] The records at Chiswick do not record such details, but the description of the daily routine provided by William Wright in the 1820s, given in Chapter 3, suggests that by this point the people at Chiswick were receiving breaks in a working day totalling two and one-half hours.[42] A rough estimate can be made using this information. Assuming average daylight of twelve hours, this would suggest a working week at Chiswick of around fifty-seven to sixty hours, which would in turn suggest that by the 1820s the population was working around 3,000 hours per year. This is well below that suggested by Higman for the early nineteenth century, but the figure does not include the work done at night in the mills. When a reasonable estimate of this workload is added, the amount would approximate Higman's lower figure. These, admittedly speculative, estimates suggest that the working hours on Chiswick may have lessened by the early 1820s, implying some possible efforts toward amelioration.

These moves, such as they were, do not seem to have had any positive effect on production. The continuous fall in production on Chiswick after 1807, shown in Tables 6 and 7, despite a gradual change in cane from Bourbon to violet, does not suggest that the amelioration measures that may have been implemented were creating a more productive workforce. Overall, the evidence regarding amelioration in the years up to 1823 at Chiswick is thin. The surviving records contain no paperwork requiring the estate's managers to send the family detailed records of the births and deaths on the estate. Such records can be found at Amity Hall where Henry Goulburn, the absentee owner, sought to understand and alter the condition of his enslaved workers through such reports. Research has shown that Goulburn 'had humane attitudes towards his estate workers' and attempted to improve worker conditions in the last decade of slavery, introducing measures such as a prohibition on night work, restricted physical punishments, and the encouragement of family relationships. Even in this case these measures were a response to labour shortages rather than derived from any enthusiasm for amelioration.[43]

Although it may be the case that such records were made at Chiswick but did not survive, there is no hint of them being asked for in the estate correspondence until the issue of compensation arose in 1833. As we shall see later, unlike the situation at Amity Hall, there is no evidence that night work was ever restricted at Chiswick and reports from third parties suggest a punishing work routine was in place on the estate during the late 1820s and 1830s. Likewise, later discussion from the attorneys was matter of fact about punishments, which were presented as essential, and bemoaned

sion and Religious Instruction and Education of the Negro Slaves in the British West India Islands* (The Society, 1826).

[41] Higman, *Slave*, p. 188; Higman, *Plantation Jamaica*, p. 225.

[42] NRO/MC1519/1/813X9, William Wright to Susanna Wright, Chiswick, 15 May 1825, p. 5.

[43] Brian Jenkins, *Henry Goulburn 1784–1856: A Political Biography* (Liverpool: Liverpool University Press, 1996), pp. 247–48, at p. 288; Turner, 'Planter', pp. 232–52.

the limits placed on discipline because of abolition and apprenticeship.[44] Overall, therefore, the balance of evidence suggests that, while the Burtons may have engaged to some extent with amelioration policies in respect of diet and provisions, they did so half-heartedly. Placed in the wider picture that has been developed regarding the Burton family's detachment from the enslaved people on their property, a limited level of engagement with amelioration is not surprising. The family's indifference to the estate's operation and their enslaved workers seems to have mitigated any concerted effort towards amelioration. The issue was, once again, that the family appear to have remained completely uninterested in any details of their workforce.

In England there was new turbulence when Frederick Burton died suddenly in October 1818.[45] Since Frederick was unmarried and died intestate, his share in the estate went to his oldest brother, Thomas. This meant that Thomas now owned two-sevenths of the two-thirds of the Chiswick estate that was held in trust under his father's will.[46] More significantly, only a month later Leonard Burton died, aged seventy-eight. Leonard had no children and left £500 to his sister-in-law, Elizabeth Burton. He bequeathed £100 to each of the Burton sisters and placed his assets in Northamptonshire and Devon in a trust, which was to provide a lifetime annuity of £100 per year for Elizabeth, with the rest of the income going to Charles and Thomas Burton and their descendants.[47]

Moreover, Leonard bequeathed his one-third share in Chiswick to Thomas Burton, making the mathematics of the ownership of Chiswick mind-bendingly complex.[48] Two-thirds of Chiswick remained divided into equal shares amongst Maria, Harriet, Caroline, Charlotte, Charles, and Thomas, who now also owned the share he had inherited from Frederick. In addition, under Leonard Burton's trust, Thomas controlled the remaining third of Chiswick. This gave Thomas the largest proportion of the shares in Chiswick – 11/21 to be precise – while the rest of his siblings had a smaller proportion of 2/21 each. The practical effect of this distribution was that, from November 1818 onwards, Thomas Burton became the central figure in decision-making.

The problem was that Thomas was uninterested in Chiswick. Previously, he had sufficient income coming from the trust that he did not need to pursue a professional career, and he had not chosen to do so. Now, with a large income from extensive estates in Northamptonshire and Devon, he was a very wealthy man and was even less inclined to manage his existing assets with the aim to nurture them and enhance

---

[44] BLO/MSS.W.Ind.s.18, fol. 87, Townson to Pitcairn & Amos, 13 October 1833.

[45] NRO/Bishop's transcripts, Film number 1278920, Burial of Frederick Burton, 14 October 1818; *Norfolk Chronicle*, Saturday 10 October 1818, p. 2.

[46] BLO/MSS.W.Ind.s.17, fol. 33, Stevens, Wood and Wilkinson to Mayhew, 4 February 1829.

[47] PROB/11/1610/156, Will of Leonard Burton of Ringstead, Northamptonshire, 12 November 1818; *The Monthly Magazine* (London: R. Phillips, 1818), p. 91; Francis Whellan and Co., *History, Topography, and Directory of Northamptonshire* (London: Whittaker & Company, 1874), pp. 924–25. For Leonard as a freeholder, see Northamptonshire Record Office, QS/F/8/1795/8, Northamptonshire Freeholders 1795–1797, September 1795 and 1797; his burial is recorded in Bishops Transcripts B0205, Leonard Burton, Holy Trinity, Denford, 17 June 1818, *Bury and Norwich Post*, Wednesday 28 August 1822, p. 3.

[48] BLO/MSS.W.Ind.s.17, fol. 33, Stevens, Wood and Wilkinson to Mayhew, 4 February 1829.

their value. As his brother Charles told Farr, Thomas was often very difficult to tie down for long enough to get him to engage with matters of business, meaning that Charles 'was obliged to wait an opportunity of catching my brother, which is not an easy task. He is out early of a morning and goes to bed with the cocks and hens.'[49] In general, Thomas was far more interested in spending his money than earning it and was content to let others manage his wealth for him. Since Thomas was now the majority shareholder of Chiswick, this detachment from the management of the estate made it even more difficult to address the long-term issues facing it.

In 1818, Caroline Burton married a solicitor from Beccles named John Lee Farr.[50] Farr was also a substantial landowner, owning both North Cove Hall and Rushmere Hall, and was linked by marriage and commerce to the Dashwoods.[51] He had experience in the operation of landed estates gained from his family's land-holdings and also from his professional expertise as a solicitor, where he acted for a number of estates, such as the manor of Earl Soham.[52] Farr was appointed as an extra trustee for the estate, a move that was probably a consequence of the Burton brothers' lack of interest in the finer detail of Chiswick's management.[53] There is no evidence, however, that his appointment resulted in any change in the management of the estate.

In retrospect, the most significant change had occurred a year before Leonard Burton's death, in 1817, when the youngest sister, Maria, married the Reverend Thomas Sayers.[54] Sayers was one year older than his bride, being born on 29 August 1790.[55] He attended Pembroke Hall, Cambridge, and was ordained in Norwich in December 1814 before gaining several appointments around Great Yarmouth, at Thurne and Clippesby.[56] These livings provided a comfortable income, but not one that allowed for great extravagance. In the marriage settlement Sayers provided a former stable and adjoining premises in Quay Street, Great Yarmouth, which had been transferred to him by his father the previous year, for Maria's use for life.[57] The settlement was short and made no mention of Chiswick but, as her husband, Thomas

[49]   BLO/MSS.W.Ind.s.17, fol. 160, C. FOL. Burton to Farr, 8 March 1831.
[50]   NRO/Y/WE/1-67, Marriage of Caroline Burton and Farr, Great Yarmouth, 10 September 1818; *Morning Post*, 12 September 1818, p. 4.
[51]   Alfred Suckling, *The History and Antiquities of the County of Suffolk: Volume 1* (Ipswich: W. S. Crowell, 1846), pp. 47–52; *London Gazette* (London: T. Neuman, 1815), p. 49; *Bury and Norwich Post*, 20 April 1814, Farr, 'Solicitor of Beccles'; Suckling, *The History*, pp. 47–52, 288; SRO/FAA/23/23/183, Marriage Licence Bond: Jarrett Dashwood and Lorina Farr, 7 November 1771; John A. Dunlap, Reports of Cases Decided in the High Court of Chancery (New York: Gould, Banks & Company, 1847), Farr v Sheriffe – Dykes v Farr, pp. 511–28, at p. 525.
[52]   Dunlap, *Reports*, pp. 511–38; *Suffolk Chronicle*, 27 November 1819, p. 2.
[53]   BLO/MSS.W.Ind.s.17, fol. 131, Pitcairn & Amos to Mayhew, 17 April 1830.
[54]   NRO/PD/28/72, Marriage of Maria Burton and Thomas Sayers, 22 December 1817.
[55]   NRO/PD/28/18, Baptism of Thomas Sayers, 31 August 1790.
[56]   Church of England Clergy Database: Person: Sayers, Thomas (1813–1821): CCEd Person ID: 115075 CCED: Persons Index (theclergydatabase.org.uk), accessed 19 December 2022.
[57]   BLO/MSS.W.Ind.s.17, fol. 33, Stevens, Wood and Wilkinson to Mayhew, 4 February 1829; NRO/Y/D/19/52-64, Abstract of Settlement on marriage between the Revd Thomas Sayers and Maria Burton, 1817; NRO/Y/D/19/52-64, Title No. 11, Row 95, being one of two dwell-

gained a life interest in Maria's share, which he was, no doubt, expecting to increase his annual income substantially.[58]

Such expectations were not to be realised since the income from Chiswick declined ever faster from 1816, averaging around 42 per cent of that in the previous decade, a substantial fall in income for all concerned. From 1816 to 1822, using the estimated average overall income of £2,131, Thomas Burton received around £703 in consequence of the one-third of the estate he had inherited from his uncle. After Frederick's death, the remaining two-thirds was divided six ways. Since Thomas had inherited Fredrick's share, he received another £476, while his siblings received £238 each. Additionally, Thomas Burton now had extensive income coming from his late uncle's English estates, and Charles also appears to have received an income from these.

The family was now clearly divided into two groups, the two wealthy brothers, and the four sisters and their spouses, whose income had halved between 1805 and 1822. The degree to which this falling income affected the sisters and their husbands varied, however. It seems that Harriet Dashwood found it difficult to rein in her spending as the receipts from Chiswick deteriorated and incurred debts that required her husband to pay from his funds.[59] Since Dashwood had a good income from his own resources, however, the fall in his wife's income was an annoyance, rather than a major issue. The same was true for John Lee Farr, who had his extensive family estates and was a practising solicitor and so, at this stage, he and Caroline appear to have been feeling no pressure financially.

In contrast, from 1816 it appears that James and Charlotte Willins faced increasing financial difficulties. The income from Chiswick had always provided far more revenue to the couple than had James Willins' livings, and the accelerating reduction in funds arriving from Chiswick caused the couple to incur debt. Eventually, at some point in the 1820s, with Charlotte's mother adamant that her daughter's interests needed to be protected, a trust was arranged under the trusteeship of Thomas Burton and the Norwich solicitors, Francis & Turner, using collateral of Charlotte's shares in Chiswick, with the income from the estate being used to pay off the debt gradually.[60] A continuing stream of income from the estate was, therefore, essential for the couple's continuing financial stability, yet this flow of funds was diminishing with each year. Later events suggest that Maria and Thomas Sayers were in a similar situation, insofar as their household income was largely reliant on Maria's shares, which had provided far more funds than the livings of her husband. With Maria's income now faltering, the Sayers needed to cut their cloth accordingly, or find an alternate way of earning money. This situation would have major repercussions for the entire family in the period after 1822.

---

inghouses converted by 1865 from a stable described as being in Brook's or King the Baker's Row; Conveyed by James Sayers to Revd. Thomas Sayers his eldest son in 1816.

[58] BLO/MSS.W.Ind.s.17, fol. 58, Pitcairn & Amos to Mayhew, 8 April 1829.

[59] BLO/MSS.W.Ind.s.19, fol. 167, Steward to Mayhew, 22 January 1844; BLO/MSS.W.Ind.s.19, fol. 142, Jarrett Dashwood to Mayhew, 12 June 1840.

[60] BLO/MSS.W.Ind.s.17, fol. 6; Mayhew to Farr, (May?) 1829; BLO/MSS.W.Ind.s.18, fol. 9, Thomas Burton to Mayhew, 29 July 1832.

The period from 1815 to 1822 had seen important and, largely undesirable, changes in the commercial situation at Chiswick and the Burtons' income streams. The end of the Napoleonic Wars had removed the firm sugar prices which had masked the consequences of the continuous decline in production from 1807 onwards. This decline in production was, primarily, a consequence of the fall in slave numbers that had begun after the abolition of the slave trade. This process was, however, a subtle one and identifying it would have required an astute businessman, who was closely engaged with the commercial operation of the sugar estate. The family needed such a figure, but instead had continued to act as absentees with a decidedly 'hands-off' style of control. As the problems became clearer between 1816 and 1822 the Burtons failed to respond in any decisive manner. Of course, the Burtons and their managers could do nothing about the level of sugar prices, but there were other areas that had been within their ability to address. No plan was devised to respond to the issue of declining worker numbers, while amelioration policies had been implemented half-heartedly and with no consideration of the potential benefits they might bring to the estate's productivity.

The upshot of this was that, nearly twenty years after Thomas Burton's death, the Burton family was facing a challenging situation. Chiswick's productivity was stuck at far lower levels than it had been previously and the incomes that some of the family had become reliant upon had begun to decline markedly. The commercial situation of Chiswick from 1805 to 1815 had also been one of steady deterioration, but the slow nature of that process allowed the Burtons to disregard it – they could always hope that the next year would get better. After 1816 this became more difficult. Ironically, their ability to ignore matters at Chiswick for so long was a result of their father's successful management. By clearing the debts of the estate in his period of ownership Thomas Burton had protected his children from the pressure of indebtedness that faced many sugar estate owners in the early 1800s. With no creditors draining away profits, the estate had yielded relatively decent returns for many years. If the Burton children had been needing to pay £2,000 per year in interest every year from 1805 to 1822, they might have been forced to think about the problems facing Chiswick at a much earlier date. Instead, the family had been able to carry on spending the money the estate produced without paying much attention to its operation for a long time. That period of easy money had now come to an end, and by the end of 1822 it was clear that something needed to be done. At this juncture Thomas Sayers stepped forward and proposed a remedy. His idea was to take commercial operations firmly under his control and for him to run Chiswick in a manner that had not been seen since the days of John and Thomas Burton.

6

'LOOKING FORWARD TO GREAT THINGS BEING DONE': A NEW PLAN, 1823–1828

Sayers' plan was to arrest the estate's declining production and so increase the family's income, without requiring any work from his relatives. His suggestion was that he should purchase the shares in Chiswick that Thomas Burton had inherited from his father and brother, which amounted to 4/21 of the estate.[1] This purchase would make Sayers a proprietor in his own right, as opposed to being so via his wife's shares, and allow him to take on a significant management role in the commercial operation of the estate. Thomas Burton would remain the largest shareholder, retaining the one third (7/21sts) of Chiswick he had gained from his uncle – but the deal would make Sayers the second largest shareholder, while the other siblings would continue to own 2/21 each. When added to his wife's 2/21 of the estate, Sayers would control nearly as much as Thomas and his influence would become significant.[2] In return, Sayers offered to take full operational control of Chiswick, from Norfolk, and was 'looking forward to great things being done with the Chiswick Estate'.[3]

Although it is not stated overtly in any of the paperwork, the timing of this change seems suggestive that it was, as least in part, prompted by the British government's amelioration programme, drawn up in 1823 and supported by the West India interest in London, which proposed reforms on estates and attempted to codify improvement. These included the ending of the flogging of women, the cessation of the use of whip as a symbol of authority and flogging only in the presence of an overseer who would record the details. Other measures considered included the abolition of Sunday markets, property rights for the enslaved, expanded magisterial oversight and religious instruction.[4] While many of these proposals came to naught, they were indicative of growing pressure at home, of which the Burtons cannot have remained unaware. Sayers may, therefore, have suggested that his management of operations would allow the family to respond, finally, to this changing political situation.

Sayers' plan to improve the estate's profitability was based on several ideas. First, he wanted to increase the number of enslaved workers, by making purchases from

[1]   BLO/MSS.W.Ind.s.17, fol. 86, '(Copy) Rev Thomas Sayers and Chiswick Estate' Debt to Messrs R & J Mitchell & Co', 22 July 1829; BLO/MSS.W.Ind.s.17, fol. 33, Stevens, Wood and Wilkinson to Mayhew, 4 February 1829.
[2]   BLO/MSS.W.Ind.s.17, fol. 9, Pitcairn & Amos to Farr, 13 January 1829.
[3]   BLO/MSS.W.Ind.s.17, fol. 40, Mayhew to Farr, 8 February 1829.
[4]   See Turner, 'Planter', pp. 232–52; Ragatz, Fall, pp. 410–15.

within the island's internal economy and so help arrest the decline in production levels by adding more labour to the estate. Second, to further improve productivity he proposed bringing new agricultural methods from Norfolk to the estate, specifically ploughing, which would make up for the gradual fall in slave numbers.[5] Finally, he wanted to improve the estate's financial bottom line by cutting the business' fixed costs.[6] The combined effect of these changes would, it was hoped, be increased productivity and a revival of the income stream for all the proprietors.

Alongside his income from his share of the estate, the arrangement also promised Sayers an annual income of £100 or 10 per cent of the profits, whichever was higher.[7] Sayers was, therefore, guaranteed an income of £100 per year for himself, whatever the yield of the estate, with a bonus in good years. Later events suggest that this guaranteed income was the major reason for Sayers' proposal. He enjoyed being part of the bustling social life of Yarmouth and revelled in the races. The revenue from his livings was moderate, however, and as Maria's income from Chiswick declined it appears that money was becoming tight.[8] In August 1831, it was suggested that his and Maria's shares were worth less than £3,592, an estimate that valued Chiswick at £12,572.[9] This suggests that the 4/21 he purchased in 1823 would have cost Sayers at least £2,300. While details are sparse, later events suggest that he may have borrowed the bulk of the money required from merchants in London, using the stable in Yarmouth and, possibly, Maria's share in Chiswick as collateral.[10] With the purchase made, Sayers began to get to work.[11]

He commenced by changing the management, declaring the attorney, Mackenzie, 'wretched' and replacing him with Charles Anderson. A new overseer, a Welshman named George Prosser, was also appointed.[12] Anderson was an active attorney on the island, managing the estates of various owners, including Andrew Gregory Johnston, who owned the Anchovy Valley estate in the parish of Portland.[13] Johnston was originally from Hempnall, Norfolk, and along with owning Anchovy Valley, was a merchant in Jamaica, where he was in partnership with William Pitcairn.[14] In 1819, Johnston had purchased the manor of Fritton and Fritton Hall,

5   NRO/MC/1519/1,813X9, William Wright to Susanna Wright, 10 April 1825, fol. 6.
6   BLO/MSS.W.Ind.s.17, fol. 137, Charles Burton to Mayhew, 9 May 1830.
7   BLO/MSS.W.Ind.s.17, fol. 10, Pitcairn and Amos to Farr, 13 January 1829.
8   Druery, *Historical*, p. xii; *Norwich Mercury*, 23 August 1823, p. 4.
9   BLO/MSS.W.Ind.s.17, 1829–1831, fol. 186, Pitcairn & Amos to Mayhew, 12 August 1831.
10 For the debt, see NRO/Y/D 19/52-64, Release of stable and premises in Great Yarmouth, 2 January 1829.
11 The exact date of the sale is not known. The deed of conveyance is mentioned in BLO/MSS.W.Ind.s.17, fol. 86, '(Copy) Rev Thomas Sayers and Chiswick Estate' Debt to Messrs R & J Mitchell & Co', 22 July 1829. Sayers' shares are detailed in BLO/MSS.W.Ind.s.17, fol. 10, Pitcairn and Amos to Farr, London 13 January 1829 and BLO/MSS.W.Ind.s.18, fol. 163, Pitcairn & Amos to Mayhew, 4 September 1834.
12 NRO/MC1519/1/813X9, William Wright to Susanna Wright, 10 April 1825, fol. 9; *Cheltenham Chronicle*, Thursday 5 January 1832, p. 4.
13 NA/T71, Office of Registry of Colonial Slaves and Slave Compensation Commission: Records; Piece Number: 153.
14 *Royal Gazette of Jamaica*, 3 January 1818, p. 27.

which lies only six miles from Yarmouth, and lived there in the 1820s, making him a neighbour of the Burtons in Norfolk.[15] He presumably became acquainted with Thomas Sayers and advised him to employ Anderson. Finally, a Kingston merchant, James Forsyth, became involved with the estate, shipping the produce to Britain and organising supplies. Forsyth ran a merchant house, Forsyth & Co., and worked with several other plantation owners, such as the owners of Belvedere estate in St Thomas-in-the-East, as well as for the government.[16] By 1832 he was recorded as managing five estates, one pen, and three plantations with 1,177 slaves under his control.[17] Forsyth provided supplies for the estate, while the cultivation of the crop was left to Anderson.[18]

The key managerial modification that Sayers was making was not, however, just changing the attorney and overseer. It was that he would be working closely with Anderson and Forsyth in managing the estate. It appears that Sayers was a charming and likeable man, and he struck up very good relations with both Anderson and Forsyth. Indeed, so friendly was the relationship that Forsyth invited Thomas and Maria to come and stay in Jamaica at one of his houses if they so wished.[19] Forsyth, Anderson, and Prosser soon treated Sayers as the owner of Chiswick, and in March 1826 the crop returns ceased calling Chiswick 'the said estate' and described it as 'the property of Thomas Sayers'.[20] Furthermore, Sayers removed the long-standing agents, Ede & Bond, and arranged for the produce to be consigned directly to him.[21] From this perspective it appeared that Sayers had implemented far tighter managerial control of Chiswick than had been the case for two decades, with all operations relating to the estate apparently being brought under his oversight. The success of this manoeuvre depended, however, on the reality of Sayers' ability to operate in the world of plantation slavery while living in Norfolk. Events would prove that obtaining actual operational control as an absentee was far more difficult than making plans to do so.

The next move made under Sayers' new regime was to purchase extra workers. In 1823 Chiswick's people numbered 179 and this had increased to 194 in 1826, despite twenty-one having died since the previous return and only five children having been born. This increase was a result of Sayers and Anderson having purchased thirty-one people between 1823 and 1826, in three groups. First, there was a group of young

---

[15] Suckling, *The History*, pp. 352–59; Palmer, *Perlustration*, p. 317; Edward Mogg, Daniel Paterson, *Paterson's Roads* (London: Longman & Company, 1824), p. 342; Johnston had returned to Jamaica to become a resident planter sometime by 1829; Society for the Conversion and Religious Instruction and Education of the Negro Slaves in the British West India Islands, *Report for the year 1829* (1829), p. 24.

[16] *Royal Gazette of Jamaica*, Saturday 30 December 1826, p. 22, 19 January 1828, p. 7, and Saturday 26 January 1828, p. 22. 'James Forsyth', *Legacies of British Slavery* database, http://wwwdepts-live.ucl.ac.uk/lbs/person/view/13987, accessed 20 October 2023.

[17] Higman, *Plantation*, pp. 66–67.

[18] BLO/MSS.W.Ind.s.17, 1829–1831, fol. 54, Forsyth to Thomas Sayers, 14 February 1829.

[19] BLO/MSS.W.Ind.s.17, fol. 53, Forsyth to Thomas Sayers, 14 February 1829.

[20] See crop returns for 1824 and 1825 JA/1B/11/4/61, fol. 104; 1B/11/4/63, fol. 9.

[21] See crop returns JA/1B/11/4/61, fol. 104; 1B/11/4/63, fol.8; 1B/11/4/65, fol. 155; 1B/11/4/67, fol. 77.

men in their late teens or early twenties – George Taylor, Thomas Walker, Anthony Fulford, and William – all of whom came originally from New Providence in the Bahamas and had been registered in the island by a man named William Gibson around 1823. Second, there was a lone teenager named Sam, who had been imported from Long Island and was registered originally by a man named Michael Major.[22]

The rest of the new arrivals, including several families, were purchased from the executors of Alan McDonald, who had owned another estate in St Thomas-in-the-East, Gilmore Hill, from 1820 to 1824.[23] There were seven men – Thomas Brydie, James Brown, John Colquhoun, Robert Boswell, Jared McCrea, John Rock, and John Rusworm – all of whom were Africans and aged between thirty-seven and forty-nine. There were also four teenagers – William Francis, Richard Brydie, Edward Thomas, and Samuel Pryce – and six boys under ten – James McDonald, Henry Thomas, Alick Thomas, Sam Mitchell, George Rock, and Joseph McDonald. These men and boys were accompanied by five African women – Margaret Colquhoun, Jane Brydie, Ann Brydie, Mary Rock, Elanor Colquhoun, and Eliza Brown – and three children under ten – Polly McDonald, Janet Rock, and Christian Brydie.[24]

Clearly, Sayers had several aims with these purchases. One was to address the imbalance of sexes on the estate and increase the number of male workers. The second was to improve the birth rate on Chiswick by purchasing families. Finally, he may have felt that bringing younger people onto the estate would strengthen the longevity of the workforce. With no new enslaved Africans arriving on the island, the death of every child was felt as a major economic blow. As Forsyth put it in 1829 on the death of a two-year-old child on the estate, 'This is a loss we regret because the children as so very few and so soon grow to be useful.'[25] Without the ability to import slave labour, estates were in competition to buy enslaved workers from the internal market, but the pool available to buy on the island was extremely limited, and the prices were high – in 1825, William Wright noted '£120 to £140 being given a good effective negro'.[26] The price paid for the new people is not recorded, nor is it clear where the funds for these purchases came from, but it may be that the collapse in returns seen since 1815 allowed Sayers to convince his fellow proprietors to forego their income and allow capital investment.

The purchases had a material effect on the birth rate, but not enough to turn the tide. From 1823 to 1826 there were twenty-nine deaths and five births.[27] Between 1826 and 1829 there were twenty-six deaths and twelve births, therefore the birth rate had doubled, but remained far below the replacement rate. In 1829 Chiswick still only had a population of 181 people overall.[28] This highlights the tremendous difficulties faced in trying to arrest the issues of an aging and shrinking workforce

---

[22] NA/T71/148, Slave Registers 1826, fols 59–60.
[23] NA/T71/146, Slave Registers 1820, fols 277–278. McDonald had purchased the estate from the executors of the previous owner, John Colquhoun.
[24] NA/T/71/148, Slave Registers 1826, fols 59–60.
[25] BLO/MSS.W.Ind.s.17, fol. 126 Forsyth to Pitcairn and Amos, 20 December 1829.
[26] NRO/MC1519/1/813X9, fol. 3, William Wright to Susanna Wright, 9 September 1825.
[27] NA/T71/148, Slave Registers 1826, fols 59–60.
[28] NA/T71/149, Slave Registers 1829.

in this period. Even with this substantial purchase Sayers had not managed to return the number of Chiswick's enslaved workers to those of 1817, never mind the ideal numbers of the 1790s when at least 280 enslaved people laboured on the estate. There were still too few workers and Chiswick continued to employ at least two jobbing gangs at harvest.[29]

Having purchased extra workers, the next element in Sayers' plan for improving the estate was cutting Chiswick's overheads. Substantial amounts of supplies were sent out from England each year to provide food and provisions for the overseers, bookkeepers, and the workforce. To these costs were added those of the 'island expenses' for the estate. The cost of these provisions was generally around £2,000 per annum, and Sayers had decided to reduce this. In a shift in strategy that seems contrary to ideas of amelioration, the task of 'victualling the negroes' was placed under 'under a proper system of economy' with the attorney instructed to bring expenses down.[30] This economy was extended to the provisions for the free workers on the estate as well, with 'salt provisions' being cut back and bread at dinner being replaced by yams and plantain. Where 'most estates get fresh beef once or twice per week', Chiswick no longer did so, and the overseer and bookkeepers were required to eat locally caught fish and 'land crabs', or pork, mutton, and poultry. Sayers also cut back on the amount of porter sent out to the estate and stopped the wine that had been provided 'when times went well'.[31] The result was a fall in estate expenses, which were £1,727, £1,052, and £1,526 in 1826, 1827, and 1828 respectively.[32]

The social consequence of this policy shift would seem to have been greater hardship for the enslaved workers at Chiswick. There is, unfortunately, no detail of the ration sizes given to the enslaved population. Likewise, there are no records to indicate how productive the provision grounds at Chiswick were. We can use evidence from other estates to help assess the situation, however. Higman suggests that the area of provision grounds in Jamaica peaked around 1800, where the average was 366 acres, with a decline thereafter to an average of 137 acres in the 1820s.[33] The limited evidence from Chiswick supports this finding. In Chapter 2 it was suggested that, using Higman's estimates, the provision grounds at Chiswick may have reached 333 acres in size around 1800 and, when added to estimated woods of 138 acres and 46 acres of ruinate, the area totalled 517 acres. Higman's figures suggest in the 1820s around 14 per cent of a plantation was woods, 8 per cent ruinate and 14 per cent provision grounds, making a total for these areas at Chiswick of 412 acres. In the 1830s his figures would suggest a further fall in this total area to 367 acres.[34] A letter from 1833 records the total area of the estate in use

---

[29] NRO/MC1519/1/813X9, William Wright to Susanna Wright, 9 September 1825, fol. 3.

[30] BLO/MSS.W.Ind.s.17, fol.137, Charles Burton to Mayhew, 9 May 1830.

[31] NRO/MC1519/1/813X9, William Wright to Susanna Wright, 10 April 1825, fol. 1.

[32] BLO/MSS.W.Ind.s.17, fol. 125, Pitcairn & Amos to Mayhew, 6 March 1830.

[33] Higman, 'The Spatial', p. 26; R. A. McDonald, *The Economy and Material Culture of Slaves: Goods and Chattels on the Sugar Plantations of Jamaica and Louisiana* (Baton Rouge, LA: University of Louisiana Press, 1993), pp. 27–28; M. Mulcahy, *Hurricanes and society in the British Greater Caribbean, 1624–1783* (Baltimore, MD: The Johns Hopkins University Press, 2006), pp. 192–93.

[34] Higman, 'The Spatial', p. 26.

for those purposes as 348 acres, only 19 acres below Higman's estimated average for the decade, which suggests that using Higman's estimates is a reliable guide for these areas at Chiswick.[35] This data is presented in Table 8 and suggests that the provision areas on the estate had fallen since 1800 and that by the 1820s there were only 161 acres of provision grounds at Chiswick.

Table 8.   Estimated acres of provision ground in relation to people of the Chiswick estate, 1800–1833.

	Number of people	**Estimated area of provision grounds**
1800	280	333
1810	245	333
1817	201	282
1826	174	161
1833	169	172

This reduction may not, however, have been a conscious decision on the part of the Burtons and their managers, but rather a consequence of the falling numbers of enslaved people on the estate. A letter from 1832, detailing the arrival of new enslaved workers on the estate explained that the new arrivals 'must be made comfortable in being provided with a good house, garden, and grounds' and that they would need to be 'maintained' until their garden began yielding food.[36] The established position appears to have been that the enslaved workers received a house, garden, and grounds. A comparison of the numbers of enslaved people on the estate from the 1790s to the 1830s and the estimates of area of provision grounds suggests that there was a rough correlation of about one acre per person at Chiswick (Table 8). These numbers would suggest that the average area per enslaved person at Chiswick was around one acre throughout the century and that the drop in overall area was a consequence of falling numbers of enslaved people. Nonetheless, one might be tempted to speculate that the sharp fall in area between 1817 and 1826, if correct, might indicate that part of Sayers' programme involved reducing the provision grounds from a larger area to one more in line with the numbers of people on the estate.

Evidence from elsewhere reinforces the idea of growing hardship. Correspondence suggests that these provision grounds were barely adequate, since it was part of the settled operation of the estate that the enslaved workers were left to forage for their 'principal support' in the Great Morass, with consequent problems in regularity of food supply.[37] The suggestion that the provision grounds were insufficient for normal purposes is augmented by reports from the attorney in 1833 that the provision grounds produced badly in poor weather and that this caused great hardship.[38] Moreover, later records suggest that the managers at Chiswick knew that the provi-

---

[35]   BLO/MSS.W.Ind.s.18, fol. 73, Townson to Pitcairn & Amos, 5 August 1833.
[36]   BLO/MSS.W.Ind.s.18, fol. 43, Forsyth to Pitcairn & Amos, 12 November 1832.
[37]   BLO/MSS.W.Ind.s.18, fol. 36, Forsyth to Pitcairn & Amos, 12 July 1832.
[38]   BLO/MSS.W.Ind.s.18, fol. 80, Townson to Pitcairn & Amos, 2 September 1833.

sion area was inadequate and were, in fact, utilising scarcity as a means of enforcing discipline on the estate. In 1835 the attorney, James Townson, stated that he had 'calculated that in consequence of the poverty of provision grounds at Chiswick, that the people would have eagerly embraced the offer of working for wages'.[39] Although from a later period, Townson's nonchalance in his discussion of this point indicates that this was a settled piece of knowledge among the estate's managerial class and, since he had been involved there since 1829, the use of scarcity to enforce discipline was a policy that pre-dated abolition and apprenticeship. This situation is reminiscent of Mary Turner's suggestion that in the eighteenth-century estate owners 'presided over a seasonal hunger cycle' which caused serious labour unrest. She found that the grounds at Amity Hall were 'minuscule' and that this reflected a general reluctant approach to engage with amelioration there.[40]

The final element in Sayers' plan was to modernise the operations of Chiswick by introducing new agricultural methods, specifically the use of ploughing. It may be that he had got this idea from discussions with Andrew Johnstone or with their neighbours, the Arcedeckne family, who owned Golden Grove and lived at Glevering Hall in Suffolk.[41] Ploughs were being used in operations at Golden Grove in this period, and so the families may have discussed the option of using ploughing to improve Chiswick's productivity.[42] It also may be that the introduction of ploughing was part of a response to the pressure from abolitionists to reduce female labour on estates. Since Chiswick, in line with most Jamaican estates, relied upon women to work in the fields, as pressure to lessen their workload grew ploughing was seen by some as a means of achieving this aim.[43]

To assist in ploughing operations Sayers decided to recruit a Norfolk farmer with experience of such matters who wished to go out to the island. The job was advertised and, after listening to 'a letter we heard read at the *Norfolk Hotel*', a twenty-two-year-old named William Wright decided to try his luck and apply for the job.[44] Wright could produce the required references and had the necessary experience.

---

[39] BLO/MSS.W.Ind.s.18, fol. 145 Townson to Pitcairn & Amos, 29 June 1835. For Townson, see 'James Townson', *Legacies of British Slavery* database, http://wwwdepts-live.ucl.ac.uk/lbs/person/view/21751, accessed 20 October 2023.

[40] Mary Turner, 'Slave Workers, Subsistence and Labour Bargaining: Amity Hall, Jamaica, 1805–1832', in *The Slaves' Economy: Independent Production by Slaves in the Americas*, ed. Ira Berlin and Philip D. Morgan (London: Frank Cass, 1991), pp. 92–106, at pp. 94–95.

[41] Simon Taylor managed the Golden Grove estate until his death in 1813 and has been studied in exceptional depth. For example, Higman, *Plantation*, pp. 127–51 and 166–226; SRO/HB/26/412/1595, Sale Particulars of Golden Grove Estate, 1891. For the family, see 'Chaloner Arcedeckne', *Legacies of British Slavery* database, http://wwwdepts-live.ucl.ac.uk/lbs/person/view/2146640845, accessed 27 October 2023; 'Andrew Arcedeckne', *Legacies of British Slavery* database, http://wwwdepts-live.ucl.ac.uk/lbs/person/view/24517, accessed 20 October 2023; Nicolas Kingsley, '(162) Arcedeckne of Glevering Hall', *Landed Families of Britain, and Ireland*, https://landedfamilies.blogspot.com/2015/04/162-arcedeckne-of-glevering-hall.html, accessed 25 March 2019.

[42] BLO/MSS.W.Ind.s.19, fol. 122, Townson to Steward & Westmoreland, 8 September 1838.

[43] Turner, 'Planter', p. 241.

[44] NRO/MC1519/1/813X9, William Wright to Susanna Wright, 10 April 1825, fol. 6.

Critically, he was desperate for work and could not find it in Norfolk. Indeed, Wright's decision to travel to slaveholding Jamaica in 1824 helps us understand why people still travelled to Jamaica to work on the plantations, even as the abolition campaign increased in fervour. He came from Watton, a small market town lying twenty-one miles south-west of Norwich. Like the rest of East Anglia in the early nineteenth century, Watton was experiencing considerable economic difficulties, with rising poverty and rents, and a growth in the workforce as men returned from the wars.[45] Wright's move to Jamaica was driven, therefore, by brutal economic reality. As he put it, 'if I could have gained a living by any endeavours without being a burden to anyone, I should never have left Norfolk'.[46]

In early 1825 Wright travelled to Jamaica to take up his post. His letters to his mother in Watton reveal that, even at this early stage of Sayers' grand scheme to turn the estate around, things were not going well. In fact, the situation at Chiswick was far more difficult than the Burtons understood, and Wright's letters show clearly that the central problems for absentee landlords were their lack of actual control of their estate and minimal understanding of operations on the ground in Jamaica. Wright explained that any instructions to the island, and information from it, were seriously delayed and, even then, the implementation of absentee orders was dependent on the degree to which the overseer and attorney agreed with them. Although Sayers had told Wright that 'I was to have the management of the agricultural part of the Concern', on arrival Wright discovered that this was not the case.[47]

The overseer, Prosser, and Charles Anderson did not consider Wright's knowledge of ploughing and Norfolk's agricultural techniques to be any use at all. It transpired that Anderson was merely going along with the plan to please Sayers. Wright discovered that ploughing had been tried at Chiswick before and had been abandoned. 'The first thing that took my attention on the Estate', he wrote soon after arriving, 'was an old plough as long and clumsy as ever you saw anything in your life.' Further enquiries revealed 'the system had been tried on the Estate but did not succeed' and that the opinion of the managers was 'very much against its being any use now'.[48] Wright hoped to attempt a trial but, despite the plan being part of Sayers' instructions, the overseer and attorney failed to support it and Wright found that he had 'no more authority to make any alteration than I had to have my Uncle Philip's Great pasture ploughed up'.[49] Prosser told him that any experiment was impossible during harvest because 'he cannot possibly spare any oxen to try it in the Season of making Sugar' and termed the project 'ridiculous'.[50]

[45]   G. E. Mingay (ed.), *The Agricultural State of the Kingdom, 1816* (Bath: Adams and Dart, 1970), pp. 190–92, 197, 301, 325. For wider discussion of these economic circumstances and their consequences for the rural population, see J. Bohstedt, *The Politics of Provisions Food Riots, Moral Economy and Market Transition in England, c. 1550–1850* (Farnham: Ashgate, 2010).

[46]   NRO/MC1519/1,813X9, William Wright to Susanna Wright, 13 January 1825, fol. 4.

[47]   NRO/MC1519/1/813X9, William Wright to Susanna Wright, 15 May 1825, fol. 2.

[48]   NRO/MC1519/1/813X9, William Wright to Susanna Wright, 14 February 1825, fol. 5.

[49]   NRO/MC1519/1/813X9, William Wright to Susanna Wright, 15 May 1825, fol. 2.

[50]   NRO/MC1519/1/813X9, William Wright to Susanna Wright, 14 February 1825, fol. 6.

The enslaved workers concurred and provided expert local knowledge to justify their view. In a rare record of the words of one of Chiswick's people, Wright recorded a conversation with one of the drivers, who remembered the previous experiment: 'You no plough on Chiswick Massa. Why? said I. Because the ground to tiff [*sic*] and the Cane roots break plough Massa.'[51] Wright did not dismiss the driver's statement but accepted that his view was based on sound knowledge of Chiswick's geography, climate, and methods of sugar cultivation. For example, Wright found that 'lifting in this situation' was difficult since 'after the rains […] it becomes nearly a morass from which the oxen could not draw their feet'. Conversely, waiting for the rains to finish did not improve the situation, since within days of any rain ending the intense heat 'bakes the soil' making the land too hard to work successfully and 'like a road at the bottom'. In any case, because Chiswick was not 'the well cultivated fields of Norfolk', the estate was completely unprepared for the plough to be used and was covered in 'large rock stones' and tree stumps.[52]

As the unnamed driver stated, if the climate and landscape were not problematic enough, the existing techniques of sugar cultivation also made ploughing deeply challenging. Wright noted that because the cane 'never stands for less than three years', and in that time 'the land is never stirred except on the top', the roots became 'most firmly fixed and something like a furze shrub'. Wright's assessment was that this would damage the ploughs as 'the shares will stand an uncommon poor chance when they come into contact with them'. Moreover, because the ground was covered in 'dead trash' laid 'several inches thick' to protect it from drying out, the trash would 'certainly drive before the cutter and keep the plough going into the ground'. Further enquiries revealed that these problems were to be found elsewhere in the area, with the 'mountainous' terrain making ploughing 'totally impracticable' on two-thirds of the estates that he had seen.[53] The estates where it did occur, such as Golden Grove and Winchester, had better soil than Chiswick. Wright noted that, 'They plough on Golden Grove 4 miles from hence, but it is a nice loose black soil.'[54] Even there, the process was tricky. Golden Grove and Winchester used 'eight oxen to a plough and 6 negros', could plough no more than half an acre a day, and the resulting trenches were not of the correct depth or width.[55]

Wright was finally able to attempt his 'trial', but only in June after the sugar crop had been gathered and it was now too late in the season. Initially he used eight oxen, but even when he increased the number to twelve, it was 'entirely useless' and he broke the head of the plough. The 'tremendous rains' that had fallen meant that the soil was 'a complete mass of nasty red clay' and made ploughing impossible. When he tried again after a dry spell, he found that he 'might as well try a turnpike', much to Prosser's amusement. The effort required five enslaved workers to 'steer the oxen' and to clear the 'cane thrash' ahead of the team. Wright and Prosser agreed that the problem was that English techniques were designed for a climate where there was

---

51 NRO/MC1519/1/813X9, William Wright to Susanna Wright, 10 April 1825, fols 6–7.
52 NRO/MC1519/1/813X9, William Wright to Susanna Wright, 10 April 1825, fols 6–7.
53 NRO/MC1519/1/813X9, William Wright to Susanna Wright, 15 May 1825, fol. 2 and 8.
54 NRO/MC1519/1/813X9, William Wright to Susanna Wright, 10 April 1825, fol. 7.
55 NRO/MC1519/1/813X9, William Wright to Susanna Wright, 12 July 1825, fol. 3.

'frost in winter and a good shower of rain at intervals in summer', but the climate in Jamaica, with long spells of dry weather and then 'heavy downfalls', meant the techniques needed adaptation.[56]

In the 1830s, however, ploughing was introduced successfully on the estate because the attorney was willing to support the process.[57] It seems, therefore, that the key problem was that the managers of Chiswick during the 1820s were unwilling to adapt their operations and chose not to implement Sayers' orders. Wright's ploughing experiment shows that, even when absentee owners attempted to improve their estate's operations, they faced an uphill struggle. Without an actual physical presence Sayers could not push the incumbent managers to change their existing mode of operation. Even his delegated expert, Wright, was unable to exert pressure on the managers to change matters. This reluctance was probably partially because of an indisposition to change, but also because of the shortage of labour which meant the estate's managers were unwilling to divert scarce labour resources away from the core activity of making sugar to support Wright's experiment.

Wright's letters record other examples which reinforce the impression of poor management at the estate that the Burtons' absentee status prevented them from dealing with. For example, Wright was upset at the quality of animal husbandry. The working oxen on the estate were 'too small' and in very poor condition, as were the mules. The animals were being overworked, because they were kept in use 'day and night' and were fed poorly. When they were worked, he noted that 'the method of drawing is shocking', since the techniques used placed the weight of the wain on their necks causing them serious health problems. While these issues could have been dealt with by redesigning the harnesses, no-one was interested. Wright believed that improving the animals' diets by increasing the available pasture was crucial to better animal husbandry and would improve the estate's profitability since it would cut the high replacement costs for the animals. Once more, such changes needed Sayers to take decisive action, but Wright doubted he was even aware of the situation. The gap between the ideas of Sayers in Norfolk and the reality of Jamaica was clear for Wright, who saw no evidence that Anderson had told Sayers about any of these issues.[58]

In any case, cutting the costs of the livestock operation by growing more food for the animals on the estate would have required more investment because the existing pastures at Chiswick were in a very poor state. Most of the fodder was provided by Indian corn, which was planted between the cane plants. There were two pastures planted with Guinea grass but most of the potential pasture was 'wide open waste covered with bushes and weeds and good for but little'.[59] Wright argued that these pastures needed to be cleaned and fed, but Prosser told him that the means to clear

---

[56] NRO/MC1519/1/813X9, William Wright to Susanna Wright, 12 July 1825, fols 1–2.
[57] WM/SC/01621, Townson to Mayhew, 24 September 1838; BLO/MSS.W.Ind.s.19, fol. 82, Pitcairn & Amos to Mayhew, 12 October 1837; fol. 121, Steward & Westmoreland to Mayhew, 18 October 1838; fol. 122, Townson to Mayhew, 8 September 1838.
[58] NRO/MC1519/1/813X9, William Wright to Susanna Wright, 10 April 1825, fols 3–4, 5–6.
[59] NRO/MC1519/1/813X9, William Wright to Susanna Wright, 10 April 1825, fol. 6; 15 May 1825, fol. 3.

and fertilise them were not available. Because all the focus of operations was on the sugar cane, this had first call on the available manure, and as there was 'not half enough for the cane land', all available manure was used there.[60] Once again, the managers at Chiswick appear to have been unwilling to innovate and the absentee Burtons had no understanding of the issues. While purchasing manure from a nearby pen would have been an extra cost, in the longer-term Wright's proposal would have reduced expenses. Anderson and Prosser seem to have been focused only on short-term profit maximisation, rather than long-term planning.

This was indicative of a general malaise at Chiswick, which was obvious to a man of Wright's experience. Alongside the problems with the livestock and the pastures, the estate was in a general state of disrepair. The fences were 'dilapidated' and need to be fixed to allow the estate to be improved but this could not be done with sufficient speed, for the same reason that the pastures were not cleared, and the animals were overworked, the lack of available labour. With most of the estate's produce being shipped from Port Morant, some twelve miles away, Chiswick's own wharf had been 'permitted to fall into total ruin'; although the 'little house' attached to it was rented out to provide extra income for the estate.[61] As Wright explained, 'Mr Sayers forgot to tell us one thing when he projected so many improvements and that was that he was very short of hands.'[62] The lack of understanding in Norfolk was clear, the Burton family had still not grasped the impact of the shortage of labour in Jamaica.

Moreover, Wright's letters suggest that under Sayers' new management the working regime had become more arduous. Some historians have proposed that in response to falling sugar prices during this period estate owners may have sought to increase the volume of production through increased work regimes.[63] This appears to have been the case at Chiswick, where Wright recorded that night work was continuing apace, with the workers being pulled into the works after field labour throughout the crop. Wright also made it clear that corporal punishment appears to have been used widely to contain unrest among the workers. He noted the prevalence of the use of the whip across the estate, 'a black driver is always with them with a whip' he noted in respect of the great gang and note how the overseer would point out 'slow' workers in the field to the driver who 'reminds them of it in the same manner as your barrow boys do when told his horses walk too slow'. The use of violence was endemic. For example, in April 1825 Wright described how Chiswick had a 'fisherman' who had to provide the overseer and bookkeepers with fish, and that 'if he fails for 2 or 3 days no matter from what cause he is sure to get a flogging'.[64]

This impression is confirmed by the case of an elderly worker on the estate named Joseph Marriot. In a pamphlet of the period written by the powerful planter

---

[60] NRO/MC1519/1/813X9, William Wright to Susanna Wright, 10 April 1825, fol. 6; 15 May 1825, fol. 3.

[61] NRO/MC1519/1/813X9, William Wright to Susanna Wright, 13 January 1825, fols 5–6; BLO/ MSS.W.Ind.s.18, fol. 111, Forsyth to Pitcairn & Amos, 29 June 1834.

[62] NRO/MC1519/1/813X9, William Wright to Susanna Wright, 10 April 1825, fol. 6.

[63] J. E. Candow, 'A Reassessment of the Provision of Food to Enslaved Persons, with Special Reference to Salted Cod in Barbados', *Journal of Caribbean History* Vol. 43 (2009), pp. 265–81, p. 271; Craton, *Searching*, p. 138.

[64] NRO/MC1519/1/813X9, William Wright to Susanna Wright, 10 April 1825, fols 1, 7–8, 12–13.

Alexander Barclay, Marriott was described as 'an old Negro belonging to Chiswick estate'.[65] Around 1828, Marriott was able to purchase the freedom of his wife, named Sophy, and her four children aged between five and fourteen, who were from Barking Lodge estate. The manumission was eventually agreed at a cost of £300 currency, or £200 sterling. Most of the money for this manumission was provided by Sophy's sister, Sarah, who had received it in consequence of her liaison with the overseer of Barking Lodge, who had freed her and provided her with property. Marriott may have provided some of the funds, however. Soon after the manumission was completed, Marriott, who remained enslaved at Chiswick, was sent to the workhouse for disobedience. Marriott died soon after his release.[66]

This tale reinforces the impression from Wright that discipline at Chiswick was severe. Nonetheless, it also shows that Marriott was able to become involved in the affairs of Barking Lodge estate, which lay around ten miles to the west of Chiswick, confirming that the estate's people were able to interact in meaningful ways with those of other estates. Marriot had also been able to earn some of the money required for the manumission, proving that Chiswick's workers were able to engage in the sale of their own produce within the island's markets. Wright noted that the workers at Chiswick were allowed twenty-six days per year to 'till their grounds' and these sources make it clear that the people of Chiswick were engaging in the barter economy as best they could. This activity was under pressure in these years, however, since Wright stated that it was not really allowed during crop, which meant that on most Saturdays for the rest of the year the bookkeepers had no work to do, since the people were in their provision grounds.[67]

A few months after arriving, having surveyed the situation at Chiswick Wright was furious with Sayers. He was not able to do the work he had been promised, he was not managing livestock, nor running ploughing operations. Rather he was working as a bookkeeper, a role he had 'no inclination to engage with'. Wright concluded initially that Sayers had been deceiving him when he was recruited, since 'if he knew anything of West India affairs' he would have realised that there was no management position for Wright.[68] After further consideration, Wright changed his view and concluded that Sayers was largely operating from ignorance and lack of understanding of the conditions at Chiswick.[69] Sayers may have hoped to bring the estate under closer control, but the drawbacks of absentee ownership had not been overcome. Without visiting Jamaica, and with no local connections on the island to rely on, the Burtons were completely dependent on second-hand information about their property and its operation.

---

[65] *The Barbadian*, 22 June 1830, pp. 3–4. Marriot would seem to have been 'Joseph Marrion' who was recorded as a sixty-year-old 'Creole' in the register of 1817, NAT/71/145, Slave Registers 1817, fol. 850. For Barclay, see 'Alexander Barclay', *Legacies of British Slavery* database, http://wwwdepts-live.ucl.ac.uk/lbs/person/view/15549, accessed 20 October 2023.
[66] *The Anti-Slavery Reporter*, 1 October 1832, pp. 265–68.
[67] NRO/MC1519/1/813X9, William Wright to Susanna Wright, 10 April 1825, fol. 8.
[68] NRO/MC1519/1/813X9, William Wright to Susanna Wright, 10 April 1825, fol. 11.
[69] NRO/MC1519/1/813X9, William Wright to Susanna Wright, 15 May 1825, fol. 4.

Even Wright, who worked in English agriculture and came from a farming family, only grasped the reality of plantation agriculture after travelling to Jamaica and living at Chiswick. Before arriving in Jamaica, Wright had no more than a generalised impression of the situation on the island, despite apparently having some degree of contact with Norfolk emigres living there. Although literate and reasonably well educated, he seems to have expected something akin to the mixed farms he would have been used to in Norfolk; focused on providing both livestock and produce for sale in local markets, with high quality livestock managed in a humane fashion, and using familiar farming techniques. Wright's letters reveal his gradual comprehension that this was a different agricultural operation entirely and that nothing mattered on the estate except sugar, which was cultivated using totally alien techniques based around large amounts of enslaved labour. He soon came to grasp that the dependence upon, and brutal exploitation of, that labour made the estate less like a Norfolk farm and more like a factory with dependent workers, and that in this circumstance, 'the grand thing is the management of the Negroes'.[70]

The Norfolk farmer's pre-arrival level of understanding was probably equivalent, if not superior, to the level of understanding of Sayers and the Burtons. Sayers had not spoken with a wide group of people before making his plans and had no experience of land management or farming. He might have spoken to the Arcedeckne family about ploughing, but they ran a very different estate and even there, ploughing was not a panacea, and the opinion was that their use of ploughing was inefficient and 'they take near as much time as if it were not ploughed at all'.[71] Otherwise, Sayers had only spoken to Anderson, who seem to have confirmed what Sayers suggested, before ignoring Sayers' instructions anyway. Wright told his mother that 'the letter we heard read at the Norfolk hotel certainly came from the attorney' and would seem to have described the situation at Chiswick in a flattering light.[72]

Wright's perceptive analysis confirms that, so long as they chose to stay in England, absentee owners such as Sayers and the Burtons could only have a general awareness of the operations of their estates, and this made any significant change to operations difficult. Their information was derived from second-hand sources, the most crucial of which were the attorney's letters from the island. The problem was that such letters were never complete in detail, nor were they, necessarily, completely frank. Even if he had been minded to, Anderson could not provide sufficiently detailed accounts of the operations of the estate to enable Sayers and the other Burtons to make informed decisions.

Moreover, since he was receiving an excellent income from his work at Chiswick, Anderson was naturally inclined to present the situation under his management in the best possible light. As Wright put it, the attorney was 'the same as the owner here, and at the present price of sugar in many cases much better off for he gets a handsome salary, good crop or bad one, there are many of the attorneys making fortunes while the estates are running deep in debt'. The attorney seems to have pretended to support Sayers' ideas to gain his position. 'I suspect', Wright wrote, 'he

<hr />

[70] NRO/MC1519/1/813X9, William Wright to Susanna Wright, 10 April 1825, fol. 8.
[71] NRO/MC1519/1/813X9, William Wright to Susanna Wright, 15 May 1825, fol. 3.
[72] NRO/MC1519/1/813X9, William Wright to Susanna Wright, 10 April 1825, fol. 6.

has gulled both Mr Sayer[s] and myself to give him a little recommendation on first taking charge of the estate and as he bore no part of the expense of it was a matter of little consequence to him whether it succeeded or not.'[73] In such a situation, there was little incentive for Anderson to be frank in discussing the estate's problems, especially when he had no solutions.

On top of this, communications with Jamaica took a long time. Even if a letter was sent by the fast packet it took at least a month to arrive. Allowing for time to research and write a response and for the return voyage for that reply, a simple conversation took three months to take place. This timeframe made gathering information both time-consuming and tedious, even if any of the Burtons had been interested in doing so. It also made detailed management from a distance extremely difficult unless the owner was willing to spend a great deal of time and energy doing so. Thomas Mayhew would do this in the 1830s, but Thomas and Charles Burton were certainly not interested in doing so and, probably, Thomas Sayers did not put in the necessary hours.

Moreover, most of the attorney's letters were mediated via the London agents, who copied the extracts from them that they considered most useful for the proprietors to see, and so edited the picture presented to the Burtons even more tightly. The family were not completely without knowledge of the estate, but without visiting it regularly it was impossible for them to truly understand Chiswick. Wright's letters from Chiswick show that absentee owners who had never visited their estates, like the Burtons, were at a significant disadvantage to planters who continued to live in Jamaica, or even those who had returned to England having made their fortunes. Such planters understood the island far more clearly than those who had never seen it. The Burtons had never looked at Chiswick's cane fields, touched its soil, witnessed a torrential downpour on its fields, felt its heat, been bitten by its mosquitoes, watched the process of harvest and sugar production, or seen one of their enslaved workers being whipped. The result of choosing to live in Norfolk and farm in the Caribbean was that the Burtons had very little understanding of what sugar cultivation based on slavery entailed in practice.

The was a similar situation to that documented by Turner at Amity Hall, where she argued that the owner, Henry Goulburn, was completely dependent on his attorney to provide him with information that he might use to rebut charges of cruelty on the estate being made against him by Zachary Macauley. As she pointed out, the reality was that the attorney provided Goulburn with information that placed the situation on his estate in the best possible light. The difference between Goulburn and the Burtons was that Goulburn was a serving MP and the situation on his estate was used to criticise him, forcing him to conduct his own investigation into matters. Even then, he only made minimal improvements on the estate.[74] There was no such external pressure on the Burtons and because they appear to have had no real interest in the situation, the implementation of changes that might have helped Chiswick deal with the rapidly altering situation of the 1820s did not occur.

---

[73] NRO/MC1519/1/813X9, William Wright to Susanna Wright, 10 April 1825, fols 6, 9–10.
[74] Turner, 'Labour', pp. 244–48.

Table 9. *Estimated net profit of the Chiswick estate, 1823–1827.*[*]

Crop year	Hogsheads of sugar sold in London (puncheons of rum in brackets)	Estimated price per hogsheads of sugar (£ sterling)	Estimated gross income (£ sterling)	Insurance costs at 7% (£ sterling)	Factor costs at 2½% (£ sterling)	Freight (9s per cwt) (£ sterling)	Estimated net profit on sugar (after fixed expenses)	Net profit (with rum at £15 per puncheon)
1823	167 (60)	25	£4,175	(£292)	(£104)	(£1,269)	(£20)	£880
1824	137 (60)	25	£3,425	(£240)	(£86)	(£1,041)	(£472)	£428
1825	110 (54)	30	£3,300	(£231)	(£83)	(£836)	£423	£1,233
1827	150 (66)	27	£4,050	(£284)	(£101)	(£1,139)	£1,474	£2,464
1828	177 (85)	16	£2,832				£527	£1,295

[*] Sources: JA/1B/11/4/61, fol. 104; 1B/11/4/63, fol. 8; 1B/11/4/65, fol. 155; 1B/11/4/67, fol. 77; BLO/MSS.W.Ind.s.17, fol. 116, Pitcairn & Amos to Farr 28 January 1830. The return for 1826 has not been located. Tierces have been converted at the ratio of 1½ tierce to 1 hogshead.

The disappointing commercial outcome of Sayers' changes to Chiswick's commercial operations from 1823 onwards is shown in Table 9. The results for 1828 have been taken from estate records, so the estimated figures have not been used. The prices for sugar, apart from that for 1828, have been taken from Ragatz.[75] The fixed expenses are known exactly for 1826, 1827, and 1828 and these are applied.[76] For 1828 no deductions are made for insurance, shipping, and factor costs, as the figures provided from the records are net of these after this date.[77] The fall in expenses showed that Sayers' efforts had been effective in that specific area and made a positive difference to the net profit until 1828. Yields remained disappointingly low, however, and the continuing softness of sugar prices meant that profits remained unremarkable. The average production of sugar was 147 hogsheads, around the 149 hogsheads achieved from 1816 to 1824 and far below the 236 hogsheads per year attained in the years 1803 to 1815. In comparison, Amity Hall produced an average of 205 in the same period.[78] The average profit for the period was £1,260 per year, £871 less than that of the years from 1815 to 1822. Overall, Sayers' experiment had been a failure.

While this was unwelcome news for all the family, it was most problematic for Sayers, who needed to increase the income stream coming from the estate immediately. Indeed, the driving force behind Sayers' enthusiasm for improving Chiswick was not an interest in agriculture, or the well-being of the family, but desperation. Thomas Sayers was in increasing financial difficulty. In 1827 he had lost his livings, reducing his annual income by over £140.[79] In a similar fashion to the situation with James and Charlotte Willins, he and Maria had asked for help from their family and a trust was arranged for them, via a Yarmouth solicitor, James Booth, with Thomas Burton and a Yarmouth barrister, Robert Alderson, as trustees.[80] It seems that Sayers continued to borrow money and at some point around 1828, he took 'advances' of around £1,600 from 'Norwich bankers' which were secured against the future income from Chiswick. At the same time, he 'retained' around £2,400 from the 1828 crop due from Chiswick.[81] What exactly this 'retention' involved is unclear, but it was done without the knowledge of the other proprietors and would seem to have been needed to be repaid before the end of the year, possibly so that the Burtons did not find out about it. This was feasible since Sayers had ensured that all the produce was consigned to him directly, meaning that there was no third party in London to check on the exact numbers coming from Jamaica. Whether malfeasance was always intended cannot be said, but it seems that as Sayers got deeper into financial trouble, this arrangement allowed him to begin manipulating the records concerning the arrival of produce from Jamaica. This may have meant that the other proprietors had

[75] L. J. Ragatz, *Statistics for the Study of British Caribbean History* (London: Bryan Edwards Press, 1927), pp. iii–iv.
[76] BLO/MSS.W.Ind.s.17, fol. 125, Pitcairn & Amos to Mayhew, 6 March 1830.
[77] BLO/MSS.W.Ind.s.18, fol. 58, Pitcairn & Amos to Mayhew, 6 June 1833.
[78] Turner, 'Planter', p. 242.
[79] CCEd: Location: Parish (Church): Thurne, CCEd Location ID: 20041; Location: Parish (Church): Clippesby CCEd Location ID: 19530.
[80] BLO/MSS.W.Ind.s.17, fols 13–14, Thomas Burton to Mayhew, 16 January 1829; Charles John Palmer, *The History of Great Yarmouth* (1856), p. 349; Palmer, *Perlustration*, pp. 339–40.
[81] BLO/MSS.W.Ind.s.17, fol. 29, Pitcairn & Amos to Mayhew, 30 January 1829.

received less income per year than the estimated figures in Table 8 suggest. Although there is no direct evidence, it is probable that this was done with the assistance of Charles Anderson.

In mid-1828 Sayers borrowed a further £3,000 from Messrs W. R. & S. Mitchell & Co., 'a very old and highly respectable' firm of merchants who had offices in Lime Street, London.[82] Mitchells were willing to lend Sayers the money he asked for, but they required security in the form of a mortgage against Chiswick. Critically, this mortgage agreement allowed Mitchells to act against all of Chiswick, although the other proprietors had neither borrowed money from them, nor had they even agreed to the mortgage.[83] On 24 July 1828, Mitchells loaned £3,000 to Sayers and the mortgage was recorded in September.[84]

This loan only postponed Sayers' problems and he soon found himself short of cash. In December 1828 he approached another firm of London merchants, Pitcairn & Amos, requesting a loan of £350. He convinced Maria to co-sign a written agreement which promised that their shares of the upcoming crop from Chiswick would be applied to repay Pitcairn & Amos and received the funds on 9 December.[85] He then returned to Mitchells and borrowed a further £700 from them, by promising that they would be repaid using the profits of his share of 1828's crop, which had already been promised to Pitcairn & Amos.[86] Presumably realising that this charade would come to light as soon as the crop was shipped, Sayers set off for London in December 1828, without Maria, before fleeing to Calais.[87] Left behind in Yarmouth by her husband, Maria finally turned to her brothers and told all she knew. The Burton family had been caught out by their absentee status and their inattention to the affairs of Chiswick and were now facing the prospect of foreclosure. Finally, the Burtons had to take direct action.

---

[82] For details of Mitchells, see *The Times*, Monday 20 September 1841, p. 5; 'Advertisement for the Estate of Anthony Gutzmeyer (Deceased)', *Morning Herald (London)*, Tuesday 1 March 1831; London Metropolitan Archives, MS11936/520/1086989, 'Insured Messrs W R and S Mitchell and Co, 46 Lime Street, merchants', 18 February 1829.

[83] BLO/MSS.W.Ind.s.17, fol. 53, Pitcairn & Amos to Mayhew, 6 April 1829.

[84] BLO/MSS.W.Ind.s.18, fol. 116, Stevens, Wood, Wilkinson, and Satchell to Pitcairn & Amos, 14 November 1834; BLO/MSS.W.Ind.s.17, fol. 69, Forsyth to Pitcairn & Amos, 16 March 1828.

[85] BLO/MSS.W.Ind.s.17, fol. 15-16, Stevens Wood & Wilkinson to Mayhew, 19 January 1829; fol. 99, Pitcairn & Amos to Farr, 11 September 1829; BLO/MSS.W.Ind.s.17, fol. 45, Pitcairn & Amos to Mayhew, 31 March 1829.

[86] BLO/MSS.W.Ind.s.17, fol. 9, Pitcairn & Amos to Farr, 13 January 1829.

[87] BLO/MSS.W.Ind.s.17, fol. 31, Mayhew to Farr, 30 January 1829.

7

'A STATE OF INSUBORDINATION': WORKER UNREST AND FINANCIAL CRISIS, 1829–1834

The years 1829 to 1834 were marked by a series of major challenges for Chiswick. The most immediately pressing problem was dealing with the financial fallout from Sayers' malfeasance. This was made doubly difficult because of the impact of the depressed sugar market on profit margins.[1] Furthermore, the complex financial negotiations that took place over these years were affected in substantial ways by the activity of the enslaved people on the estate, who were described in April 1829 as being 'in a state of insubordination' and who pushed the boundaries of their situation for the entire period.[2] Finally, there was the growing threat, which became a reality in 1833, that the British government would emancipate the enslaved workers across the Caribbean. Dealing with these issues was made doubly difficult by the family's absentee status, which continued to weaken their ability to discover what was happening on the estate. For example, in January 1829 the Burtons knew about the mortgage debt to Mitchells but did not know if Sayers had mortgaged the property to any different parties in Jamaica.[3] Moreover, because Sayers owned 4/21 of the estate, the possibility existed that he would go to Jamaica and move into the great house at Chiswick. The fact of the family's absentee status made this option potentially devastating. If Sayers went to Jamaica he could 'exert his rights as resident proprietor' and 'do more mischief to the property than any legal proceedings that may be initiated by Mitchells'.[4] Sitting in Norfolk, the family were powerless to stop him from doing so, and it was only his decision not to go to the island that prevented them losing control of the estate. The precarious nature of absentee ownership was on full display.

Rather than taking charge personally, however, the trustees – Charles and Thomas Burton and John Lee Farr – appointed Farr's brother-in-law, Thomas Mayhew, to act as their legal advisor.[5] A successful and well-respected solicitor, Mayhew was

---

[1] BLO/MSS.W.Ind.s.17, fol. 190, Pitcairn & Amos to Mayhew, 31 August 1831.
[2] BLO/MSS.W.Ind.s.17, fol. 49-50, Pitcairn & Amos to Mayhew, 4 April 1829.
[3] BLO/MSS.W.Ind.s.17, fol. 20, Pitcairn & Amos to Farr, 20 January 1829.
[4] BLO/MSS.W.Ind.s.17, fol. 15, Stevens, Wood, & Wilkinson to Mayhew, 19 January 1829; fol.22, Stevens, Wood, & Wilkinson to Mayhew, 24 January 1829.
[5] SRO/FAA/23/41/12, Marriage Licence Bond: Thomas Mayhew and Susanna Farr, 9 November 1814.

thirty-eight years old, and lived in the town of his birth, Saxmundham.[6] Although 'hands-off' management by the Burton brothers had produced lacklustre results since 1805, and had then failed spectacularly under Sayers, it was still the case that the brothers would not become deeply involved in Chiswick's business affairs and the matter was left largely to Mayhew. Fortunately for the Burtons, Mayhew was competent and honest and set to work shoring things up.[7] Wisely, he appointed the creditors Pitcairn & Amos to be the family's new London agents, replacing Sayers, thereby bringing one creditor onside. Mayhew then moved to minimise the possibility that Thomas Sayers could cause further 'mischief' and when it became clear that Sayers was not going to Jamaica but was remaining in France, Mayhew acted.[8] He took steps to prevent Sayers selling his equity of redemption in the mortgage to a third party to raise money and altered the trust settlement.[9] Having done so Mayhew had 'exclude[d] Mr Sayers effectually from all interference' in the affairs of Chiswick.[10]

Mayhew then established what proportion of Sayers' debts were secured against Chiswick by mortgage, and to whom mortgages had been given.[11] James Forsyth made enquiries in Jamaica that revealed another debt of £600, ostensibly secured against Maria Sayers' share of the estate, but by mid-March 1829 he confirmed, to everyone's relief, that this had not been recorded within twelve months of being dated and was non-enforceable. Forsyth also established that there were no other deeds affecting Chiswick recorded in the island.[12] By April 1829, therefore, Mayhew had determined the full extent of the secured debts agreed by Sayers. There was a

---

[6]   Suffolk Baptism Index 1538–1911 (Part 1), Baptism of Thomas Mayhew, 9 January 1791.

[7]   BLO/MSS.W.Ind.s.17, fol. 31, Mayhew to Farr, 30 January 1829.

[8]   For discussions of Sayers' location, see BLO/MSS.W.Ind.s.17, fol. 11, Pitcairn & Amos to Thomas Burton, 13 January 1829; fol. 22, Stevens, Wood, and Wilkinson to Mayhew, 24 January 1829; BLO/MSS.W.Ind.s.17, fol. 28, Thomas Burton to Mayhew, 30 January 1829; fol. 31, Mayhew to Farr, 30 January 1829; fol. 52, Thomas Sayers to Stevens, Wood, and Wilkinson, 4 April 1829.

[9]   Before 1926 a mortgage was commonly effected by the transfer of the mortgagor's interest in the property to the mortgagee. Under the equity of redemption, the mortgagor continued to be the true owner of mortgaged property throughout a mortgage despite lacking legal title. A mortgagee's interest was mere security for a debt; and a mortgagor was thus entitled to redeem the property at any time – irrespective of the terms of the mortgage – until his or her equity of redemption was declared foreclosed by a court; D. P. Waddilove, 'Why the Equity of Redemption?', in *Land and Credit: Mortgages in the Medieval and Early Modern European Countryside*, ed. Chris Briggs, and C. J. Zuijderduijn (Palgrave Studies in the History of Finance) (Cham, Switzerland: Palgrave Macmillan, 2018), pp. 117–48, at 117–18. BLO/MSS.W.Ind.s.17, fol. 15, Stevens, Wood, & Wilkinson to Thomas Burton, 19 January 1829; BLO/MSS.W.Ind.s.17, fol. 63, Stevens Wood & Wilkinson to Mayhew, 16 April 1829; fol. 72, Stevens Wood and Wilkinson to Mayhew, 24 April 1829; fol. 76, Thomas Burton to Mayhew, 18 May 1829; fol. 80, Pitcairn & Amos to Mayhew, 15 June 1829.

[10] BLO/MSS.W.Ind.s.17, fol. 96, Pitcairn & Amos to Farr, 2 September 1829; fol. 100, Pitcairn & Amos to Mayhew, 14 September 1829; fol. 110, White & Barrett to Mayhew, 28 January 1830.

[11] BLO/MSS.W.Ind.s.17, fol. 19, Pitcairn & Amos to Farr, 24 January 1829; fol. 22, Stevens, Wood, & Wilkinson to Mayhew, 24 January 1829.

[12] BLO/MSS.W.Ind.s.17, fol. 69, Forsyth to Pitcairn & Amos, 16 March 1829.

£3,000 loan from Mitchells, which was secured against Chiswick by mortgage, along with a second loan from them for £700, and another loan of £350 from Pitcairn & Amos, both secured against the Sayers' joint share of the 1828/9 crop.[13] There was also a £1,600 'advance' that Sayers had arranged with 'Norwich bankers' in 1828, but the papers do not specify how this was secured.[14]

The next difficulty was the fact that some of the crop had already been shipped from Jamaica under instructions from Sayers to send it directly to Mitchells in lieu of his debts.[15] Applications were prepared to the Court of Chancery for an injunction to prevent Mitchells from disposing of any produce they received.[16] In late March 20 hogsheads of sugar and 9 puncheons of rum arrived at the docks on the *West Indian*, consigned to Mitchells.[17] Negotiations resulted in the sugar and rum held by Mitchells being purchased by Pitcairn & Amos for £734, with the costs being added to the proprietors' joint account. The final, and most difficult, task was to reach an agreement with Mitchells and avoid legal action in Jamaica – including potential receivership – which 'would prove ruinous to all parties' if it occurred.[18] Mitchells had a formidable reputation for enforcing their debt collection and, as Mayhew told Farr, 'the estate has been within a hair of a serious lawsuit abroad on the part of Mitchells which would have caused mischief almost ruinous to the whole property'.[19]

The immediate response to the crisis caused by Sayers exposes, therefore, the fundamental problems that had hampered the operation of Chiswick since Thomas Burton's death in 1805; family disinterest and lack of commercial acumen, exacerbated by absentee status. Since their father's death, no Burton had engaged properly with the estate's management. While, of course, this can happen to any family business, the negative effects of this lack of engagement were hidden from the family because they lived 4,000 miles away and did not understand Jamaica. Their detachment meant that the proprietors' fortunes were dependent on the capacity of the people they chose to manage the estate on their behalf, but the ability of these managers was not assessed in any meaningful manner and, as has been seen, since Lumsden's death, Chiswick's managers had been mediocre. In 1829 Mayhew was chosen primarily because he was Farr's brother-in-law, not because he had any knowledge of sugar estates. As luck would have it, Mayhew was competent, honest, and learned quickly. Nonetheless, his ability to manoeuvre was constantly constrained by the family's insistence that they did not want to pay the debts incurred by Sayers from their personal portions of the profits, which tied his hands, while at the same time

[13] BLO/MSS.W.Ind.s.17, fol. 33, Stevens, Wood & Wilkinson to Mayhew, 29 February 1829.
[14] BLO/MSS.W.Ind.s.17, fol. 29, Pitcairn & Amos to Mayhew, 30 January 1829.
[15] BLO/MSS.W.Ind.s.17, fol. 19, Pitcairn & Amos to Farr, 24 January 1829.
[16] BLO/MSS.W.Ind.s.17, fol. 8, Pitcairn & Amos to Farr, 5 January 1829; fol. 25, Mayhew to Farr, 26 January 1829; fol. 37, Stevens, Wood, & Wilkinson to Mayhew, 7 February 1829.
[17] BLO/MSS.W.Ind.s.17, fol. 45, Pitcairn & Amos to Mayhew, 31 March 1829.
[18] BLO/MSS.W.Ind.s.17, fol. 66, Pitcairn & Amos to Farr, 20 April 1829.
[19] For Mitchells in litigation, see their action against Milligan, Robertson & Co, 19 January 1828, *The London Gazette* (London: T. Neuman, 1828), p. 148; BLO/MSS.W.Ind.s.17, fols 5–6; Mayhew to Farr, (May?) 1829.

they continued to avoid detailed engagement with the sugar estate's commercial operations and environment.[20]

The consequence was that the next few years saw a long, and wearing, game of shadowboxing involving Mayhew, Pitcairn & Amos, and Mitchells, with infrequent, but problematic, interference from the Burtons. In line with his employers' instructions, Mayhew's overall thrust was to get Mitchells to agree to allow the estate to carry on operating as normal and to accept that they should receive payment only from the share of the profits earmarked for Thomas and Maria Sayers.[21] Mayhew guessed, correctly, that Mitchells would prefer an agreement and were 'endeavouring to extort all the Chiswick London business from the co-proprietors by threat of a lawsuit', rather than risk the uncertainty of actual litigation.[22] Consequently, Mayhew played for time.

In the middle of all this argument, however, were the enslaved people of Chiswick. The letters make it clear that all parties involved were concerned that any legal proceedings on the island would become known to the enslaved workforce and cause further problems. As Pitcairn & Amos put it when advising an early settlement with Mitchells, 'By the arrangement we propose an end would be put to all law proceedings – both here and in Jamaica, and there would be an end to all fear of the minds of the negroes becoming unsettled.'[23] This comment reveals a remarkable fact that became increasingly apparent over the next few years. This was that the estate's people could influence the thinking of the Burtons in Norwich and Yarmouth, Thomas Mayhew in Saxmundham, and Pitcairn & Amos and Mitchells in London. All parties involved in the negotiations had to take cognisance of the reality that, although the workers at Chiswick were enslaved, they might act in ways that could, and did, disrupt the plans being devised by the estate's owners and managers.

One way the workers could do this was by well-timed activities such as 'desertion'. In 1817 there was one 'runaway' listed at the estate, a twenty-eight-year-old 'creole' man named Duke. Duke had run away from Chiswick on 14 February 1814 and would not be returned until 1819, when he was found in the Spanish Town workhouse.[24] Duke appears to have been a repeat runaway and would be purchased out of the Morant Bay workhouse between 1826 and 1829.[25] The Chiswick papers have frustratingly little information on runaways such as Duke, which is unfortunate, since there is much that can be learnt about conditions on estates from runaway patterns.[26]

[20] See, for example, BLO/MSS.W.Ind.s.17, fol. 106, Charles Burton to Mayhew, 3 December 1829; fol. 120, Charles Burton to Mayhew, 19 February 1830; fol. 129, Thomas Burton to Mayhew, 28 March 1830; fol. 135, Thomas Burton to Mayhew, 24 April 1830.

[21] BLO/MSS.W.Ind.s.17, fol. 16, Stevens, Wilkinson and Wood to Mayhew, 19 January 1829; BLO/MSS.W.Ind.s.17, fols 11–12, Pitcairn & Amos to Thomas Burton, 13 January 1829; fol. 33, Stevens, Wood, & Wilkinson to Mayhew, 4 February 1829.

[22] BLO/MSS.W.Ind.s.17, fol. 23, Pitcairn & Amos to Mayhew, 24 January 1829; BLO/MSS.W.Ind.s.17, fol. 19, Pitcairn & Amos to Farr, 24 January 1829.

[23] BLO/MSS.W.Ind.s.17, fol. 12, Pitcairn & Amos to Thomas Burton, 13 January 1829.

[24] NA/T/71/146, Slave Registers 1820, fol. 85.

[25] NA/T/71/149, Slave Registers 1826, fols 59–60.

[26] G. Heuman, 'Runaway Slaves in Nineteenth-Century Barbados', in *Out of the House of Bondage: Runaways, Resistance and Marronage in Africa and the New World*, ed. G.

Nonetheless, there are a few other examples in the newspapers. Richard Hope was a 'creole' born at Chiswick in 1807. Originally named Hamlet, his mother was Susan Vernon. Hope deserted Chiswick in 1826 and had to be purchased from the work-house.[27] In mid-1827 another man, William Shand, was convicted for running away and 'having twenty pounds weight of meat in his possession'. He received thirty-nine lashes and was sentenced to six months hard labour.[28] Likewise, 'Davy, a Mungola' was held in the Kingston workhouse during September 1827, bearing 'marks of a recent flogging'.[29]

One key issue with these deserters were that they were men of prime working age, a group that Chiswick was already short of and could ill afford to lose and the considerable problems such deserters could cause was exemplified by John Vernon, who deserted in late 1827.[30] He was listed in the 1817 return as a thirty-five-year-old 'creole', whose mother was Mary Clair, and whose previous name was Scipio.[31] In 1828 he was being held in the workhouse with 'marks of recent flogging on his back', suggesting that he had been recently disciplined at Chiswick. He muddied the waters by saying his surname was 'Vernal', and claiming he was 'formerly of Chiswick' but now belonged to 'Mr Lumsden' of Ludlow estate, St Andrews. This was clearly false, since William Lumsden had died in 1807, the Ludlow estate was in Clarendon, and was owned by an absentee named Samuel Poole.[32] Nonetheless, Vernon's strategy was successful and meant that he remained in the workhouse until early March 1828, while matters were decided upon, depriving Chiswick of a much-needed worker for most of the period of the harvest.[33]

In early 1829 Forsyth revealed the extra costs incurred by Anderson when implementing Sayers' instructions to maximise the 1828 crop. There had been 'great loss of stock last year in taking off the crop which will swell the contingent account of this year; you will observe that £424 has been paid and charged for cattle, and there will be £266.13.4 to be provided for next month'. Forsyth stated candidly that these costs were 'unquestionably too large', implying that Anderson had been defrauding the owners, and in April Anderson was sacked.[34] The timing of the dismissal suggests that Mayhew agreed with Forsyth's conclusion and may have decided that Anderson had been colluding with Sayers in arranging the mortgage with Mitchells. Forsyth continued to focus on shipping Chiswick's produce, buying the stores required for the estate's operations, and keeping the accounts. The cultivation of the crops and running of the

Heuman (London: Frank Cass, 1986), pp. 95–111. Once again, the Mesopotamia records contain the best dataset on runaways from 1762 to 1832; Ward, 'Economic', p. 1207.
27   *Royal Gazette of Jamaica*, 28 October 1826, p. 17.
28   *Royal Gazette of Jamaica*, 7 July 1827, p. 19.
29   *Royal Gazette of Jamaica*, 8 September 1827, p. 24.
30   *Royal Gazette of Jamaica*, 24 November 1827, p. 14.
31   NA/T/71/145, Slave Registers 1817, fol. 850.
32   'Samuel Poole', *Legacies of British Slavery* database, http://wwwdepts-live.ucl.ac.uk/lbs/person/view/21001, accessed 8 March 2023.
33   *Royal Gazette of Jamaica*, 15 March 1828, p. 6.
34   BLO/MSS.W.Ind.s.17, fol. 53, Forsyth to Thomas Sayers, 14 February 1829; fol. 86, '(Copy) Rev. Thomas Sayers and Chiswick Estate debt to Messrs R & J Mitchell & Co', 22 July 1829; BLO/MSS.W.Ind.s.17, fol. 49, Pitcairn & Amos to Charles Anderson (copy), 18 April 1829.

estate now became the responsibility of his business partner, James Townson, who would remain in this role until the mid-1840s.[35] Although a small operation, Townson and Forsyth appear to have been acting for several other absentees.[36]

The disquiet on the estate worsened as time progressed and affected Mayhew's negotiations. In April 1829 Forsyth stated, 'I am concerned to acquaint you that the negroes are in a state of insubordination, they have been refractory since Christmas, an investigation will take place next week before the magistrates, which I trust will restore matters to their usual order.'[37] Alongside the general unease on the estate caused by the threat of litigation, it seems that the workers were chafing against the heavy workload that had been enforced upon them under the regime implemented by Sayers and Anderson. As Pitcairn & Amos pointed out, 'the negroes and cattle have been overworked, producing the large crops at the expense of the capital'.[38] This overwork had exacerbated the problems resulting from Sayers' programme of economy in relation to supplies for the workers. Anderson had reduced provisions but had not reconsidered this reduction in the face of shortages on the island during 1828 to 1829, when 'provisions of all kinds have been very scarce'. These shortages had caused prices to rise, with flour, for example, costing £10 per pound. The consequence had been great hardship, and growing discontent among the people.[39]

In the autumn of 1829 there was an outbreak of dysentery.[40] This was a continual problem at the estate, with another outbreak in 1833, and seems likely to have been related to high workloads and poor diet, as well as the overall dilapidation of the estate.[41] Matters improved as the shortage of food resulting from Sayers' programme of economy was dealt with, both because prices had now eased, and because Forsyth had 'recommended them to cultivate papaya which is genial to a poor, dry soil and more productive that cocoa and yams'.[42] With the estate reeling from the dysentery outbreak, and also in an apparent attempt to deal with the unrest and problems among the workers, in September 1829 Forsyth and Townson decreased the enslaved workers' workload by making significant alterations to the programme of cultivation. Having looked at the number of workers available, they decided to reduce the sugar planting area by five acres since 'to apply the labour and manure on 40 acres in place of 45 acres which will make the land more productive and save much labour'.[43]

Nonetheless, life at Chiswick remained hard and resistance from the workforce continued. In August 1830 Forsyth averred that discipline had been re-established after an unnamed male slave who 'had practiced *obeah* (witchcraft)' – a form of spiritualism which was associated by slave-owners with insubordination and insur-

[35]   WM/SC/01621, fol. 1, Townson to Mayhew, 7 January 1833.
[36]   'Jamaica St Thomas-in-the-East, Surrey 439 (Middleton Estate)', *Legacies of British Slavery* database, http://wwwdepts-live.ucl.ac.uk/lbs/claim/view/12043, accessed 18 October 2023.
[37]   BLO/MSS.W.Ind.s.17, fols 49–50, Pitcairn & Amos to Mayhew, 4 April 1829.
[38]   BLO/MSS.W.Ind.s.17, fol. 66, Pitcairn & Amos to Farr, 20 April 1829.
[39]   BLO/MSS.W.Ind.s.17, fol. 103, Pitcairn & Amos to Mayhew, 14 September 1829.
[40]   BLO/MSS.W.Ind.s.17, fol. 103, Pitcairn & Amos to Mayhew, 14 September 1829.
[41]   BLO/MSS.W.Ind.s.18, fol. 73, Townson to Pitcairn & Amos, 5 August 1833.
[42]   BLO/MSS.W.Ind.s.17, fol. 103, Pitcairn & Amos to Mayhew, 14 September 1829.
[43]   BLO/MSS.W.Ind.s.17, fol. 98, Forsyth to Pitcairn & Amos, August 1829; fol. 103, Forsyth to Pitcairn & Amos, 5 September 1829.

rection – was 'tried and sentenced to six months hard labour with a flagellation on going into and coming out of confinement, which we hope will have good effect'.[44] The issue of *obeah* is complex, but Paton has argued that prosecutions for it tended to occur in situations where enslaved workers had been oppositional, and so it seems that this case is an example of Forsyth and Townson instilling discipline on workers who had been causing problems.[45] The unnamed worker's punishment was, at one level, proof that the opposition had failed. However, it can also be seen as indicative of the continuing pressure being exerted by the workers. The move to use a prosecution for *obeah* suggests that Forsyth and Townson were finding it necessary to explore new ways of controlling the, increasingly recalcitrant, workforce.

Having dealt with this matter, on 2 August 1830 Townson was bullish, stating that 'The seasons are very fine and the prospects look uncommonly well', but only five days later a hurricane struck Jamaica, affecting Chiswick badly.[46] Forsyth reported that 'Fortunately the negroes and cattle are safe' but there was considerable damage to the canes, 'particularly those that are forward, broken and twisted in a way that hardly leaves any hope of recovery'.[47] It also appears that the 'coppers' in the factory were damaged, along with the windmill, and repairs were only completed by January, which delayed the production of the crop.[48] There was considerable damage to the workers' housing, '14 negro houses were blown down and others considerably injured'.[49] The hurricane also damaged the provision crops, and the drought that followed saw new shortages of food for the workers that continued into mid-1831. The food shortages became so bad that Forsyth reported he had 'been obliged to send a few barrels of meat by way of assistance for old, the young, and the infirm' on the estate.[50] The drought conditions gradually eased and by autumn 1832 Forsyth told his employers that 'the gardens are very promising' and that provisions were 'abundant' with the result that the 'people are doing well'.[51]

The news of the Baptist War of December 1831 to January 1832 caused great consternation for the Burton family, but Chiswick was unaffected. The Baptist War was the largest uprising by enslaved people ever to take place in the British Caribbean and was led mainly by enslaved converts to the Baptist Church. While the rebellion was contained on the other side of the island, in the parish of St James, Thomas Burton wrote that 'The accounts from Jamaica are of such a serious complexion, as to paralyse the feelings of the proprietors unfortunately connected to that island'.[52] Pitcairn & Amos told the family that the rebels were 'desperate fellows', who were 'deluded' and explained that the deaths of 200 enslaved people, who were killed by the regulars

---

[44] BLO/MSS.W.Ind.s.17, fol. 148, Forsyth to Pitcairn & Amos, 2 August 1830.

[45] D. Paton, *The Cultural Politics of Obeah: Religion, Colonialism and Modernity in the Caribbean World* (Cambridge: Cambridge University Press, 2015), p. 115.

[46] BLO/MSS.W.Ind.s.17, fol. 148, Forsyth to Pitcairn & Amos, 2 August 1830.

[47] BLO/MSS.W.Ind.s.17, fol. 148, Forsyth to Pitcairn & Amos, 13 August 1830.

[48] BLO/MSS.W.Ind.s.18, fol. 12, Forsyth to Pitcairn & Amos, 15 January 1832.

[49] BLO/MSS.W.Ind.s.17, fol. 148, Forsyth to Pitcairn & Amos, 13 August 1830

[50] BLO/MSS.W.Ind.s.17, fol. 166, Forsyth to Pitcairn & Amos, 13 March 1831.

[51] BLO/MSS.W.Ind.s.18, fol. 43, Forsyth to Pitcairn & Amos, 10 October 1832.

[52] BLO/MSS.W.Ind.s.18, fol. 9, Thomas Burton to Mayhew, 29 February 1832; see also fol. 11, Pitcairn & Amos to Mayhew, 4 March 1832.

and militia, and more than 340 who were captured and later executed, were 'dreadful but necessary examples [which] will soon restore peace and quiet as the other parts of the country are all quiet and at work'.[53] There was great relief among the Burtons when Forsyth reported that there had been no problems at Chiswick and that 'the people are behaving extremely well and appear perfectly happy and contented'.[54] The incident confirmed, therefore, the continuing lack of interest on the part of the Burtons in the lives and conditions of their enslaved workforce. Their letters about the rebellion focused on their investment and on their concern that they would lose money. The family did not spend any time considering why the enslaved people of Jamaica might have revolted.

Although Forsyth told the Burtons in his letters that the people of Chiswick were 'contented', it seems that the working regimen was ferocious. In 1832 a report of a court case in Jamaica involving the planter Alexander Barclay detailed an accusa-tion in the *Christian Record* about shifts at various estates in St Thomas-in-the-East, including Chiswick. The accusation was that the shifts at Chiswick during the crop involved 'two spells […] which relieve each other every twenty-four hours at midday' meaning that 'of every forty-eight hours each slave works during thirty-six hours'. If correct, the report reveals that, even at this late stage, during crop the people of Chiswick rose at 6 a.m., worked at cutting canes until midday, then went on a spell in the mills for twenty-four hours before working another six hours in the field. The *Christian Record* placed the blame for this staggering workload on the lack of workers on the estate. They provided evidence, therefore, of the way the insoluble problem of the declining workforce bled into every aspect of the estate's operation and how the solutions to declining productivity inevitably involved greater hardship for the people. The caveat to relying on this report is that the court found that the accusation against Barclay was libel and that such shift patterns were not used at his estate, the Rhyne, which he managed for Sir E. H. East.

On balance, however, the *Christian Record*'s claims seem likely to be correct for several reasons. First, the accusations against Chiswick were not taken to court and so were not tested there. Second, the impartiality of the verdict is questionable, since it appears that the court was determined to prove the wealthy and influential Barclay was innocent.[55] Third, the report is so detailed that it seems unlikely to have been a concoction. Fourth, there is evidence of sleep deprivation among the workers in the letters from Townson, who reported in 1833 that 'A valuable good man fell asleep on the wain […] a few days ago while carrying canes for the mill and in this state, he fell off and the loaded wain passed over and killed him'.[56] Finally, the descriptions in the *Christian Record* bear strong resemblance to the routines outlined by William Wright in the mid-1820s, adding actual timings of shifts to Wright's more general-ised description. Therefore, the *Christian Record*'s account seems to provide solid evidence on which to assess the work regime on the estate. It seems that Townson and Forsyth were working the enslaved people at a severe rate.

---

[53]   BLO/MSS.W.Ind.s.18, fol. 7, Pitcairn & Amos to Mayhew, 21 February 1832.
[54]   BLO/MSS.W.Ind.s.18, fol. 12, Forsyth to Pitcairn & Amos, 15 January 1932.
[55]   *Morning Post*, Saturday 20 October 1832, p. 2.
[56]   BLO/MSS.W.Ind.s.18, fol. 129, Townson to Pitcairn & Amos, 22 January 1835.

The death of the estate's overseer, George Prosser, on 26 October 1831, aged thir-ty-one, led to the only documented manumissions on Chiswick. Prosser had 'formed a connection with one of the women on the estate', Celia Darby, who was twen-ty-three years old. Prosser had made provision of 'ample means' in his will to pay for her freedom and that of their two surviving children, Janet, and Charles, who were aged three and five. His executors arranged for the payment of £143 sterling to the Burtons for the family's freedom in 1832. Forsyth stated that Celia had 'been much indulged for many years' and had become 'troublesome' and argued that her manumission was the best result in the circumstances.[57]

The money received from Prosser's estate was then used to purchase six more people in 1832, the last purchase of human beings made by the Burtons. These people cost £315 (£225 sterling), or £45 each (£32 sterling). Where they came from is not recorded, but comprised Alick McLune, who was about forty-five years old, Char-lotte McGilney, aged forty-three, Will Lund, aged thirteen, Nancy Thomas, aged eighteen, Lewis Thomas, aged eleven, and Susannah McLune, aged fifteen. Forsyth explained that, since they were all in good health, their purchase had not affected the average value of the estate negatively. Nonetheless, Chiswick's ageing population now contained 'many cripples and invalids that reduce the average value & lately we doubt if they would average more than £35 currency pound (£25 sterling)'.[58]

Once settled in, the new workers would be required to 'set their shoulders to the wheel for the general benefit' and Forsyth urged that, if more could be purchased, this would be 'great relief to the others, particularly in their night spells'.[59] His comments would, therefore, seem to provide further support for the claims in the *Christian Record* about workloads at Chiswick. Although the attorney said that 'There never can be a more favourable period to purchase labourers than the present, as every description of property is at the very lowest ebb', no other workers were purchased. Forsyth's advice reflected his concern that even the reduced crop was too large for the existing workforce to deal with and illuminates the degree to which shortage of workers had now become critical.[60] As he noted elsewhere, 'the gradual falling off offers no hope at present of amendment'.[61] Mayhew could seek to deal with Sayers' debts, Forsyth and Townson could alter crop patterns and increase pastureland, and Pitcairn & Amos could try to maximise the sale price of the estate's crop, but the weakening of Chiswick's workforce remained insuperable. At the existing rate of decline, in a decade there would be less than one hundred and fifty enslaved workers on the estate, too few to cultivate it.[62]

Townson seems to have attempted to arrest the fall in numbers by implementing measures to improve welfare, with a new nursery being constructed for the young children near the overseer's house, so he could ensure that they were 'kept clean'.

57   BLO/MSS.W.Ind.s.18, fol. 36, Forsyth to Pitcairn & Amos, 12 July 1832; fol. 56 Pitcairn & Amos to Mayhew, 17 May 1833.
58   BLO/MSS.W.Ind.s.18, fol. 43, Forsyth to Pitcairn & Amos, 10 October 1832.
59   BLO/MSS.W.Ind.s.18, fol. 43, Forsyth to Pitcairn & Amos, 12 November 1832.
60   BLO/MSS.W.Ind.s.18, fol. 36, Forsyth to Pitcairn & Amos, 12 July 1832.
61   BLO/MSS.W.Ind.s.17, fol. 117, Forsyth to Pitcairn & Amos, 15 November 1829.
62   NA/T/71/149, Slave Registers 1829, fols 179–80.

[63] This was, however, a measure born of desperation rather than any real expectation, and the incidence of child mortality at Chiswick remained high. Between
1829 and 1832 the deaths of six children were recorded. They were all girls – Nelly
Francis, aged ten, Sarah Stuart, aged two, Jenney, aged seven, a fourteen-year-old
named Ann, the four-year-old Antoinette Anderson and the 'mulatto' daughter
of the overseer, Mary Ann Prosser, aged three.[64] A smallpox outbreak in mid-1831
had made 'great havoc in town' but was stated not to have affected the workers at
Chiswick who had 'all been vaccinated'. Nonetheless, Forsyth reported the death
of one 'very old' person at Chiswick, and one 'young – the last we think was likely
to be from worms, which are common and troublesome to children and frequently
produce convulsions and death'.[65]

In 1832 there was a serious incident when 'one of the wainmen […] stuck his boy
such a blow that he is supposed to have died from it'. Since it could not be proven
that the beating had been the cause of death, the man was tried and received 'hard
labour in the workhouse for six months'.[66] Unfortunately, the boy and man were not
named, and it appears that the event happened after the 1832 return, so their names
are unknown. Other deaths included ten men and women over fifty, all Africans –
the oldest of whom was Phebe, who was eighty-eight. Among workers aged between
twenty and fifty, the twenty-nine-year-old Bahamian named Thomas Walker died, as
did two other men and one woman. With only eleven births, by September 1832 the
estate had a population of 169, comprising eighty-five men and eighty-four women.[67]
In 1833, outbreaks of dysentery and whooping cough led to the deaths of three children and an 'old invalid'.[68] Overall, the numbers of men and women at Chiswick
were now nearly equal, eighty-four men and eighty women, which was somewhat
unusual, as women tended to outnumber men on estates by this date.[69] The population at Chiswick was aging, with nearly 8 per cent too old to work, and a very small
proportion of children, only 9 per cent.[70] All this meant that, as on other estates,
the working gang was deteriorating in efficiency. As Forsyth stated bluntly, the large
number of elderly and infirm among Chiswick's workforce meant 'they are by no
means an effective gang'.[71]

Aside from the human suffering involved, this situation created commercial risk.
News of the unrest and problems at Chiswick caused Pitcairn & Amos to become
concerned that they might not be paid money owed to them by the proprietors.
The consequence was that Pitcairn & Amos altered their assessment of the value
of Chiswick itself, stating it had 'even our estimate of its value has been too high',

[63] BLO/MSS.W.Ind.s.17, fol. 148, Forsyth to Pitcairn & Amos, 2 August 1830; fol. 191 Forsyth
      to Pitcairn & Amos, 10 July 1831.
[64] NA/T71/150, Register 1832, fols 183–84.
[65] BLO/MSS.W.Ind.s.17, fol. 166, Forsyth to Pitcairn & Amos, 13 March 1831.
[66] BLO/MSS.W.Ind.s.18, fol. 43, Forsyth to Pitcairn & Amos, 10 October 1832.
[67] NA/T71/150, Register 1832, fols 183–84.
[68] BLO/MSS.W.Ind.s.18, fol. 67, Forsyth to Pitcairn & Amos, 7 July 1833.
[69] See, for example, Dunn, *A Tale*, pp. 42–43, Appendix 9, and Appendix 10.
[70] BLO/MSS.W.Ind.s.18, fol. 86. Pitcairn & Amos to Mayhew, 4 December 1833; fol. 88;
      Pitcairn & Amos to Mayhew, 30 December 1833.
[71] BLO/MSS.W.Ind.s.18, fol. 43, Forsyth to Pitcairn & Amos, 12 November 1832.

and that they would not lend money to the Burtons as they had previously offered to do.[72] Worker pressure in Jamaica had, therefore, created commercial uncertainty which had, in turn, caused a material change in the valuation of the worth of the Burton family and soured relations with Pitcairn & Amos.[73]

This pressure caused a period of ill-tempered disagreement in London which was only concluded when Pitcairn & Amos forced the Burtons to provide a promissory note to cover forthcoming expenses, personally guaranteed by the Burton brothers and Farr.[74] The use of such promissory notes became the norm for the business thereafter. Remarkably, therefore, although 4,000 miles away and enslaved the actions of the workers at Chiswick, such as Duke, Richard Hope, and John Vernon, in the context of long-term demographic trend of declining worker numbers, materially affected the negotiations and calculations being taken in London and Suffolk in the years after 1829. As we shall see, this remote influence upon English decision-making by the workers at Chiswick would continue, and grow stronger, over the next two decades.

This situation is reminiscent of Turner's findings in her classic study of labour relations in Saint Thomas-in-the East. Looking at the Blue Mountain and Grange Hill estates, she argued for a history of low-level worker resistance and managerial accommodation that stretched back into the eighteenth century. She also found that 'the *results* of these struggles were facilitated by long term trends' which included the 'diminution in the labour force' and this describes the situation at Chiswick at the end of the 1820s rather well. With the managerial team weakened and under pressure, the worsening labour situation allowed the workers turn the Burtons' problems to their advantage.[75]

The financial situation at Chiswick in this period is laid out in Table 10. From 1829 to 1833, average sugar production was 156 hogsheads per annum. This was marginally above the averages achieved from 1816 to 1828, which suggests that Townson's reduction of cultivated areas had worked. Nevertheless, it was nearly 100 hogsheads per year below the average from 1803 to 1815. For most of these years the estate's rum was sold in the island and used to immediately cover part of Forsyth and Townson's expenses, as this was argued to bring in higher prices than shipping to London and was, therefore, missing in the accounts.[76] Bad weather and the general unrest on the estate caused a fall in production to 140 hogsheads in 1830, the worst crop since 1826.

[72] BLO/MSS.W.Ind.s.17, fol. 49, Pitcairn & Amos to Mayhew, 4 April 1829.

[73] BLO/MSS.W.Ind.s.17, fol. 60, Pitcairn & Amos to Mayhew, 10 April 1829; BLO/MSS.W.Ind.s.17, fol. 56, Pitcairn & Amos to Mayhew, 7 April 1829; fol. 66, Pitcairn & Amos to Farr, 20 April 1829; fol. 81, Pitcairn & Amos to Mayhew, 15 June 1829; fol. 82, Pitcairn & Amos to Mayhew, 26 June 1829.

[74] BLO/MSS.W.Ind.s.17, fol. 94, Pitcairn & Amos to Mayhew, 22 August 1829; fol. 131, Pitcairn & Amos to Mayhew, 17 April 1830; fol. 133, Pitcairn & Amos to Mayhew, 24 April 1830; fol. 139, Thomas Burton to Mayhew, 30 June 1830.

[75] Mary Turner, 'Chattel Slaves into Wage Slaves: A Jamaican Case Study', in *From Chattel Slaves to Wage Slaves: The Dynamics of Labour Bargaining in the Americas*, ed. Mary Turner (Kingston: Ian Randle, 1995), pp. 33–47, at pp. 44–47.

[76] BLO/MSS.W.Ind.s.18, fol. 111, Forsyth to Pitcairn & Amos, 29 July 1834; fol. 105, Forsyth to Pitcairn & Amos, 25 June 1834.

Table 10. Produce and finances of the Chiswick estate, 1829–1833. *

Crop year	Hogsheads of sugar sold (London and Jamaica)	Gross income from sugar	Puncheons of rum sold (London and Jamaica)	Gross income from rum (£ sterling)	Expenses (£ sterling)	Net profit (loss) (£ sterling)
1829	173	£1,705	85	£600	(£2,150)	£155
1830	140	£1,300	78		(£1,305)	(£5)
1831	147	£1,417	78		(£1,148)	£264
1832	150	£2,112			(£1,785)	£326
1833	185	£3,287	68	£718	(£1,601)	£2,404

* Sources: JA/1B/11/4/68. fol. 58: BLO/MSS.W.Ind.s.17, fol. 125 Pitcairn & Amos to Mayhew, 6 March 1830: fol. 176, Pitcairn & Amos to Mayhew, 8 June 1831: BLO/MSS.W.Ind.s.18, fol. 168, Pitcairn & Amos to Mayhew, 4 November 1835. Levels of rum production have not been recorded for 1830, and 1832, and there are no rum income figures for 1830–1832 and 1834/1835 as the rum was sold on the island and used for expenses directly.

Matters were then made worse by the 'long and continued' drought which lasted into May 1831, which meant 'the country is most deplorably dry', damaging the following crop considerably.[77] It was not until the crop of 1832 that there was an improvement, with the weather that year proving uncommonly mild.[78] This meant that the 1832 crop was the best for many years, at 193 hogsheads, although 43 hogsheads were not sold until 1833 because they could not be sold at a high enough price.[79]

Continuing depressed sugar and rum prices meant that prior to 1833 profits were negligible, however. As Pitcairn & Amos put it, 'every fluctuation of a shilling seriously affects the interest of the proprietor' and in this period the fluctuation was, generally, downwards.[80] Part of this was a consequence of the competition offered to Jamaican sugar from other locations, especially Mauritius, which lowered prices 'leaving very little for the planter'. Pitcairn & Amos told Mayhew that 'at the present miserable prices we fear it will do little more than cover the expenses of management'.[81] Prices rose somewhat in 1833 when the crop was 'short in some parts of the island' but even then, prices for Chiswick's lower-quality sugar remained low.[82]

The average annual profit for the period was £599 yielding, in theory, around £100 to each of the proprietors, but no-one received a penny. In fact, the family was building up new debts to Pitcairn & Amos to cover the expenses incurred just keeping the estate running.[83] Interest payments had to be made to Mitchells, to keep them from taking legal action, and these were being added to the proprietors' account, notwithstanding the Burtons' objections.[84] In 1830 aggregate claims against the estate were £4,840 and increasing, while prices and production were falling. The expectation was that output would 'scarcely pay for the Jamaican expenses and London supplies'.[85] The London merchants vented their spleen against the government and 'the tide of popular prejudice continuing to flow as strong as ever against West India property'.[86] Even when sugar prices improved from 1832 onwards no money was received in profits, as any money made went immediately to pay the family's existing debts to Pitcairn & Amos and Mitchells. Had no debt been attached to the property then the crop of 1833 would, theoretically, have yielded a profit of around £1,450 after all normal expenses had been paid. This would have meant £483 going to Thomas

---

[77] BLO/MSS.W.Ind.s.17, fol. 162, Forsyth to Mayhew, 14 March 1831; fol. 166, Forsyth to Pitcairn & Amos, 14 March 1831.

[78] BLO/MSS.W.Ind.s.17, f. 208, Forsyth to Pitcairn & Amos, 16 October 1831.

[79] BLO/MSS.W.Ind.s.18, fol. 90, Pitcairn & Amos to Mayhew, 22 January 1834.

[80] BLO/MSS.W.Ind.s.17, fol. 104, Pitcairn & Amos to Mayhew, 12 November 1829; fol. 108, Pitcairn & Amos to Mayhew, 1 January 1830.

[81] See, for example, BLO/MSS.W.Ind.s.17, fol. 84, Pitcairn & Amos to Mayhew, 22 July 1829; fol. 176, Pitcairn & Amos to Mayhew, 8 June 1831.

[82] BLO/MSS.W.Ind.s.18, fol. 53 and fol. 54, Pitcairn & Amos to Mayhew, 8 April 1833 and 29 April 1833.

[83] BLO/MSS.W.Ind.s.17, fol. 104, Pitcairn & Amos to Mayhew, 12 November 1829; fol. 108, Pitcairn & Amos to Mayhew, 1 January 1830.

[84] BLO/MSS.W.Ind.s.17, fol. 103, Pitcairn & Amos to Mayhew, 14 September 1829.

[85] BLO/MSS.W.Ind.s.17, fol. 104, Pitcairn & Amos to Mayhew, 12 November 1829; fol. 108, Pitcairn & Amos to Mayhew, 1 January 1830.

[86] BLO/MSS.W.Ind.s.17, fol. 118, Pitcairn & Amos to Mayhew, 22 March 1830.

Burton and £138 to the other siblings, with the Sayers' combined share going to pay their debts to the family. In the event, no money reached any of the Burtons since the outstanding promissory notes to Pitcairn & Amos, due in July 1834, totalled £2,017 and another £875 had to be paid to Mitchells to clear their outstanding claim.[87]

This worsening situation seems to have caused financial problems for the Burtons. Maria and Thomas Sayers were living hand to mouth in Paris and pestering their relatives with begging letters.[88] Their pleas fell on deaf ears, however, as the general financial situation for the family deteriorated. The Burtons had problems repaying a loan they had incurred with the Norwich bank, Tompson, Barclay & Ives in 1829.[89] Although wealthy enough to deal with it himself, Thomas Burton required each family member to pay £298 16s 5d to clear the debt. His brother and Harriet Dashwood could do so, but the Willins had to borrow the sum from him, while Caroline and John Lee Farr had to ask for more time.[90] The Farr's financial situation was deteriorating rapidly and the declining income from Chiswick added to, but was not the cause of, financial difficulties that saw them lease and then sell North Cove Hall and various other properties during the 1830s.[91]

As finances became more strained during 1831, Charles and Thomas Burton were finally forced to pay Mitchell's loan from their own funds, by providing promissory notes to clear the debt in staged payments over three years.[92] The pressure of the situation was summed up by Thomas Burton who asked Mayhew to 'endeavour all in your power to get us out of the hands of the Mitchell & Co'.[93] By 1833 debts had risen to a value of £2,017 and led to problems with bankers such as Esdaile & Co. when they were not paid on time.[94] Moreover, the Burtons were also forced to purchase the Morass to the south of the estate under threat of litigation, which cost a further

---

[87]   BLO/MSS.W.Ind.s.18, fol. 90, Pitcairn & Amos to Mayhew, 22 January 1834.

[88]   BLO/MSS.W.Ind.s.17, fol. 110, White & Barrett to Mayhew, 28 January 1830; BLO/MSS.W.Ind.s.18, fol. 82, White & Barrett to Mayhew, 11 November 1833.

[89]   BLO/MSS.W.Ind.s.17, fol. 106, Charles Burton to Mayhew 3 December 1829; BLO/MSS.W.Ind.s.17, fol. 29, Pitcairn & Amos to Mayhew, 30 January 1829; BLO/MSS.W.Ind.s.17, fol. 120, Charles Burton to Mayhew, 19 February 1830; fol. 129 Thomas Burton to Mayhew, 28 March 1830.

[90]   BLO/MSS.W.Ind.s.18, fol. 158 James Palmer to Mayhew, 16 October 1835; BLO/MSS.W.Ind.s.17, fol. 137, Charles Burton to Mayhew, 8 May 1830.

[91]   BLO/MSS.W.Ind.s.17, fol. 26, Mayhew to Farr, 26 January 1829; *London Gazette*, Dissolution of partnership between John Lee Farr and Robert Fiske, 'Farr and Fiske, Attorney at Law and Solicitors', 8 September 1829, p. 1672; *Norwich Mercury*, 19 September 1829, p. 2; BLO/MSS.W.Ind.s.17, fols 114–115, Mayhew to Farr, 27 January 1830; *Suffolk Chronicle*, 15 May 1830, p. 2; *Warwick and Warwickshire Advertiser*, 27 November 1830, p. 3; *Norwich Mercury*, 4 October 1834, p. 4.

[92]   BLO/MSS.W.Ind.s.17, fol. 180, Stevenson, Wood, Wilkinson and Satchell to Mayhew, 29 July 1831; fol. 195, Pitcairn & Amos to Mayhew, 27 September 1831.

[93]   BLO/MSS.W.Ind.s.18, fol. 18, Thomas Burton to Mayhew, 15 April 1832.

[94]   BLO/MSS.W.Ind.s.18, fol. 68, Pitcairn & Amos to Mayhew, 30 August 1833; BLO/MSS.W.Ind.s.17, fol. 203, Pitcairn & Amos to Mayhew, 5 November 1831; fol. 279, Pitcairn & Amos to Mayhew, 8 November 1831.

£196 sterling.[95] To recoup these funds the brothers required each family member to pay a portion of the debt equivalent to their share in the estate, which for Mitchells' debt meant that each share required a payment of £238 1s 11d.[96] This fell heaviest on Thomas Burton, who was required to pay his own £1,584 and also £833 for Maria and Thomas Sayers' shares, which was added as a debt to their account.[97] Some respite was offered by the £10,000 left to the family in the will of Elizabeth Burton, who died in late 1831.[98] Amid tense family argument, the Willins were required to use their share from this inheritance to repay their debt to Charles and Thomas. The same was true for Maria, whose inheritance was used to clear some of the debt that had been gradually accruing since 1829.[99]

As pressure grew 'the great precariousness of West India property' was made worse by the prospect of emancipation and the general antipathy towards planters being exhibited in Britain.[100] In 1830 Pitcairn and Amos had judged that the ideal outcome was to sell Chiswick and that 'the proprietors were well quit of the estate', but then summed up the problems which prevented any sale being likely. Chiswick needed investment since 'we fear it will never become productive without a considerable extra outlay', but the overall political and economic situation made such investment inadvisable because, as the merchants explained, 'there is such a powerful evil spirit abroad machinating against West India planters and so little dependence can be placed on the permanency of government measures respecting the Islands'.[101] The Burtons explored the possibility of a sale but, as the prospect of abolition caused estate prices in Jamaica to fall further, Chiswick became less and less valuable and they decided against it.[102] By November 1832, Forsyth declared that he thought that the value of the enslaved workers would not be more than £21 each if the estate was broken up, because they had ceased to be 'an effective gang'. In 1832 he considered that the maximum price achievable for Chiswick would be £3,571, less than the entire debt the family owed to Pitcairn & Amos.[103]

As 1833 began Townson reported that 'the people enjoy the blessings of abundance' and that cultivation was going well.[104] Sugar prices remained low, however, and the prospect of emancipation now loomed.[105] The rebellion of 1831 had strength-

---

[95] BLO/MSS.W.Ind.s.18, fol. 43, Forsyth to Pitcairn & Amos, 11 November 1832; fol. 56, Pitcairn & Amos to Mayhew, 17 May 1833.

[96] BLO/MSS.W.Ind.s.17, fol. 193, Jarrett Dashwood to Mayhew, 20 September 1831; fol. 195, Pitcairn & Amos 27 September 1831; fol. 198, Pitcairn & Amos to Mayhew, 28 September 1831; fol. 203, Pitcairn & Amos to Mayhew, 5 November 1831.

[97] BLO/MSS.W.Ind.s.17, fol. 201, George Wells to Pitcairn & Amos, 29 October 1831.

[98] BLO/MSS.W.Ind.s.17, fol. 193, Jarrett Dashwood to Mayhew, 20 September 1831; BLO/MSS.W.Ind.s.18, fol. 1, Burton to Mayhew Yarmouth, 16 January 1832; fol. 9, Thomas Burton to Mayhew, 29 February 1832.

[99] BLO/MSS.W.Ind.s.18, fol. 70, Thomas Burton to Mayhew, 13 September 1833.

[100] BLO/MSS.W.Ind.s.17, fol. 116, Pitcairn & Amos to Farr, 28 January 1830.

[101] BLO/MSS.W.Ind.s.17, fol. 143, Pitcairn & Amos to Mayhew, 28 July 1830.

[102] BLO/MSS.W.Ind.s.17, fol. 129, Thomas Burton to Mayhew, 28 March 1830.

[103] BLO/MSS.W.Ind.s.18, fol. 43, Forsyth to Pitcairn & Amos, 12 November 1832.

[104] WM/SC/01621, fol. 2, Townson to Mayhew, 2 February 1833.

[105] BLO/MSS.W.Ind.s.18, fol. 46, Pitcairn & Amos to Mayhew, 11 March 1833.

ened the demands of abolitionists that the entire system of slavery be ended, and the passage of the Reform Bill in 1832 resulted in a new Parliament that was determined to do so. The protracted negotiations surrounding emancipation caused mounting tension both in Jamaica and England. In April Forsyth argued that if the compensation was inadequate then the result would be 'anarchy, confusion and bloodshed' as the goodwill of planters was lost.[106] This hyperbole continued as the year progressed and what Forsyth termed the 'awful experiment' unfolded. The planters' hope now was for 'the right to property being upheld by a fair compensation to the proprietor' and compensation to be paid to them for their impending losses.[107] As every twist and turn of the discussion was poured over, the blame was placed on the Westminster government and the abolitionists. From Forsyth's perspective the problem was that 'the people in England are ignorant of the necessary details of the subject' and did not understand that the way the enslaved workers were treated in Jamaica was a consequence of their lack of 'manners', since 'The government want things done for a people of more civilised habits than our labourers while we are obliged to be governed by what is right and proper for them.'[108]

On 28 August 1833, the Slavery Abolition Act was given Royal Assent, with emancipation set for one year later, on 1 August 1834, and compensation promised for the owners.[109] Writing shortly afterwards, Thomas Burton showed little empathy with the people at Chiswick, comparing the stress caused to himself and the family by the process with that of those held in slavery. 'Happy shall we feel ourselves', he wrote, 'when our compensation and emancipation take place.' Aside from this, Burton made no mention of the enslaved workers on the estate and was, instead, focused immediately on ensuring that his sister, Maria, would not receive any of the compensation money until all the debts she and her husband owed to the rest of the family had been paid.[110] As had been the case from 1788, the Burton family continued to be myopically focused on personal material gain, even in the midst of the arguments about the end of slavery.

While the Burtons fixated on their compensation, in Jamaica Townson worried over the consequences for Chiswick. Despite concerns about order, which resulted in troops being deployed around the island, by late December 1833 Townson reported that 'Everything is peaceful, quiet, and orderly', yet he was greatly concerned about the approaching year. Once again, the response of the workers on the estate to the new situation became the central factor in planning. While they were said to be 'very orderly and quiet for the present although under very great excitement', the letters from Jamaica contain hints of growing recalcitrance. Key in this was the people's response to the concept of apprenticeship, which was to be introduced under the new system as a transitional stage between slavery and full freedom for enslaved people. The system would involve the people continuing to work for their former owners in exchange for necessities such as food and shelter. Forsyth noted that this was an

[106] BLO/MSS.W.Ind.s.18, fol. 59, Forsyth to Pitcairn & Amos, 27 April 1833.
[107] BLO/MSS.W.Ind.s.18, fol. 56, Pitcairn & Amos to Mayhew, 17 May 1833.
[108] BLO/MSS.W.Ind.s.18, fol. 67, Forsyth to Pitcairn & Amos, 7 July 1833.
[109] The Slavery Abolition Act 1833 (3 & 4 Will. IV c. 73).
[110] BLO/MSS.W.Ind.s.18, fol. 70, Thomas Burton to Mayhew Yarmouth, 13 September 1833.

unwelcome move from the workers' perspective who, were 'quite disappointed at the idea of serving 12 years – they expected if free they were no longer to work'.[111]

In September 1833 the oldest person on the estate, Lucy Wallen, died at the age of ninety-six.[112] Having been transported from Africa as a young woman and lived most of her long life on Chiswick she will have heard that slavery was ending, but did not see the actual event. With her death the estate's population had shrunk to 163 by December 1833. There were fifteen children who were too young to work, while thirteen were elderly people who were too old to work. There was also one woman expecting a child, nine people who were in the hospital, while four others were in the 'yaws house' and isolated from the general population. There were also seven runaways recorded, revealing how, as emancipation approached, the decline in numbers at Chiswick had created an environment in which the people could test the regime. This left, as Pitcairn & Amos put it succinctly, 'only 109 to work'.[113] As Townson explained, 'It cannot be expected while so exciting a subject as freedom is under discussion that the people will not be affected by it.' There were increasing levels of absenteeism and less productivity, as the workers 'go away occasionally and do not go to their work as early as they used to do'. Townson's view was that 'without the fear of any punishment unless for extraordinary offences' the workers on Chiswick could no longer be controlled.[114] Pitcairn & Amos agreed and reported that workers were 'playing truant frequently under the impression that they were exempt from the usual discipline'.[115]

Low numbers combined with resistance to cause Townson to alter the disciplinary environment on the estate 'in such a way as to make it as imperceptible as possible'. He dropped the carrying and widespread use of the whip since, as he put it, 'it is right to drop authority by degrees and not to be paralysed all at once on the first of August'. Years of life in the pitiless environment of Jamaica meant, however, that Townson's idea of reduced severity was still harsh. 'No person', he explained, 'is now punished on the estate beyond twelve stripes with a switch unless under the direction of a magistrate and no driver or other person superintending any people at work is allowed to carry or use anything but a switch.'[116] Townson's words revealed the brute reality of the process of emancipation. The workers of Chiswick had been freed in principle, but the system under which they lived was altering only slowly and by degree.

Nonetheless, worker opposition had real effects on the attorney's thinking. Looking at the workers' behaviour, Townson judged that after emancipation he would not be able compel them to provide the labour Chiswick required.[117] Consequently, he decided that the 'fall plants' (that is the cane being planted for the 1834

---

[111] BLO/MSS.W.Ind.s.18, fol. 67, Forsyth to Pitcairn & Amos, 7 July 1833.
[112] Lucy Wallen's passing is mentioned in BLO/MSS.W.Ind.s.18, fol. 88; Pitcairn & Amos to Mayhew, 30 December 1833, where she is mentioned as 'Susey'. However, she is recorded as 'Lucy' in the 1817 Register, NA/T/71/145, Slave Registers 1817, fol. 852.
[113] BLO/MSS.W.Ind.s.18, fol. 88, Pitcairn & Amos to Mayhew, 30 December 1833.
[114] BLO/MSS.W.Ind.s.18, fol. 87, Townson to Pitcairn & Amos, 13 October 1833.
[115] BLO/MSS.W.Ind.s.18, fol. 89, Forsyth to Pitcairn & Amos, 23 November 1833.
[116] BLO/MSS.W.Ind.s.18, fol. 93, Townson, to Pitcairn & Amos, 21 December 1833.
[117] BLO/MSS.W.Ind.s.18, fol. 80, Townson to Pitcairn & Amos, 2 September 1833.

crop) needed to be reduced by one-quarter, to 30 acres. His aim was to 'produce more sugar from less surface employed' by more efficient manuring.[118] Townson's underlying fear was that the extra disruption to working patterns resulting from the introduction of emancipation/apprenticeship in August 1834 would exacerbate the problems already resulting from the decline in the numbers of people at Chiswick since 1807 and reduce his ability to produce sugar even further. His glum expectation was of a crop of 130 to 140 hogsheads, and worse to come.

[118] BLO/MSS.W.Ind.s.18, fol. 73, Townson to Pitcairn & Amos, 5 August 1833; fol. 89, Forsyth to Pitcairn & Amos, 23 November 1833.

8

'WHAT FREE IS THIS?'
THE CHALLENGES OF APPRENTICESHIP,
1834–1838

Between 1804 and 1834 the total number of sugar estates in St Thomas-in-the-East had fallen by nearly one-third; from ninety-four to sixty-seven. Eighty per cent of Jamaica's sugar estates were owned by absentees.[1] These remaining estates had to operate in a totally new environment as owners, managers, and workers struggled with the system of 'apprenticeship' created by the Abolition Act, which specified that formerly enslaved people would become apprentices on 1 August 1834. Full freedom would arrive for domestic workers, trades, and skilled people (*non-praedials*) in 1838 and for field workers (*praedials*) on 1 August 1840. The new system required that the apprentices would live on their existing plantations and work for their former owners without remuneration for between forty and forty-five hours per week – typically from sunrise to sunset, including Sundays and public holidays. They could, however, negotiate wages for additional labour and were to be provided with basic provisions such as clothing, food, and shelter by the estate owners. All children under six were freed on 1 August 1834. The implementation of the new system was monitored by special magistrates, appointed in Britain, who were required to be impartial in their dealings.[2]

---

[1]   Higman, *Jamaica Surveyed*, p. 17; Hall, *Free*, p. 82.
[2]   For an overview, see William A. Green, *British Slave Emancipation: The Sugar Colonies and the Great Experiment 1830–1865* (Oxford: Clarendon Press, 1976), pp. 129–61; W. L. Burn, *Emancipation and Apprenticeship in the British West Indies* (London: Jonathan Cape, 1937). For specific Jamaican plantations, see B. W. Higman '"To Begin the World Again": Responses to Emancipation at Friendship and Greenwich, Estate, Jamaica', in *Jamaica in Slavery and Freedom*, ed. Kathleen Monteith and Glen Richards (Kingston, Jamaica: University of the West Indies Press, 2002), pp. 291–306; *Montpelier*, pp. 55–60, 283–87; and *Plantation*, pp. 154–56, 227, 231–57; Kenneth Morgan, 'Labour Relations During and After Apprenticeship: Amity Hall, Jamaica, 1834–1840', *Slavery and Abolition* Vol. 33 (2012), pp. 457–78; Douglas Hall, 'The Apprenticeship Period in Jamaica, 1834–1838', *Caribbean Quarterly* (1953), pp. 142–66; Philip D. Curtin, *Two Jamaicas: The Role of Ideas in a Tropical Colony* (Cambridge, MA: Harvard University Press, 1955); Swithin R. Wilmot, 'Not "Full Free": The Ex-Slaves and the Apprenticeship System in Jamaica, 1834–1838', *Jamaica Journal* (1984), pp. 2–10; Verene Shepherd, 'The Apprenticeship Experience on Jamaican Livestock Pens, 1834–1838', *Jamaica Journal* (1989), pp. 48–55; Thomas C. Holt, *The Problem of Freedom: Race, Labor, and Politics in Jamaica and Britain, 1832–1938* (Baltimore, MD: Johns Hopkins University Press, 1992), pp. 55–112; Diana Paton, ed., *Narrative of Events, since the First of August,*

As Mathieson put it so deliciously, 'It savours of paradox to say that the Act which abolished slavery did not emancipate the slaves', but this was the case.[3] Designed as an intermediate status to ease the transition from slavery to freedom apprenticeship was meant to provide the apprentices with the opportunity to learn new skills and trades and to prepare themselves for full freedom. It was also intended to help the owners of the sugar estates to negotiate the changes imposed by London. As it turned out, apprenticeship was an 'unhappy attempt at compromise between slavery and freedom' and proved a failure, being abandoned prematurely in 1838.[4]

The period of apprenticeship is a crucial one in the history of Jamaica and Marshall has called for more case studies on the topic.[5] The paperwork from Chiswick in this period adds a valuable layer of information to our understanding and supports the picture found in contemporary magistrates' reports, and suggested by Wilmot, that this was a fractious period for labour relations in St Thomas-in-the-East.[6] As has been argued throughout this book, from 1788 onwards the Burtons had no emotional attachment to Chiswick or its people, and from the start of their ownership of the estate had cared only about making money. After the deaths of Thomas and John Burton, the second generation of Burton owners had been content to live in Norfolk and wait for the profits to come to them. Focused on profit-taking alone, they had not paid sufficient attention to the commercial operations at Chiswick and had given no thought to their enslaved workers. During the period of apprenticeship, the Burtons' approach did not change, and their attitude towards Chiswick continued to be dominated by monetary considerations, clouded by a lack of understanding,

---

1834, by James Williams, an Apprenticed Labourer in Jamaica (Durham, NC: Duke University Press, 2001); Colleen A. Vasconcellos, *Slavery, Childhood, and Abolition in Jamaica, 1788–1838* (Early American Places) (Athens, GA: University of Georgia Press, 2015); Diana Paton, *No Bond but the Law: Punishment, Race, and Gender in Jamaican State Formation, 1780–1870* (Durham, NC: Duke University Press, 2004); Henrice Altink, 'Slavery by Another Name: Apprenticed Women in Jamaican Workhouses in the Period 1834–8', *Social History* (2001), pp. 40–59; '"To Wed or Not to Wed?": The Struggle to Define Afro-Jamaican Relationships, 1834–1838', *Journal of Social History* (2004), pp. 81–111; and *Representations of Slave Women in Discourses over Slavery and Abolition, 1780–1838* (London: Routledge, 2007); Ronald V. Sires, 'Negro Labour in Jamaica in the Years Following Emancipation', *The Journal of Negro History* (1940), pp. 484–97.

[3] William Law Mathieson, *British Slavery and Its Abolition, 1823–1838* (London and New York: Longmans, Green and Co, 1926), p. 243.

[4] Hall, 'The Apprenticeship Period', p. 142.

[5] Woodville K. Marshall, 'The Post-Slavery Labour Problem Revisited', in *Slavery, Freedom and Gender: The Dynamics of Caribbean Society*, ed. Brian L. Moore, B. W. Higman, Carl Campbell, and Patrick Bryan (Kingston: University of the West Indies Press, 2001), pp. 115–32.

[6] Wilmot, 'Not', pp. 3–6; Swithin Wilmot, 'Emancipation in Action: Workers and Wage Conflict in Jamaica 1838–1840', in *Caribbean Freedom: Economy and Society from Emancipation to the Present: A Student Reader*, ed. Hilary Beckles and Verene Shepherd (Princeton, NJ: M. Wiener/London: James Curry Publishers/Kingston, Jamaica: IRP, 1996), pp. 48–53, at p. 49. For a contemporary account, see the report from E. B. Lyon, Stipendiary Magistrate, 1837 reproduced in James Armstrong Thome and Joseph Horace Kimball, *Emancipation in the West Indies* (1838), pp. 463–68.

marked by managerial idleness, and remained devoid of concern for the apprentices on the estate. From 1805 to 1834 this approach had not prevented a slow decline of the estate and in the years from 1834 to 1838 it continued to fail as the Burtons and their managers found the newly created apprentices increasingly difficult to manage.

As other research has shown, the apprentices were forced by the new system to work in sugar cultivation, but its system of subsistence plus overtime offered them no real incentive to work towards high levels of productivity. Morgan's work on Amity Hall suggests that apprentices wanted a specific set of things, and the evidence from Chiswick supports this.[7] The people sought freedom, access to land, control over their lives, and independence. They bristled against the concept of 'apprenticeship' and, unsurprisingly, resisted aspects of the new system that seemed to resemble slavery. At Chiswick the apprentices were willing and able to negotiate their working days and hours, happy to refuse to work for extra pay, failed to attend when it suited them, and withdrew their labour to pressure their managers. The apprentices appear to have believed that the allotment grounds, gardens, and provision grounds on the estate were theirs. The sceptical, but realistic, view of apprenticeship amongst the people at Chiswick over these years was summed up in a rare verbatim record of a comment made by one unnamed apprentice in early August 1834. 'What free is this', he said to Townson, 'here I am going to the fields with my hoe on my shoulder and the sun rising the same way as before.'[8] In his perceptive comment, the unnamed man had summarised the essential tensions that would characterise this new period and revealed a depth of understanding of these problems among the apprentices that eluded the Burtons in England.

Seeking an understanding of the views of the apprentices was not at the forefront of the Burtons' minds as apprenticeship began; compensation was. In 1834, when asked to provide an estimate of the value of Thomas Sayers' share of Chiswick, the 'outside value' given by Pitcairn & Amos was £800. This meant that the entire estate was now valued at a maximum of £4,000, a precipitous fall from the £12,572 that it had been thought to be worth only two years earlier.[9] This fall in capital value made the amount of compensation that would be received even more important to the family. The prospect of the compensation money was, in Thomas Burton's view, a form of 'justice' which offered what he described as 'a minor remuneration for all our anxieties'.[10] As ever, the details of making the claim were left to other parties, specifically Mayhew and Pitcairn & Amos. The latter were dealing with over ninety similar claims for other clients and soon became experts in the process.[11] There was considerable disappointment in July 1835 when Pitcairn & Amos calculated that the compensation proposed would produce a value for Chiswick's population of £19 15s. 4d. each, making the family's compensation worth around £3,163. The family reck-

---

[7]   Morgan, 'Labour', p. 459.

[8]   BLO/MSS.W.Ind.s.18, fol. 111, Townson to Pitcairn & Amos, 10 August 1834.

[9]   BLO/MSS.W.Ind.s.18, fol. 103, Pitcairn & Amos to Mayhew, 4 September 1834; BLO/ MSS.W.Ind.s.17, 1829–1831, fol. 186, Pitcairn & Amos to Mayhew, 12 August 1831.

[10] BLO/MSS.W.Ind.s.18, fol. 96, Thomas Burton to Mayhew Yarmouth, 12 April 1834.

[11] BLO/MSS.W.Ind.s.18, fol. 154, Pitcairn & Amos to Mayhew, 2 October 1835.

oned that this meant they would be receiving less than half the amount of what they felt the people were worth.[12]

The prospect of definitive compensation money made Pitcairn & Amos far more willing to advance credit.[13] This was the situation in respect of many indebted estates where, as Thomas Burton put it, 'the arms of the City merchants will be widely expanded to receive the best part of it'.[14] After some argument Thomas Sayers agreed to 'forego his claims' in return for an 'annual allowance' and did not contest the family claim.[15] The compensation finally paid was £3,118 7s. 7d.[16] This was one of the 4,260 awards over £500 made in the British Caribbean in the process, 2,121 of which were to absentees. In Jamaica 997 absentees, including the Burton family, received compensation exceeding £500.[17] When the claim was paid on 7 December 1835, it totalled £3,227 8s. 7d., including £119 interest, and was deposited at Esdaile & Co. before being used to pay the family debts to Pitcairn & Amos and Lacon & Co., to whom the family was 'saddled with a heavy interest debt'.[18] After these creditors were paid, it appears that the family received £1,600, or £76 per share.[19] The Willins' share went to Thomas Burton to repay money they owed him from 1829.[20]

While the Burtons obsessed around their compensation payment, the situation at Chiswick was extremely difficult. The financial uncertainties of the 'new order' resulting from emancipation appears to have increased the general nervousness of the Jamaican managers, and in early 1834 Forsyth moved his billing cycle forward, clearly concerned over the financial stability of his own business.[21] In England, Thomas Burton was oblivious and noted that while Sayers' actions had caused the family to 'chew the cud of bitter adversity' for some time, the news from Chiswick

---

[12]   BLO/MSS.W.Ind.s.18, fol. 140 and fol. 141, Stevens, Wood, & Wilkinson to Mayhew, 11 July 1835.

[13]   See, for example, BLO/MSS.W.Ind.s.18, fol. 90, Pitcairn & Amos to Mayhew, 22 January 1834.

[14]   BLO/MSS.W.Ind.s.18, fol. 94, Thomas Burton to Mayhew, 3 February 1834.

[15]   BLO/MSS.W.Ind.s.18, fol. 120, Pitcairn & Amos to Mayhew, 5 December 1834; fol. 134, White and Barrett to Mayhew, 25 May 1835; BLO/MSS.W.Ind.s.19, fol. 7, Pitcairn & Amos to Mayhew, 13 May 1836; Draper identifies 3,500 cases where awards were contested: Nick Draper, '"Possessing Slaves": Ownership, Compensation and Metropolitan Society in Britain at the time of Emancipation 1834–40', *History Workshop Journal* (2007), pp. 75–102, at p. 81.

[16]   *House of Commons Parliamentary Papers 1837–8* (215), vol. 48, Accounts of slave compensation claims, p. 48; NA/T/71/867, Registers of claims: Jamaica: St Thomas in the East (1834–41); BLO/MSS.W.Ind.s.18, fol. 150 and fol. 151, Pitcairn & Amos to Mayhew, 15 September 1835.

[17]   Draper found 30,000 awards in total, the majority of which went to people who owned less than five enslaved people; Draper, '"Possessing Slaves"', pp. 85–87.

[18]   BLO/MSS.W.Ind.s.18, fol. 171, Pitcairn & Amos to Mayhew, 7 December 1835; fol. 173, Thomas Burton to Mayhew, 17 December 1835; BLO/MSS.W.Ind.s.18, fol. 155a, Thomas Burton to Mayhew, 10 October 1835.

[19]   BLO/MSS.W.Ind.s.19, fol. 3, Thomas Burton to Mayhew, 15 March 1835.

[20]   BLO/MSS.W.Ind.s.18, fol. 155a, Thomas Burton to Mayhew, 10 October 1835; fol. 158, James Palmer to Mayhew, 16 October 1835.

[21]   BLO/MSS.W.Ind.s.18, fol. 92, Pitcairn & Amos to Mayhew, 23 January 1834.

was 'of such a pleasing complexion' that he was hopeful that 'we may still weather the storm which has been so long overshadowing our earnest endeavours to avoid'.[22]

His optimism was ill-founded. On Monday 4 August 1834, Chiswick's workers arrived as normal for work and Townson reported that 'The Chiswick people have behaved very well. They have attended to their work regularly since the first instant.'[23] Nonetheless, the question of working hours was contentious. The law did not define how the work of 40½ hours per week required was to be organised. Some Jamaican planters tended towards a work regime based around an eight-hour day, but this left apprentices insufficient time to cultivate their provision grounds, since Saturday was their market day, and they were not meant to cultivate their grounds on Sundays. The apprentices preferred a nine-hour day from Monday to Thursday and a half day on Fridays, which would have given them time to work their grounds, but this was generally refused.[24] At Amity Hall, the workers were allowed to operate a nine-hour day, but this does not appear to have reduced tension and disquiet.[25]

Townson implemented the eight-hour a day regime and found himself in immediate difficulty.[26] The basic problem he faced was that the people were largely uninterested in working for one moment longer than the hours mandated and this was not enough for Townson to run the estate effectively.[27] Prior to 1834, Chiswick's punishing regime had seen the mills operated from six o'clock on Sunday night and worked non-stop until daybreak the following Sunday, for six months in the year, with the workers required to 'continuous exertion from Monday morning to Saturday night', working in shifts having come directly from the fields.[28] Even using the eight-hour day, this level of production was not possible and made paid labour inevitable.

Townson proposed to pay the workers one penny per extra hour worked, however, he had settled on this figure not from any discussion with the workforce, but by looking at how much the estate could 'afford', which was a matter of his opinion rather than any quantifiable figure.[29] The attorney's approach was framed by his previous experience and tended towards exhibitions of strength rather than compromise. In July 1834, for example, he had told Pitcairn & Amos that he would be holding back the usual delivery of cloth to the workers until after 1 August, 'in order to show them that they are still dependent', a somewhat desperate attempt to pretend that he and the Burtons were still in control.[30] The reality was very different and the months following 1 August 1834 saw the work schedules of Chiswick collapse

[22] BLO/MSS.W.Ind.s.18, fol. 94, Thomas Burton to Mayhew, 3 February 1834.
[23] BLO/MSS.W.Ind.s.18, fol. 111, Townson to Pitcairn & Amos, 10 August 1834.
[24] Wilmot, 'Not "Full Free"', p. 7; Burn, *Emancipation*, pp. 170, 177–78; Curtin, *Two*, p. 94; Gad Heuman, 'Riots and Resistance in the Caribbean at the Moment of Freedom', *Slavery & Abolition* (2000), pp. 144–45, at p. 143.
[25] Morgan, 'Labour', p. 462.
[26] BLO/MSS.W.Ind.s.18, fol. 129, Townson to Pitcairn & Amos, 22 January 1835.
[27] This view was shared elsewhere; Morgan, 'Labour', p. 462; Higman '"To Begin"', p. 296.
[28] WM/SC/01621, Townson to Mayhew, 1 January 1835; Hall, 'The Apprenticeship', p. 143.
[29] BLO/MSS.W.Ind.s.18, fol. 104, Pitcairn & Amos to Mayhew, 7 August 1834.
[30] BLO/MSS.W.Ind.s.18, fol. 102, Townson to Pitcairn & Amos, 25 July 1834.

because the old way of working could not be carried on into the new system and new approaches were not explored.

Townson found out, rapidly, that the workers at Chiswick wanted more than his planned one penny a day to work outside their mandated hours. In fact, during the first few months under the new system Chiswick's workers refused to do any paid shift work at all.[31] This situation has been found on other estates that have been studied.[32] The resultant disruption to working patterns, allied with widespread absenteeism, meant that virtually no work was done on the estate before Christmas. As 1835 began Townson reported that the workforce was 'better disposed to labour', but he was putting the best gloss on the situation.[33] Production levels were nearly 40 per cent lower than they had been under enslavement, with productivity having fallen from 8 hogsheads of sugar per week to 5.[34]

The situation worsened as the year progressed. By July, Forsyth admitted that 'the remainder of the crop will not be manufactured previous of the first of August' and that there would be a 'falling off' in production in the next year because the available labour was being used to produce the crop and so the estate 'could not be attended'. The deteriorating commercial situation meant that there would be insufficient funds to pay the wage bill from Jamaican resources and an extra call was likely on the Burtons. Moreover, the lack of personnel had led to a 'loss of stock' which would require 'expense' to replace.[35] As has already been discussed, Forsyth and Townson hoped that 'the poverty of the provision grounds' at Chiswick would encourage the people to work for low wages, but this seems to have been an ineffective ploy. The workers would only do paid work for 'limited periods' and it appears that they were discussing wage rates with their neighbours at other estates and demanding similar rates.[36]

The Burtons provided no firm guidance on what was to be done. Indeed, the degree to which the family had failed to keep abreast of the situation at Chiswick was revealed in a comment made by Thomas Burton in early 1834: 'I am rather surprised at the paucity of negroes upon the property.'[37] Had Burton been keeping watch over the previous decades and requiring his attorneys to provide detailed reports on the estate, in the manner of men such as Goulburn, he would not have been surprised. His inattention to business had, therefore, prevented him from grasping the implications of the gradual reduction in worker numbers at Chiswick and his statement highlights the Burtons' lack of engagement with the detail of the estate's operation and the lives of Chiswick's people. Even at this stage, the fact that the family was thinking about the subject of worker numbers in 1834 did not relate to their desire to become more involved in its management. The only reason they were looking at the matter was because the number of people who were held on the estate was the basis

[31]   BLO/MSS.W.Ind.s.18, fol. 111, Townson to Pitcairn & Amos, 10 August 1834.
[32]   Morgan, 'Labour', p. 462.
[33]   BLO/MSS.W.Ind.s.18, fol. 129, Townson to Pitcairn & Amos, 22 January 1835.
[34]   WM/SC/01621, Townson to Mayhew, 1 January 1835.
[35]   BLO/MSS.W.Ind.s.19, fol. 2, Forsyth to Pitcairn & Amos, 18 November 1835.
[36]   BLO/MSS.W.Ind.s.18, fol. 145, Townson to Pitcairn & Amos, 29 June 1835.
[37]   BLO/MSS.W.Ind.s.18, fol. 94, Thomas Burton to Mayhew, 3 February 1834.

of calculations for compensation. Aside from this, the family remained remarkably uninterested in the operation of Chiswick in the new era.

In Jamaica, there was much discussion about the problems caused by such lack of engagement among absentee owners. Many commentators, including Governor Sligo and some stipendiary magistrates, argued that absentee owners should move to Jamaica and take personal control of their estates, suggesting that by doing so owners would be able to respond more readily to the challenges of the new situation.[38] While this idea had some merit on paper, it ignored reality. Men such as Thomas Burton had extensive business affairs in England, which they could not just leave behind. Moreover, they had a social world to which they were accustomed in England, and none in Jamaica, a cultural chasm that made such a move unlikely. Finally, this idea assumed that the presence of such owners would improve the situation on an estate but, as we have seen, one of the problems that continually threatened estates such as Chiswick was the danger of an unsuitable manager. None of the Burton family had any qualifications or knowledge which would have helped the situation at Chiswick, and this is likely to have been the case with most absentees. In the absence of a member of the family with entrepreneurial flair, the arrival of one of the Burtons in 1834 would probably have caused more harm than good.

There were other options. Some absentees responded by tightening the management of their estates, or even arranged for them to be inspected. At Amity Hall, Goulburn resolved to carry on a 'well-regulated system of apprenticeship' and allowed his attorney to adjust the work regime, for example giving workers a free day on Saturday, in addition to the Sabbath.[39] The evidence does not suggest that such moves made any difference to worker attitudes, but reveals a degree of engagement that was lacking at Chiswick, where the Burtons issued no such instructions and left Mayhew to run operations. Over the next few years, the solicitor did his best and engaged in a lively correspondence with Townson and Pitcairn & Amos, which would cover options for improvement of the estate ranging from the (re)introduction of ploughing to the provision of a library of 'practical agriculture'.[40] His efforts were stymied by the Burtons' lack of interest and their unwillingness to invest in the estate, which meant Mayhew could not engage in the radical overhaul of operations that the new situation demanded.

The Burtons' view appears to have been that the solution to the immediate difficulties after the Abolition Act was to continue with the policy, begun under Sayers, of controlling expenses. In choosing this path, they mimicked the approach of many other planters, who responded to the Act by withdrawing the customary allowances of salted provisions, rum, and sugar to their workers.[41] Even before emancipation occurred, Pitcairn & Amos had cautioned that, while the proprietors wanted economies to be made, 'in provisions and what immediately concerns the personal comfort

---

[38] Hall, 'Apprenticeship', p. 159.
[39] Morgan, 'Labour', p. 461.
[40] See, for example, BLO/MSS.W.Ind.s.19, fol. 82, Pitcairn & Amos to Mayhew, 12 October 1837.
[41] Mathieson, *British*, p. 260.

of the labourers, there must be no pinching at this crisis'.[42] The agent's advice was sensible. As Chiswick's labourers explored their new situation, the proprietors – if they were to have any real hope of keeping the estate in operation – needed to consider how they might earn the goodwill of their workforce. Providing reasonable provisions along with acceptable living and working conditions was one potential route to that end. The Burtons remained transfixed, however, upon the programme of cuts to provisions and unwilling, or unable, to think about the estate's people except as assets.[43]

By failing to take such advice and seeking only to cut costs, the family did not plan effectively for the momentous changes that began in the last months of 1834, which were a period of great unrest in Jamaica generally and Chiswick in particular. As early as October 1834, the governor, Lord Sligo, noted that 'I cannot, after two months trial of the New System, report to you, that it is working at all in a satisfactory manner.'[44] As has been said, under the terms of the Abolition Act Jamaica's apprentices were bound to give up to 45 hours of free labour to the estate owner every week, but masters and labourers alike knew that during the intense period of crop-taking, when the mills and boilers needed to be operating most of the day, this would not be enough. This meant that wages would have to be paid for overtime, but the planters as a group did not come to any agreement about wage rates. Little effort was made to discuss matters with the workers before the system of apprenticeship began, and *ad hoc* bargaining only commenced afterwards. This meant that on many estates, including Chiswick, agreement on wages had not been reached before harvest arrived. The labour required to take the crop was not, therefore, readily available. This strengthened the apprentices' bargaining position. Moreover, since all available labour was focused on the current crop, the maintenance of estates and preparation for the following year's crop was generally neglected, which meant that the future economic security of the estates was imperilled.

Townson's commentary on this situation provides a clear insight into the viewpoint of the planters in this period and gives hints of that among the workers. He explained:

> It requires the master to supply the wants of the labour upon his giving 40 ½ hours work per week – these supplies he takes as a right that belonged to him in former times – he does not think he has gained enough – he has no direct impulse to work now that the master is without control and his feeling does not stimulate him to give his 40½ hours with the goodwill of a free labourer.

From Townson's perspective, therefore, the problem was that the apprenticeship system was too generous in what it offered the workers at Chiswick. This situation meant, in his view, that because the workers saw 'freedom and idleness are synonymous terms' they could not be induced to work for more than the hours allotted under the Act, even with an offer of wages. This view would seem to have been framed by Townson's previous experience where, as part of the racialised viewpoint

---

[42] BLO/MSS.W.Ind.s.18, fol. 78, Pitcairn & Amos to Mayhew, 12 October 1833.
[43] BLO/MSS.W.Ind.s.18, fol. 94, Thomas Burton to Mayhew, 3 February 1834.
[44] Hall, 'The Apprenticeship', p. 144.

that justified enslavement, the people had been characterised as naturally workshy and requiring severe discipline.[45]

It is also clear that Townson completely underestimated the ability of the people of Chiswick to operate in a wage economy. In 1836 he commented that 'I consider it desirable to instruct them in the value of money as an exchange for labour as early as possible', indicating that he believed they did not understand the new system.[46] His comment repeated, almost word for word, one made by the attorney for Amity Hall in 1835. As Morgan points out, such comments completely 'overlooked the enslaved's long-standing immersion in Jamaica's money economy'.[47] This seems to indicate a uniformity of thought on the part of planters, which caused them to underestimate the capacity of their workforce and weakened the planters' ability to conduct successful negotiations. Townson appears to have been unable to think outside the confines of his racially configured mindset and make sound commercial decisions. Instead, he mused about unrealistic options such as the government taking measures to 'compel labour' on sugar estates after the end of apprenticeship.[48] Alternatively, he argued for a swift move to abandon the apprenticeship system and pay only wages, 'as the great stimulant to industry on every occasion when the people are inclined to work in their own time'.[49] Having lost their previous cognitive category for the people – 'slaves' – planters now sought to re-categorise the workforce and had settled upon the idea that they would become industrial labourers, whose only option was to seek wages to support themselves.

Reading between the lines, Townson's letters suggest that the workers at Chiswick adjusted to the new system more readily than their masters, whose entrenched prejudices were creating problems for them. At the most simplistic level, labour supply is determined by the number of workers willing and able to work in a particular job or industry for a given wage. Under apprenticeship it was logical for the workers to seek to maximise their return, and only work the minimum levels required by statute – which covered their basic food and lodging – before considering the alternatives available to them. In fact, Chiswick's people were managing their free time effectively and applying it to tasks that maximised their overall 'income' which was, however, potentially composed of many elements. Wages might make part of it, but there was also the option of providing necessities for themselves and for trade from their personal provision grounds, as well as using their time for, what might be termed, 'leisure'; that is activity not directly related to earning cash or growing provisions. Chiswick's workers appear to have understood the complexities of their new position better than Townson. The problem for planters like Townson was that they had not adjusted intellectually or emotionally to the fact that the workers could choose how they used their time outside the hours laid down by the Act.

---

[45] WM/SC/01621, Townson to Mayhew, 1 January 1835.
[46] BLO/MSS.W.Ind.s.19, fol. 22, Townson to Pitcairn & Amos, 24 June 1836.
[47] Morgan, 'Labour', pp. 462–63.
[48] WM/SC/01621, Townson to Mayhew, 24 September 1836.
[49] WM/SC/01621, Townson to Mayhew, 22 November 1836.

Townson's constant recourse to the stereotype of their alleged 'idleness' or inability to understand 'the value of money' was a means, probably not even perceived consciously, for him to deal with the reality that he was being pressured successfully by the people at Chiswick into ever higher rates of pay.[50] Going forward, the attorney was involved in a constant process of negotiation with Chiswick's people, who were setting parameters for their labour that revealed a good understanding of how to use the limitations of the Act for their advantage. This successful approach to collective bargaining has been identified elsewhere.[51] At Chiswick, Townson bemoaned the fact that 'on no account will they work for hire on Saturdays', but this made perfect sense as it provided a day of rest that could be used for a variety of options and could not be removed by Townson's *fiat*. Likewise, Townson faced concerted opposition in relation to the employment of children. The Act stated that children under six years were free and could only be employed with their mothers' agreement. Townson noted, ruefully, that this permission was not forthcoming despite his attempts to explain that the parents owed it to the children to teach them 'habits of industry'.[52] This blanket refusal of cooperation reveals a profound antipathy on the part of the people to the entire system, and a desire to spare their children any involvement in work that was redolent of slavery.

It also seems that the workers at Chiswick were willing to support their demands with robust action and Townson's letters contain hints of regular worker unrest. 'The great change in the [...] system of carrying on work has caused feelings amongst the people', he wrote, 'which occasionally break out in little ebullition which like the passing of a summer cloud goes off and resumes its normal cheerfulness.'[53] Townson's style was to present the news from Chiswick positively, but the wider context suggests that the 'little ebullition' to which he was referring were regular expressions of worker disquiet. Now that the disciplinary powers of managers, overseers, and bookkeepers had been largely removed, and jurisdiction passed to the new stipendiary magistrates, this disquiet could no longer be dealt with using the whip or by accusations of *obeah*.[54]

It is apparent that this shift in the disciplinary structure was extremely difficult for Townson to navigate and, along with many attorneys and owners, he was dissatisfied with the new system. When he approved of the magistrate's decisions, he judged them 'common prudence' but when he did not, they were dismissed as 'ridiculous and annoying'. Townson's dissatisfaction suggests that the magistrate system appears to have been effective in controlling his clear desire to use more stringent measures of discipline. As he put it, the requirement upon the magistrates to report on the 'character and conduct' of planters was 'a mischievous and offensive measure' that might mean an 'innocent person may be vilified and injured without cause'.[55] His approach was tempered by his desire not to be reported as being guilty of any

[50] WM/SC/01621, Townson to Mayhew, 1 January 1835.
[51] Morgan, 'Labour', pp. 461–62; Turner, 'Slave', pp. 97–102.
[52] BLO/MSS.W.Ind.s.18, fol. 145, Townson to Pitcairn & Amos, 29 June 1835.
[53] BLO/MSS.W.Ind.s.18, fol. 127, Townson to Pitcairn & Amos, 1 January 1835.
[54] Hall, 'The Apprenticeship', p. 143.
[55] BLO/MSS.W.Ind.s.18, fol. 133, Townson to Pitcairn & Amos, 29 March 1835.

infractions. Although the system of stipendiary magistrates had many, very real, failings and was unsatisfactory for all concerned, reading between the lines, Townson's comment suggests that the prospect of being reported had the very real effect of moderating planters' behaviour. The attorney was clearly tempted to impose stricter discipline but did not dare to do so because he was afraid of the personal consequences of any infraction.

Protected by the new legal framework, facing a management that was completely unprepared for the new system, and acting in unity, the people at Chiswick were able to leverage their intimate knowledge of the estate's production processes and force Townson to agree a wage scale far higher than the one penny a day he had proposed only a few months earlier.[56] While the details of the negotiations have not survived, Townson's report on the first wage agreement at Chiswick in early 1835 provides fascinating hints of these discussions. The outcome of the initial set of talks was that the workers in the mill and manufactory agreed to work an extra eight hours per day for five days per week, in addition to the eight hours they were required to do under the apprenticeship system, in return for higher wages. These wages varied according to seniority and role but were uniformly higher than Townson's initial idea of a penny a day. So, the 'boatswain' and 'head boiler' each received 1s. 8d. per day. The three 'under boilers' received 1s. a day, while the 'stoker' received 10d., as did the two 'mill feeders', the two 'cane carriers' and the three 'wainmen'. Even the boys working in both locations received 5d. per day extra. The total wage bill for a week was £5 7s. 3d., whereas Townson had initially been hoping to pay less than £1 per week.[57] Such rates approximate those reported by other studies.[58] At Amity Hall the head boilerman settled for an extra 4s. 2d. per week from Monday to Friday, less than that accepted at Chiswick, suggesting that Chiswick's people were able to use the particularly weak economic position of the estate to their advantage.[59]

Away from the mills records have not survived, but in June 1835 Townson mentioned wages of 100 s. to the head driver, Matthew Hallen, 26s. 8d. to each of the coopers, the same to the head carpenter, and 13s. 4d. to the under-carpenter. Townson calculated wages to be running at 18s. per hogshead, but the letter is unclear as to whether this included the wages for the mill and manufactory.[60] Overall levels of wages in this period are not recorded, but in 1838 Townson stated that his expectation was for the wages to average at 10d. per day for each worker over 250 days, making the wage bill for the estate around £1,145 per annum. With the workers negotiating as a collective, the Burtons had to accept a wage level that took a substantial bite out of their – already depleted – profit margin.[61]

Furthermore, the people were able to renegotiate their working structures successfully. As has already been stated, they refused to work for hire on Saturdays, and they also stuck rigidly to the time limits prescribed by the Act. Perhaps

[56] BLO/MSS.W.Ind.s.18, fol. 129, Townson to Pitcairn & Amos, 22 January 1835.
[57] BLO/MSS.W.Ind.s.18, fol. 129, Townson to Pitcairn & Amos, 22 January 1835.
[58] Hall, 'The Apprenticeship', p. 155.
[59] Morgan, 'Labour', p. 462.
[60] BLO/MSS.W.Ind.s.18, fol. 145, Townson to Pitcairn & Amos, 29 June 1835.
[61] WM/SC/01621, Townson to Mayhew, 24 February 1838.

the most visible sign of this new working dynamic was the request of Townson for a clock in late 1836, 'as we can no longer take our day's work by the rising and setting of the sun'.[62] Moreover, as has been said, the mothers exerted their right to refuse to allow their children to do any work, even when offered 5d. per week for the work, much to Townson's annoyance.[63] Of course, Chiswick's people were still working an onerous system of shifts, covering the mills and the fields in the hours of daylight, but the parameters of their cooperation had been established and Townson had to work within their limits.[64] Considering the unique character of their change in status from enslaved to apprentice, the workers at Chiswick had managed to achieve reasonable result under the new order. Of course, these wages were for hours over the mandated hours per week, and still represented a very hard burden of work. Life at Chiswick remained extremely tough for the people, but they had entered the new era with real success.

Despite the evidence provided by the wage negotiations, the Burtons do not seem to have grasped the extent of the challenges now affecting Chiswick. In early 1834, Thomas Burton wrote approvingly of the 'favourable behaviour' of the workers and stated that Townson required 'sincere congratulation'. Beyond that the family made no enquiries into the particulars of the situation, nor did they provide instructions to Forsyth and Townson. They appear to have ignored the details coming from Jamaica that showed the increased recalcitrance being shown on the estate and focused on the few lines in Forsyth and Townson's letters that described the workers as happy and well behaved. Indeed, Thomas Burton's view seems to have been that any discontent on the part of Chiswick's workforce could only be the result of external agitators and that 'should their minds not be excited by ill-disposed people the happiest results will ultimately follow'.[65]

Clearly, Burton did not understand the situation in Jamaica. In the years from 1834 to 1838 the Abolition Act created a new set of operating parameters that exacerbated the critical underlying issue at Chiswick, unchanged since 1807, the base fact of declining worker numbers. When considering the working practices imposed by the apprenticeship system and in his negotiations with the apprentices, Townson had to start from the fact that the number of workers available at Chiswick, even if they all turned up, was far too few for the estate. In 1834 the overall number included four domestics, fifteen children under six, and twelve who were classed as 'aged and infirm', none of whom could work in the fields or mills. This meant that the main gang only numbered seventy-four and the second gang forty-four, far too low for anything other than core tasks. Finally, there were only ten tradesmen to maintain the entire property, meaning only the most important jobs could be done.[66] This

[62] BLO/MSS.W.Ind.s.19, fol. 31, Townson to Pitcairn & Amos, 2 August 1836.
[63] BLO/MSS.W.Ind.s.18, fol. 145, Townson to Pitcairn & Amos, 29 June 1835.
[64] BLO/MSS.W.Ind.s.18, fol. 129, Townson to Pitcairn & Amos, 22 January 1835.
[65] BLO/MSS.W.Ind.s.18, fol. 94, Thomas Burton to Mayhew, 3 February 1834.
[66] BLO/MSS.W.Ind.s.18, fol. 150 and fol. 151, Pitcairn & Amos to Mayhew, 15 September 1835; fol. 111, Townson to Pitcairn & Amos, 10 August 1834.

resembled the structure at Mesopotamia and meant that the workforce was 'not very well designed for sugar production'.[67]

This small labour force meant that, in Townson's words, the workforce at Chiswick was 'not effective' even before apprenticeship was introduced. As the changes imposed in 1834 took effect, and the available hours that could be drawn on fell, all the estate's available workforce was needed to harvest and manufacture the crop. This meant that 'the cane fields and grass pieces are for a time neglected', with the consequence that 'the estate is turning into a wilderness and canes which out to be growing for the succeeding year will be choked in weeds and fail'.[68] This was a vicious circle since such neglect reduced future production levels and profits. The crop of 1836 to 1837 was one of the worst in living memory, with only 96 hogsheads being produced.[69]

With no new labour sources, a low birth rate, and the steadfast refusal of the workers to compromise on their hours, the only solution available was to use hired labour, but emancipation made hired gangs more expensive.[70] The exact costs at Chiswick are unclear, but one surviving document shows that in the year from 1836 to 1837 the bill for jobbing gangs provided by Bell & Barclay and Ambrose Carter totalled around £286, over 10 per cent of the total made from the sale of sugar in that year.[71] The estate was also having to pay for pasturage as it had insufficient people to look after the animals, with Phillipsfield Pen being paid £27 in 1837.[72] Added to the wage bill for Chiswick's own people, this was a significant set of costs for the proprietors to bear and Townson urged them to think of the longer term. 'The proprietors must now console themselves', he wrote, 'that although there will be great additional expense their property will not be swamped under the new system although it will be unproductive for a time.'[73]

A measles outbreak in early 1837 caused great suffering on the estate. Townson reported that 'The Chiswick people have been miserably ill with the measles; when it first appeared, it was very mild, but it has since become very fatal; three deaths occurred the week before last and upwards of twenty working patients were in the hospital.' The numbers involved possibly indicate that Townson was demanding workers attend their posts even when ill, resulting in the people mixing at a time when they should have been quarantining. Whether this was the case or not, it is clear from this letter that for Townson and the Burtons the health of the apprentices was not a matter of human solidarity but of economic exploitation. Townson's

---

[67] Dunn, *A Tale*, p. 43.
[68] WM/SC/01621, Townson to Mayhew, 1 January 1835.
[69] BLO/MSS.W.Ind.s.19, fol. 71, Townson to Pitcairn & Amos, 7 July 1837.
[70] BLO/MSS.W.Ind.s.19, fol. 30, Townson to Pitcairn & Amos, 18 July 1836.
[71] BLO/MSS.W.Ind.s.19, fol. 59, Pitcairn & Amos to Mayhew, 24 April 1837. For Bell and Barclay as 'Jobbers' in the parish, see *Royal Gazette of Jamaica*, 21 April 1827, p. 14. Carter was the joint owner of the Essex and Wilmington sugar estates; 'Ambrose Carter', *Legacies of British Slavery* database, http://wwwdepts-live.ucl.ac.uk/lbs/person/view/2146653439, accessed 20 October 2023.
[72] BLO/MSS.W.Ind.s.19, fol. 59, Pitcairn & Amos to Mayhew, 24 April 1837.
[73] WM/SC/01621, Townson to Mayhew, 18 April 1837.

report about the measles outbreak was focused on its economic cost. As he put it to Mayhew, the measles outbreak had been 'to the great hindrance of sugar making'.[74]

Faced with declining production, Townson looked for a solution in technology. In 1835, he recommended the purchase of a steam engine and horizontal mill, which he thought might allow him to 'finish the crop early' and permit the workers to cultivate the property, while cutting the costs of jobbers.[75] This was the first discussion of such a machine at Chiswick and reveals the degree to which the estate lagged behind some of its peers. For example, a steam engine had been added to Amity Hall in 1818.[76] Townson estimated that the cost of around £1,600 would take four years to defray. This was a large capital investment, and he then undermined his argument by stating that the machinery would be paid for just as apprenticeship would end on the estate. In consequence, he worried that the investment might prove to be wasted since 'according to present appearances there will be no more sugar to make'.[77] Townson's indecision was mirrored by all those involved. Forsyth argued against the idea on the grounds that a mill would not replace field labour.[78] Pitcairn & Amos also advised against it, stating that such an expense should be avoided until the owners had 'more experience of the working of the new system'.[79] This debate would carry on for several years, but fear of further financial loss hamstrung the decision-making process despite the evidence provided by Townson of 'the slow progress' of production using the cattle mill and windmill.[80] The Burtons made no decision and so, as other estates began to use such machinery with some success, what Townson called the 'heart-breaking' fall in yield at Chiswick continued unabated.[81]

This outcome was indicative of the wider situation. The Burtons' position as absentee owners limited their ability to assess and respond to the rapidly changing situation in Jamaica. Looking from Norfolk and having never engaged with the people of Chiswick in any meaningful fashion, the family were unable to understand the views and actions of the people on the estate as they changed during the period of apprenticeship. Moreover, there was also generational change taking place in the family. From around 1835, Thomas Burton, now approaching sixty, gradually disengaged from his, already nominal, involvement in Chiswick and placed oversight of his affairs in the hands of his son-in-law, Samuel Palmer, a Yarmouth solicitor.[82] Likewise, Charles Fisher Burton gradually handed over his affairs to another solicitor, Robert Cory.[83] Over the next few years, Cory and Palmer, together with

---

[74] BLO/MSS.W.Ind.s.19, fol. 60, Pitcairn & Amos to Mayhew, 19 April 1837; fol. 65, Pitcairn & Amos to Mayhew, 18 May 1837; WM/SC/01621, Townson to Mayhew, 18 April 1837.
[75] WM/SC/01621, Townson to Mayhew, 1 January 1835.
[76] Turner, 'Planter', p. 234.
[77] WM/SC/01621, Townson to Mayhew, 1 January 1835.
[78] BLO/MSS.W.Ind.s.18, fol. 129, Forsyth to Pitcairn & Amos, 20 January 1835.
[79] BLO/MSS.W.Ind.s.18, fol. 128, Pitcairn & Amos to Mayhew, 17 March 1835.
[80] BLO/MSS.W.Ind.s.19, fol. 13, Townson to Pitcairn & Amos, 18 April 1836.
[81] BLO/MSS.W.Ind.s.19, fol. 19, Townson to Pitcairn & Amos, 26 May 1836.
[82] BLO/MSS.W.Ind.s.19, fol. 11, Thos. Burton to Mayhew, 8 June 1836. NRO/PD/28/74, Marriage of Augusta Burton and Samuel Palmer, 10 May 1831.
[83] BLO/MSS.W.Ind.s.18, fol. 164, Robert Cory to Mayhew, 4 November 1835. For Cory, see *Norfolk Chronicle*, 19 July 1834, p. 3.

another lawyer named Charles Ives, took on a greater role in the oversight of financial matters relating to the estate.[84] Their arrival did not, however, alter the lack of leadership coming from England. None of these men had experience in running a sugar estate in Jamaica and they largely continued with the status quo. Mayhew was left to manage Chiswick as best he could, but no change in course was authorised.

Faced with such uninterested owners, Townson and Forsyth were unsure of what to do, as were Pitcairn & Amos. These advisors had other sources of income and did not own Chiswick, therefore the temptation to inaction was strong. In this situation the Burtons needed to be engaged and to take decisive decisions, but their absentee status deprived the family of essential commercial data that might have spurred action. For example, it was only on the death of James Forsyth in June 1836, that the family discovered his ill health had meant that he rarely left his home in Kingston, and that he had only visited the estate once since 1832, 'for a few minutes'.[85] The Burtons had been making commercial decisions on Chiswick relying on the advice of a man who had hardly left his house since before the Abolition Act was passed.

In fact, the rapidly changing situation in Jamaica from 1834 made the operation of the estate as absentees far more problematic than it had been at any time since the family had acquired the estate. From 1788 to 1833 change in Jamaica had been slow and incremental. After 1807 the Burtons had been able to rest on their laurels, since the decline in income following the abolition of the slave trade had been gradual. This slow speed of change had altered in 1834 when Jamaica had entered a new period of rapid social and economic change, but with letters from Jamaica arriving only a few times per year, the Burtons were not fully informed about their estate and lacked real understanding of the situation in Jamaica. The speed of change placed absentees at an increasing disadvantage. Pitcairn & Amos recognised this and in 1836, when the estate's overseer Mr Wilson left to rent a sugar estate, the London firm suggested that the family needed to consider letting Chiswick out for rental. They argued that when full freedom arrived, and the people could work for whoever they wished 'this must place absent proprietors under peculiar disadvantage' and urged the family to act.[86]

Despite this advice, and the mounting evidence from the accounts, no definite action was taken. The Burtons did not rent the estate out, neither did they take the necessary control of it. In the absence of strong leadership from England, Townson asked for books on the management of stock and 'agriculture' to be sent over to the estate to enable the overseer to gain the latest knowledge in these areas.[87] One small advance was made in late 1837 when Townson asked for a plough to be sent out.[88] It seems that this was after discussions with his neighbours at Golden Grove, since

---

[84] BLO/MSS.W.Ind.s.18, fol. 160, Robert Cory, Charles John Ives, Samuel Palmer to Mayhew, 26 October 1835.
[85] BLO/MSS.W.Ind.s.19, fol. 22, Townson to Pitcairn & Amos, 24 June 1836.
[86] BLO/MSS.W.Ind.s.19, fol. 13, Pitcairn & Amos to Mayhew, 9 June 1836, underlining in original.
[87] BLO/MSS.W.Ind.s.19, fol. 16, Townson to Pitcairn & Amos, 7 May 1836.
[88] BLO/MSS.W.Ind.s.19, fol. 82, Pitcairn & Amos to Mayhew, 12 October 1837; Townson to Mayhew, 7 September 1839.

he asked for the same type of plough in use there. Such moves were common across the island as managers and owners struggled to cope with declining productivity levels.[89] The introduction of ploughing was more successful in 1837 than it had been for William Wright a decade earlier, because the attorney was now engaged with the idea. Although the original Wilkies plough was broken by a large stone, the replacement – from Ransomes of Ipswich – proved more resilient and Townson judged the experiment a success.[90] An indication of the impact of such methods is provided by Ramlackhansingh, who calculated that introducing the plough and harrow reduced cultivation costs at Amity Hall by 65 per cent in this period, but no data is available to allow any such calculations to be made for Chiswick.[91]

As Table 11 shows, the introduction of ploughing had little material effect at Chiswick and production fell markedly during apprenticeship. Compared with the period from 1829 to 1833, when the average production at Chiswick had been 187 hogsheads of sugar per annum, the years of apprenticeship saw a fall of 37 per cent, to around 118 hogsheads. This was poor in comparison with the situation at Worthy Park, where production only fell by around 17 per cent and at Amity Hall, where sugar output 'did not decline significantly during apprenticeship' and averaged 230 hogsheads.[92] It may be that Chiswick's experience is representative of many absentee-owned estates in the period, where owners had not adjusted to the new regime as well as places like Worthy Park and Amity Hall. The result of this underperformance was that, even though the average price for sugar increased in this period from 29s 5d. per hundredweight in 1834 to 33s. 8d. in 1838, the profits of Chiswick continued to decline, falling 25 per cent.[93]

At the same time, however, the overall financial situation altered. From 1834 to 1836 the profits were swallowed by debt payments resulting from the Sayers debacle. As of 30 April 1834, the proprietors would have made a profit of £1,661 had it not been for debts amounting to £3,583 owed to Pitcairn & Amos and other creditors. In the event, they received nothing. A note made in May 1836 quantified the putative liability owed by Sayers to the other proprietors at £6,007 13s. 3d., showing that Thomas Sayers' debts had swallowed up all potential profits from 1830 to 1836.[94] Nonetheless, the prospect of compensation made Pitcairn & Amos noticeably more relaxed about the situation than during the previous years and the necessary loans were made.[95]

---

[89] Morgan, 'Labour', p. 464, Hall, 'The Apprenticeship', p. 154, D. G. Hall, *Free Jamaica, 1838– 1865. An Economic History* (New Haven, CT: Yale University Press, 1959), p. 47.

[90] WM/SC/01621, Townson to Mayhew, 24 September 1838; BLO/MSS.W.Ind.s.19, fol. 121, Steward & Westmoreland to Mayhew, 18 October 1838; fol. 122, Townson to Mayhew, 8 September 1838.

[91] G. S. Ramlackhansingh, 'Amity Hall 1760–1860: The Geography of a Jamaican Plantation', Master's thesis, University of London, 1966, p. 46.

[92] Craton and Walvin, *A Jamaican*, p. 209; Morgan, 'Labour', p. 460.

[93] Prices from Hall, *Free*, p. 270.

[94] BLO/MSS.W.Ind.s.19, fol. 7, Pitcairn & Amos to Mayhew, 13 May 1836.

[95] BLO/MSS.W.Ind.s.18, fol. 98, Pitcairn & Amos to Mayhew, 22 May 1834; fol. 100, 21 June 1834.

Table 11. *Produce and finances of the Chiswick estate, 1834–1838.**

Crop year	Hogsheads of sugar sold (London and Jamaica)	Gross income from sugar (after duties)	Puncheons of rum sold (London and Jamaica)	Gross income from rum (£ sterling)	Expenses (£ sterling)	Net profit (loss) (£ sterling)
1834	160	£2,409	75		(£747)	£1,661
1835	105	£2,924	46			£1,092
1836	96	£2,023	69	£828		
1837	112	£1,993				£1,245
1838	100	Not known				£2,124

* Details of rum sales only survive for 1836, and for expenses from 1834. Sales of sugar are known, and where the income for the year is not known an estimate has been made from prices estimated by Hall, *Free*, p. 270. Sources: BLO/MSS.W.Ind.s. 18, fol.167; Pitcairn & Amos to Mayhew, 4 November 1835; BLO/MSS.W.Ind.s.19, fol. 7, Pitcairn & Amos to Mayhew, 13 May 1836; fol. 22, Townson to Pitcairn & Amos, 24 June 1836; fol. 29, Townson to Pitcairn & Amos, 2 July 1836; fol. 59 Pitcairn & Amos to Mayhew, 24 April 1847; fol. 81, Townson to Pitcairn & Amos, 24 June 1837; fol. 100 Pitcairn & Amos to Mayhew, 24 January 1838; fol. 109 Pitcairn & Amos to Mayhew, 25 April 1838; fol. 117, Steward & Westmoreland to Mayhew 17 September 1838.

From 1836 onwards, however, with the debts attached to the estate finally cleared thanks to Mayhew's careful management and the arrival of the compensation money, the Burtons began to see positive returns, especially as the profits from Sayers' share of the plantation were now paid to the other proprietors.[96] Once again, the fact that Thomas Burton's management in the 1790s had left the sugar estate in the unusual position of being debt-free proved to be a benefit for his children, and the finances of the estate stabilised. The profit levels were far lower than they had been, but Chiswick was finally providing a positive return. Going forward, Townson was aiming at a steady rate of production of 120 hogsheads annually.[97]

These changes engendered optimism in Norfolk. In early 1836 Thomas Burton wrote to John Lee Farr stating, 'I not only rejoice with you at the recent favourable prospects of Chiswick, but also anticipate the future, from what has already been effected.' Despite the mounting evidence from Jamaica of deteriorating productivity and worsening labour relations, Burton was still of the view that 'after a short lapse of time the negroes will work better than they do at this present, providing that they will get the benefit arising from their own industry'. So confident was he that he argued, 'we may still live to see that West India property is more valuable than English'.[98] Optimism grew and in August 1837 Townson reported that 'Everything is doing well, the seasons are good and there is a great quantity of provisions.'[99] In September there was poor weather, including a storm, but Chiswick 'comparatively escaped', although a general shortage of provisions in the island added to estate costs.[100] Expectations grew for the crop and the eventual production for 1837 to 1838 was a, much improved, 112 hogsheads.[101]

The consequence of this optimism was that some hard currency was sent to Townson to make payments in Jamaica, where economic uncertainty was causing severe financial problems. In response, the family sent 300 sovereigns out in 1836 to cover Chiswick's intra-island transactions for the year.[102] The younger generation now running the estate also began to seek alternate financial investments and began to augment the income from the estate's produce through speculation in the bond market, where they invested £1,300 in 1837, a programme that was carried on into 1838, with an investment of £1,200.[103] The return from this speculation was described as 'handsome' by Pitcairn & Amos and, at £51 2s. 3d. in 1837 and £66 in 1838, it amounted to healthy average return on capital of around 4.7 per cent.[104] All of this meant that in 1838, after a decade of turmoil, the total profits distributed to the family were £2,124.5 1s., with £991 6s. 4d. going to Thomas Burton and £288 4s. 8d.

---

[96]   BLO/MSS.W.Ind.s.19, fol. 109, Pitcairn & Amos to Mayhew, 25 April 1838.
[97]   BLO/MSS.W.Ind.s.19, fol. 7, Townson to Pitcairn & Amos, 18 July 1836.
[98]   BLO/MSS.W.Ind.s.19, fol. 5, Thomas Burton to Farr, 15 March 1836.
[99]   BLO/MSS.W.Ind.s.19, fol. 82, Townson to Pitcairn & Amos, 25 August 1837.
[100] BLO/MSS.W.Ind.s.19, fol. 86, Pitcairn & Amos to Mayhew, 24 November 1837.
[101] BLO/MSS.W.Ind.s.19, fol. 100, Pitcairn & Amos to Mayhew, 24 January 1838.
[102] BLO/MSS.W.Ind.s.19, fol. 48, Townson to Pitcairn & Amos, 23 November 1836.
[103] BLO/MSS.W.Ind.s.19, fol. 49, Pitcairn & Amos to Mayhew, 17 January 1837; fol. 58, Pitcairn & Amos to Mayhew, 26 January 1837; BLO/MSS.W.Ind.s.19, fol. 109, Pitcairn & Amos to Mayhew, 25 April 1838.
[104] BLO/MSS.W.Ind.s.19, fol. 59, Pitcairn & Amos to Mayhew, 24 April 1837.

going to the other members of the family. This was a remarkable improvement over the period of losses from 1829 to 1835 and exceeded the average returns from 1816 to 1824, which had been £1,251 per year, meaning the siblings had received around £138 on average.

At one level, this income stream suggests that Mayhew, Pitcairn & Amos, and Townson had done well in their management since 1834. In fact, the new-found profitability of the estate rested firmly upon the efforts of the people of Chiswick, whose willingness to cooperate with the Burtons, via Townson, during the period of apprenticeship – despite their history before 1833, and their discontent with the current situation – was admirable. The apprentices had bargained hard with Townson to improve their wages and conditions, but they had also worked hard for the Burton family. From 1834 to 1838 the Burtons had failed to invest in the estate, had lacked any strategy to change its operations, and had continued to show no interest in the apprentices. The family had done nothing to deal with the fact that the numbers of workers they had available to harvest their sugar was continuing to decline. Those workers had, therefore, to produce sugar in a business with aging equipment, a run-down environment, and while affected by illness and drought. Unable to affect these wider issues, the apprentices had cooperated with Townson and the Burtons, worked hard, and produced sufficient sugar that the family was now again receiving profits.

This cooperation was about to vanish as events took a new course. In August 1838 apprenticeship was abandoned two years early. The original plan had called for the complete freedom of the non-praedial labourers in 1838, and for the praedial labourers – such as those at Chiswick – in 1840, but by 1838 the discontent with the system – across the island, the West Indies and in Britain – was such that a rapid dissolution of apprenticeship occurred. During May 1838, the governments in Barbados, Nevis, Montserrat, and Tortola, all passed Acts of general emancipation, releasing all apprentices on 1 August 1838; and other legislatures prepared to follow them. Several absentee proprietors in Jamaica foresaw the inevitable and freed their apprentices. After a short discussion the Jamaican Assembly passed an Act ending apprenticeship on 1 August 1838.

The Burtons had not developed a plan to deal with the end of apprenticeship. Townson had been warning the family since 1836 that he had 'doubts' about the willingness of the people to continue working on the estate when apprenticeship came to an end but, in the absence of any instructions from England, his planning had focused on maximising returns in the years running up to 1840.[105] With a dwindling labour force even without the end of apprenticeship, the family had failed to address reality. They had not looked seriously at the possibility for mechanisation, for example in the use of a steam engine to replace the ancient breeze mill and labour-intensive cattle mill, although Townson had raised this possibility. Neither had they considered how they might reconstruct their relations with the people of Chiswick when apprenticeship came to its scheduled end in 1840. Nor had they thought about what this would mean for work patterns, the availability of labour, the maintenance and ownership of houses and provision grounds, or what might

[105] WM/SC/01621, Townson to Mayhew, 18 April 1837.

happen to wages in a changed labour market. At the same time, the Burton family could still not bring themselves to consider selling the estate, because the price they could obtain was lower than the one they had embedded in their heads. So it was that, with those heads in the sand, the Burtons had done nothing and now, with the early end of apprenticeship, the family had to face the fact that Chiswick's people were finally free.

9

'Ruin must ensue': Freedom and the Collapse of Chiswick, 1838–1846

The years following the end of apprenticeship saw a radical shift in the economic system in Jamaica, as real emancipation flung estate owners and workers into period of further rapid adjustment. For the former apprentices a range of economic new options appeared. They could stay on estates and work on a fully waged basis. Alternatively, they could leave the estates and live in their villages, becoming what Craton has termed a 'proto-peasantry', still linked to the estate but living as free people.[1] Another option was squatting on land elsewhere, or even buying it, thereby cutting previous links entirely and establishing new living conditions. Skilled workers, such as carpenters, could set up independent businesses, and others could choose to engage in small scale-cultivation, where the farming of cash crops like coffee and cocoa offered genuine options. There was also the option to move to urban areas, the main possibility being Kingston. The newly free people across the island followed all these options over the next few years, which would see the appearance of widescale peasant agriculture, urban migration, and the establishment of free villages, along with a wage economy.[2]

The nature, timing and variety of these responses varied, and in August 1838 there was no immediate mass exodus from the island's sugar estates, including Chiswick.[3] Nonetheless, the immediate result of the ending of apprenticeship at Chiswick was

---

[1] Michael Craton, 'Proto-Peasant Revolts? The Late Slave Rebellions in the British West Indies, 1816–1832', *Past & Present* (1979), pp. 99–125; 'Reshuffling the Pack: The Transition from Slavery to Other Forms of Labour in the British Caribbean, Ca. 1790–1890', *New West Indian Guide* (1994), pp. 23–75.

[2] For discussion, see, for example, Swithin Wilmot, '"We not slave again": Enslaved Jamaicans in Early Freedom, 1838–1865', in *The Faces of Freedom: The Manumission and Emancipation of Slaves in Old World and New World Slavery*, ed. Marc Kleijwegt (Leiden: Brill, 2006), pp. 215–31, at pp. 218–19; Gad Heuman, 'Riots and Resistance in the Caribbean at the Moment of Freedom', *Slavery & Abolition* (2000), pp. 144–45; Woodville K. Marshall, '"We be wise to many more tings": Blacks' Hopes and Expectations of Emancipation', in *Caribbean Freedom: Society and Economy from Emancipation to the Present*, ed. Hilary Beckles and Verene A. Shepherd (Kingston: Ian Randle, 1993), pp. 12–20; Holt, *Problem*, pp. 55–79; O. Nigel Bolland, 'Systems of Domination after Slavery: The Control of Land and Labour in the British West Indies after 1838', *Comparative Studies in Society and History* (1981), pp. 591–619; Hilary McD Beckles, 'Freedom and Labour in the Post-Emancipation British Caribbean', *Journal of Social History* Vol. 35, No. 4 (2002), pp. 868–71; Michael Craton, 'Free Villages in Jamaica', *Social and Economic Studies* (1968), pp. 336–59.

[3] Douglas Hall, 'The Flight from the Estates Reconsidered: The British West Indies, 1838–1842', *Journal of Caribbean History* Vols 10–11 (1978), pp. 7–24.

the near collapse of the work regime. In early October Townson reported that until 1 August the labourers at Chiswick had 'conducted themselves in an orderly, praise-worthy manner', but since emancipation 'not one had appeared for field work'.[4] This was a common complaint across the island as, not unexpectedly, the people on the plantations took stock of their new situation and considered how to respond to it. Townson was definite that this 'indisposition to labour' had resulted in 'the great injury of many properties' on the island.[5] This lack of labourers at Chiswick in the last few months of the year meant that grass and weeds began to choke the canes, and there was insufficient pasture for fodder, which meant that the livestock was less able to help gather the crop and work the mill. Moreover, and most worryingly for Townson, the shortage of labour meant that the preparations normally undertaken for next year's crop, including planting the thirty acres needed to ensure the normal rotation, had been delayed, 'to the great prejudice of the next crop and the estate generally'. Looking forward, Townson feared this would become a self-reinforcing pattern, which would drive production on the estate to zero. As Townson put it, 'if idleness is much longer permitted, ruin must ensure'.[6]

The attorney blamed the fact that 'whole cane fields are now covered with grass' on the governor who, he felt, was too gentle in his approach. The example Townson used was that 'Our Governor very unfortunately because our Slave Law exempted women from Hard labour who had families, said all women are not to labour, and they declare it is Governor's Law and will not'.[7] This response of the women was problematic because of the gendered division of labour on Chiswick, where women had been heavily involved in cutting cane at crop time, while the men had attended the stock, dealt with the wains, and boiled sugar. The women's new willingness to assert their rights troubled Townson, and he had no answer to it.

Townson was also concerned about the activity of Baptist and other Christian preachers in the area.[8] He reported that the Baptists had been distributing leaflets among the workers advising that they should ask for '2/6 if not 3/4 a day' as wages, far higher than the wages he proposed to pay. The problem was, Townson felt, that such policies, statements, and leaflets had combined with the lack of 'proper meas-ures' on the part of the government to create a 'feeling which in some places is decidedly against cultivating canes again'. He then linked this feeling to one of his favoured characterisations of Chiswick's people, what he characterised as a penchant for 'idleness' on their part, which he felt was 'the source of mischief'.[9]

By pointing his finger at the governor and the Baptists, however, Townson was failing to give Chiswick's people sufficient credit and, once more, his inability to tran-

---

[4]   BLO/MSS.W.Ind.s.19, fol. 123, Steward & Westmoreland to Mayhew, 3 October 1838.
[5]   BLO/MSS.W.Ind.s.19, fol. 119, Steward & Westmoreland to Mayhew, 2 October 1838.
[6]   BLO/MSS.W.Ind.s.19, fol. 120, Townson to Steward & Westmoreland, 25 August 1838.
[7]   BLO/MSS.W.Ind.s.19, fol. 120, Townson to Steward & Westmoreland, 25 August 1838.
[8]   BLO/MSS.W.Ind.s.19, fol. 123, Townson to Steward & Westmoreland, 8 September 1838. For a useful discussion of the hostility towards Baptists and non-conformists in general, see Sharon Grant, 'The Reverend Thomas Pennock, Wesleyan Methodist Missionary in Nineteenth Century Jamaica: A Case Study of Acculturation, Enculturation, Or Something Else?', *Wesley and Methodist Studies* (2012), pp. 117–28.
[9]   BLO/MSS.W.Ind.s.19, fol. 120, Townson to Steward & Westmoreland, 25 August 1838; fol. 122, Townson to Steward & Westmoreland, 8 September 1838.

scend the ideas he had developed in the era of slavery prevented him from doing his job effectively. The attorney identified that there was 'no doubt strong feeling against field labour', yet he dismissed this as a 'prejudice' among the people that 'a free man is degraded by doing the work formerly done by a slave'. So, while Townson recognised the sentiments among the people at Chiswick against working on the estate because of its association with slavery, he lacked the ability to empathise with the estate's workers and realise that this was a logical, and rather inevitable, consequence of the history of the estate and the island. His inability to shift his entrenched presuppositions meant that his strategy, which was not opposed in England, was to 'break down this feeling' rather than work with it. The tool Townson chose to respond to the workforce as they tried to navigate their new situation was not negotiation, the restructuring of operations, or a new payment system, but economic coercion. This involved 'proper instruction and fair wages, with a threat of discharge in case of persevering obstinacy'.[10] By 'fair', he appears to have meant the lowest he could manage to pay.

The degree to which such methods could be deployed was limited, however, since the workers at Chiswick appear to have understood the new situation rather better than Townson. Although Townson highlighted their 'agitation' and their 'unsettled' nature, examination of the people's actions suggest they were engaged in a measured and informed approach to work and wage negotiations. When the governor suggested the minimum wage level for able field labourers should be 1s. 8d. per day, this was the level Chiswick's people asked for, rather than the higher levels Townson bemoaned the Baptists were encouraging.[11] Despite Townson's bluster, his attempts to pay 'fair' wages failed. In fact, in the tight labour market in Saint Thomas in this period, wage levels were driven up. Hall found that the average daily wages of estate workers increased from 9d. per day in October 1838 to 1s. 6d. per day in December 1834, and emphasised that these were minimums, and could be exceeded on task work by threepence to sixpence.[12] Across the island there was a 'lack of sustained work and requests for high wage rates' generally.[13]

Although he could now recruit from a wider labour pool, Townson was unable to 'entice the labourers' from nearby estates such as Plantain Garden to work at Chiswick. While he stated that this was because these estates were more 'fertile' and so could afford higher wages, the more mundane reason was that he and the Burtons refused to pay higher levels that could match their competitors.[14] It was also a legacy of the lack of interest in the workforce shown by the Burtons since 1788. This was a moment when an entirely new set of working relationships were being worked out from scratch. The final vestiges of the old slave regime had been demolished and new relations had to be constructed between worker and estate owner. No longer forced to work at Chiswick, the people could now choose where they worked and, since the Burtons had never shown any interest in them, there was little loyalty to the family. In the absence of such loyalty, choosing to work at Chiswick on any day was a judge-

[10] BLO/MSS.W.Ind.s.19, fol. 122, Townson to Steward & Westmoreland, 8 September 1838.
[11] WM/SC/01621, Townson to Mayhew, 24 September 1838.
[12] Hall, *Free*, pp. 44–45.
[13] Morgan, 'Labour', p. 467.
[14] WM/SC/01621, Townson to Mayhew, 24 September 1838; BLO/MSS.W.Ind.s.19, fol. 126, Townson to Steward & Westmoreland, 3 December 1838.

ment made in response to a wide and changeable set of factors. The people had to consider what wages were available, the distance they wanted to travel to work, their options in relation to their own produce, what they hoped to do in in the short and longer term, how they felt, family commitments, the weather and so on. Indeed, in some ways, as 'proto-peasantry' the people had more options than the urban poor in England, who did not have provision grounds on which they could fall back and who were tied into an industrial economy without alternatives. In this new environment Townson and the Burtons needed to act decisively, but they did not.

Somewhat belatedly, Chiswick's overseer, William Whitehouse, attempted to improve the situation and inculcate loyalty by means of 'tact and good temper' in his relations with, what were termed, the 'faithful' people on the estate. This improved the supply of labour and raised Townson's hopes that the crop might be got off. This small example reveals that there were options for the family even at this late juncture, if they had been willing and able to change their approach. This was not to be, and any increase in crop without such changes could only be achieved by abandoning the preparation of next year's plants and by paying the wages required by the workers. The people were quite willing and able to change employers, and Townson found that any attempt to pay under the norm for the area caused them to travel to the 'rich estates' nearby. Knowledge of this appears to have strengthened the resolve of the people to refuse to work for lower wages and Townson was forced to pay the average of 1s. 8d. per day, which he described as 'ruinous' and amounted to around £1,571 for the year.[15] Matters worsened after the Christmas holidays, when 'the whole parish was at a standstill'. In consequence, although the crop had been harvested, sugar making had not commenced as January reached its end.[16]

It did resume but then, in March 1839, Chiswick was affected by a strike. Although details are sparse, it seems that with the crop taken off and sugar making finally underway the people attempted to force Townson to pay more than 1s. 8d. per day. Townson reported that there was 'no satisfying them' and when he refused their demand the people withdrew their labour, and 'sugar-making is at a standstill'.[17] The exact outcome of the conflict is unclear and in May Townson reported that 'most' of the people who had 'kept back from work' were now returned.[18] This, somewhat evasive, comment needs to be linked to a separate request for an extra £300 to pay wages. Townson explained to the owners that 'proximity to the rich estates on the river is such a temptation for the people to go there that it is difficult to get hands to work at the cattle mill', yet the nearness of the request for extra money to the date of the strike is suggestive.[19] The new London agents, Steward & Westmoreland of Winchester House, Broad Street, London, who had replaced Pitcairn & Amos when the latter dissolved their partnership on 30 April 1838, were worried.[20] At such high

---

[15]   BLO/MSS.W.Ind.s.19, fol. 126, Townson to Steward & Westmoreland, 3 December 1838.
[16]   BLO/MSS.W.Ind.s.19, fol. 130, Townson to Steward & Westmoreland, 18 January 1839.
[17]   BLO/MSS.W.Ind.s.19, fol. 132, Townson to Steward & Westmoreland, March 1839.
[18]   BLO/MSS.W.Ind.s.19, fol. 135, Steward & Westmoreland to Mayhew, 6 May 1839.
[19]   BLO/MSS.W.Ind.s.19, fol. 133, Steward & Westmoreland to Mayhew, 2 April 1839.
[20]   BLO/MSS.W.Ind.s.19, fol. 92, Pitcairn & Amos to Mayhew, 13 December 1837. For Steward
       & Westmoreland, see Sir Erskine Perry, *Sir Henry Davison, Reports of Cases Argued and
       Determined in the Court of Queen's Bench* (1839), pp. 514–19.

wage levels they felt that there would be 'little or no return from the estates' and Chiswick would struggle to turn a profit, as would many estates across the island.[21]

Further comments about the slowing work rates, which had dropped to 2 hogsheads per week, and the fact that the people 'work when they want' indicate that Townson had been forced to capitulate to worker demands to some extent.[22] We know that such industrial action had occurred elsewhere on the island before the 1830s, but this is the first strike mentioned in the Chiswick correspondence.[23] As we have seen, worker absenteeism had been a problem at Chiswick previously and we can assume malingering had also been used as a method of resistance. Whether the man sentenced for *obeah* a few years before had been trying to organise such action cannot be known, but in the new era the whip and incarceration were no longer an option to deal with such activity. Instead, the workers had to be paid.

Eventually the crop of 70 hogsheads was shipped to London and, just over a year after the ending of apprenticeship, Townson gave a summary of the situation to Mayhew. His overall tone was downbeat: 'I have had little to communicate that could give you pleasure' but he tried to find positive news where he could. The people of Chiswick were, and had been, 'peaceable and orderly' he noted but they were simply not providing enough labour to operate the estate, resulting in 'the great falling off in the yielding of the canes'. With insufficient labour to produce the sugar, he had been unable to get on with the planting for next year, while the fields had not been maintained and the attorney had no expectation that matters would improve in 1840. His only hope was that by 1841 the worst might be over and that, as 'this wonderful change' worked itself out, the people would realise 'the advantage money gives in purchasing better food and more luxuries' and would provide more regular labour.[24] To cut costs, Townson experimented with growing fodder, and tried lucerne (alfalfa) and mangelwurzel, but had found that guinea grass was the best option. Townson suggested that the Burtons should 'sink some little money' into the estate to help with the management of the transition and, while he clearly wanted a steam engine because 'the expenses are great and the return small', he had no expectation of such investment. He accepted that the traditional methods of power used for a century at Chiswick – 'our Breeze mill and cattle' would have to continue.[25]

It was a morose letter and revealed that Townson had little expectation of the Burtons being capable of saving Chiswick. True, events generally in Jamaica from August 1838 to the late 1839 reveal that the swiftness of the move to full emancipation was a challenge, but other owners tried to respond. The overseer at Chiswick, Whitehouse, was extremely interested in improvements and later published a series of letters in the Jamaican newspapers, under the pseudonym 'Agricola', in which he

[21]   BLO/MSS.W.Ind.s.19, fol. 123, Steward & Westmoreland to Mayhew, 7 January 1839 and BLO/MSS.W.Ind.s.19, fol. 131, Steward & Westmoreland to Mayhew, 16 March 1839.
[22]   BLO/MSS.W.Ind.s.19, fol. 135, Steward & Westmoreland to Mayhew, 6 May 1839; fol. 137, Steward & Westmoreland to Mayhew, 13 June 1839.
[23]   Turner, 'Planter', p. 249; Turner, 'Slave', p. 99.
[24]   WM/SC/01621, Townson to Mayhew, 7 September 1839.
[25]   WM/SC/01621, Townson to Mayhew, 7 September 1839.

discussed new approaches to planting in detail.[26] Whitehouse appears to have seen that some other planters had sought to respond to the new situation. There were, for example, experiments with cane-cutting machines and even intra-estate railways.[27] An estate such as Chiswick, unencumbered by debt as it was, was a primary candidate to be able to weather the storm, but this would only happen with an engaged ownership. As the old system collapsed, the family needed a member with the entrepreneurial spirit that could be seen elsewhere in the nineteenth-century economy and radically alter the way the estate was run, but no-one came forward.[28]

Instead, the men trusted by the Burton brothers to take control of their affairs – Cory, Palmer, and Ives – were cautious. They were all solicitors in Yarmouth and did nothing to respond directly to the new situation in Jamaica. The ownership became even more complicated when, on 1 September 1838 Charles Burton fell from his horse while out riding, dying the following day.[29] With no children of the blood, he left a series of large bequests to his wife's children, nephews, and nieces, and his assets were placed in a trust for his sister, Charlotte, and her children. Two new trustees were added, both solicitors – John Baker of Yarmouth and George Weller-Poley of Boxted Hall, Suffolk.[30] Chiswick had, therefore, gained two more people in its management team who had no experience of the sugar business, and no direct interest in the estate's success. There was no incentive for such trustees to take the radical decisions necessary to respond to the changing situation in Jamaica. Indeed, their natural tendency was to act in a conservative fashion. The only move made by the new trustees was to put Charles Burton's 2/21 share of Chiswick for sale in December 1839. Unsurprisingly, given the parlous nature of sugar planting at that point, and the complexity of Chiswick's ownership, no buyers came forward.[31]

The result of this inaction in England was disillusionment in Jamaica, with Townson displaying increased frustration and Whitehouse leaving Chiswick in late 1839 to move to a 'larger plantation'.[32] From 1839 to 1841 Jamaica was affected by a prolonged drought, although Chiswick's coastal position mitigated the effects somewhat.[33] The crop of 1840 was 'a very small crop indeed', only 33 hogsheads, which was the smallest output from Chiswick since the Burton family inherited it, a pathetic 10 per cent of the average achieved in the 1790s.[34] The drought's consequences were

---

[26] W. F. Whitehouse, *Agricola's Letters and Essays on Sugar-Farming in Jamaica* (Kingston, Jamaica, 1845).

[27] Hall, *Free*, pp. 49–50 and 59–60.

[28] For example, Nicholas J. Morgan and Michael Moss, '"Wealthy and Titled Persons" – The Accumulation of Riches in Victorian Britain: The Case of Peter Denny', *Business History* (1989), pp. 28–47.

[29] *London Evening Standard*, Friday 7 September 1838, p. 4.

[30] NA/PROB/11/1906/204, Will of Charles Fisher Burton of Great Yarmouth, Norfolk, 15 February 1839. Henry Barrett, Great Yarmouth corporation, *A report of the investigation before his majesty's municipal commissioners, appointed to examine into the corporate affairs of this borough* (1834), p. 10; William Paley Baildon, *The Records of the Honourable Society of Lincoln's Inn* (Lincoln's Inn, 1896), p. 366.

[31] *Morning Herald (London)*, Friday 6 December 1839, p. 1; *Norfolk Chronicle*, 23 October 1847, p. 1; *Saint James's Chronicle*, 15 December 1836, p. 3.

[32] WM/SC/01621, Townson to Mayhew, 7 September 1839.

[33] WM/SC/01621, Townson to Mayhew, 30 September 1840.

[34] WM/SC/01621, Townson to Mayhew, 29 June 1840.

exacerbated by the lack of labour which had prevented planting for the following season, meaning that Chiswick had an unusually low area in plant. The proportionally lower area of crop meant that while the drought left the ratoons 'yielding a mere nothing' this poor yield was not compensated for by a larger planting area. The lower levels of planting resulting from the lack of labour had increased, therefore, the vulnerability of the estate to weather variations, reducing the resilience of operations. Furthermore, although the people were 'uncommonly civil' they were still not providing sufficient labour to manufacture sugar and rum, and the rate of production was only 3 hogsheads per week, less than half of that achieved before 1834.[35]

Although the profit/loss figure for the year is not recorded, with average prices of sugar in London (excluding duty) of 39s. 2d. the 33 hogsheads would have yielded around £1,367, since lack of production meant that sugar prices increased sharply to 49s. 1d. per hundredweight.[36] Costs for the year were around £1,428 thousand pounds, and salaries, taxes, and capital replacement – mainly for cattle – amounted to around £714, meaning the Burtons probably made a loss of around £775.[37] The following crop, of 1841, was improved – 72 hogsheads – because Townson managed to plant thirty acres in 1840, around what he was planting during the period of apprenticeship, and the weather was also more kind.[38] Greater production across the island meant, however, that sugar prices fell, so the Burtons' profits were only £235, around £39 per proprietor.

With such poor results, Townson was clearly worried that his managerial ability was under scrutiny and pointed out that such outcomes were general across the island. He emphasised that, although the lack of rain had affected the crops, it was the 'total neglect of all the duties that belong to the labouring class' consequent upon emancipation that were the root of the problems.[39] Based on his experience in 1839 where the availability of labour had increased, if only marginally, Townson expressed a hope that 'the wants of the people are increasing with their means', but this did not mean anything more than the hope that they would provide sufficient labour for future years so 'we shall not fall back into a wilderness'. Alternatively, he mentioned the hope that 'emigration from Africa or the Blacks of the United States' might increase the labour pool.[40]

This was very similar to the experiences being reported by other attorneys across the island in this period, where there was a rapid deterioration in labour relations and productivity.[41] Nonetheless, the attorney's news was not received well in England. The shocking fall in production and the consequent suggestion from Mayhew that some 'cash in hand' should be held back from distribution to the family to cover contingencies, finally spurred some interest from the Burtons at the annual meeting of the proprietors.[42] Their responses only revealed their ignorance of the situation, however. Ignoring the fundamental issue of labour that was crushing the profitability

[35] WM/SC/01621, Townson to Mayhew, 18 April 1840.
[36] Sugar price from Hall, *Free*, p. 270.
[37] WM/SC/01621, Townson to Mayhew, 30 September 1840.
[38] WM/SC/01621, Townson to Mayhew, 20 January 1841.
[39] WM/SC/01621, Townson to Mayhew, 29 June 1840.
[40] WM/SC/01621, Townson to Mayhew, 18 April 1840.
[41] Morgan, 'Labour', p. 468.
[42] BLO/MSS.W.Ind.s.19, fol. 144, Harriet Dashwood to Mayhew, 12 June 1840.

of the estate, Jarrett Dashwood wrote to Mayhew that he 'should have thought the locality of Chiswick Estate would have rendered advantages over many others' and argued that the 'great, expenditures over many years past by the proprietors for uten-sils & improvements' should have placed it in a strong position. He appears to have been unable to grasp that the reason insufficient crops had been planted in 1838 was because there was no-one willing to work on the estate and instead asked why there had not been 'substitution of crops?'[43]

A year earlier Dashwood had been unable to find the time to attend the annual meeting organised by Mayhew, and his lack of knowledge was exposed as his concern over the loss of income for his wife grew. Dashwood focused on one detail in Town-son's letter, that the attorney had visited the estate twice in one month. Dashwood was appalled by this information, '<u>only twice</u>', he wrote, apparently unaware that this had been the norm for the attorneys for many years. With complete lack of irony, the absentee Dashwood – who had hitherto shown no interest in Chiswick or its people, other than to help his wife spend the estate's profits – complained that Townson's visiting schedule was like a 'gentleman farming his estate at a distance'. The rhetorical question he followed this comment with summarised, in many ways, the underlying problem for Chiswick, and estates like it, during this period of rapid and radical change in Jamaica. 'Is it probable', Dashwood asked, 'an estate so managed can be satisfactorily productive?'[44] This was a question that the absentee Burtons might have asked more usefully thirty years earlier.

Under pressure from the owners, in September 1840, Townson emphasised that costs had been increased because 'the drought' had required flour to be imported and had led to the loss of cattle from thirst. Desperate to paint a positive picture, he waxed lyrical and told Mayhew the rain had now arrived and 'like the enchanter's hand has given the appearance of the most beautiful vegetation to what was arid parched and miserable land' while the people were 'daily becoming more truly a labouring and well conducted peasantry'. Given protection from the government and time by the Burtons, he assured Mayhew, the future looked promising. Indeed, he argued that 'I think we shall find our new system will be in time much more profitable to the proprietors.' In the interim, however, he told his employers that they would have to accept 'some sacrifice to obtain it'.[45]

Townson's stated aim was to increase production to 100 hogsheads per year, the level achieved under apprenticeship, but he was unable to provide any detail of how this might be achieved. The problem of labour remained insuperable and, as Townson phrased it, 'the hand of the industrious labourer is wanted to reap the fruits'.[46] Under apprenticeship, Townson had been able to achieve levels around 100 hogsheads with a workforce compelled to work for 40½ hours per week for no pay. To increase productivity to these former levels Townson had to find sufficient labourers to provide those hours. Even if he did this, the wage bill would rise and

---

[43] BLO/MSS.W.Ind.s.19, fol. 142, Dashwood to Mayhew, 12 June 1840.
[44] BLO/MSS.W.Ind.s.19, fol. 142, Dashwood to Mayhew, 12 June 1840, underlining in original.
[45] WM/SC/01621, Townson to Mayhew, 30 September 1840.
[46] WM/SC/01621, Townson to Mayhew, 18 September 1841.

so undercut the effect of increased production. In letter after letter, Townson had no solution other than vague hopes 'that better times are sure for us'.[47]

Along with many planters, Townson placed some hope in immigration.[48] Some new labour arrived on the estate in late 1841, when fifteen 'Africans from Sierra Leone' were employed, and were joined at some point by 'eight African boys' from St Helena.[49] Although the new workers were 'obliging' and spoke English, they were unused to work on a plantation and so 'by no means so handy on our plantations as the Creoles'. Moreover, while Townson seems to have hoped to employ them at under the norm for the area, they were soon demanding wages and conditions on par with the existing workforce.[50] By early 1842 Townson stated that the newcomers were now 'getting as insolent as the others' and the new workers joined their fellows when the estate was affected by another strike for higher wages. Townson recounted how the people had looked at the higher yield coming from the field, which he had hoped might achieve 100 hogsheads, and so had asked for higher wages; 'because they thought I must give it'. He claimed that he had successfully refused to increase their pay and that after a period of no labour they had gradually returned to work. Nonetheless, their productivity was low and so the crop had not yielded as he had expected.[51]

With only Townson's side reported, we must guess at the thinking among the people of Chiswick, but it seems that, once more, they were making reasonable decisions based on a good understanding of the business. By this date, diligent workers were able to make £2 to £3 pounds per week from selling provisions at markets, and so had a cushion to allow them to negotiate for wages from a position of strength.[52] Chiswick's people knew that Townson was under pressure after the previous poor harvest and was desperate to maximise production. Recognising a situation of leverage, they had asked for more money and had then withdrawn their labour when he refused. Even after returning to work, they had not increased production. This conflict revealed the true state of the situation at Chiswick, where Townson was unable to find a route around the labour issue. The workers were fully aware that the labour market in the parish was tight and that this meant they could push for higher wages. They appear to have been united in their approach to negotiating; even the new workers from Sierra Leone joined the strike. Moreover, it seems that Townson had been forced to pay higher wages, since the wage bill for 1842 rose to £1,611.[53] It seems, therefore, that the strike had worked but, even with higher wage levels, productivity remained low. Matters were at an impasse, Townson needed to

---

[47] WM/SC/01621, Townson to Mayhew, 20 January 1841.
[48] For discussion of schemes to use European migrants on the island, see Carl H. Senior, 'German Immigrants in Jamaica 1834–8', *Journal of Caribbean History* (1978), pp. 37–38; Douglas Hall, 'Bountied European Immigration into Jamaica with Special Reference to the German Settlement at Seaford Town', *Jamaica Journal* (1974), pp. 48–54, and (1975), pp. 2–9; Hall, *Free*, pp. 21–22.
[49] WM/SC/01621, Townson to Mayhew, 8 December 1841, and 16 January 1843.
[50] WM/SC/01621, Townson to Mayhew, 8 December 1841.
[51] WM/SC/01621, Townson to Mayhew, 14 February 1842.
[52] Curtin, *Two*, p. 142.
[53] WM/SC/01621, Townson to Mayhew, 16 January 1843.

pay more, but could not afford to do so because of the pressure from England to keep wages down.

Townson's analysis and actions revealed that his approach to managing the estate remained mired in the racially demarcated ideas of the period before 1833. Townson's words and actions laid bare a fundamental weakness of the approach of most managers in Jamaica and owners in England. With minds locked in the old, racially constrained, manner of thinking they were unable to reconfigure their operations to survive in the new era. Harvesting, in this view, was the job of 'the people' and the methods to be used were those of the previous 100 years. This inability to reconfigure their manner of approach to the business then combined with financial uncertainty to prevent any capital investment, such as in a steam engine, ensuring that the cycle of decline continued. As with so many other declining industries, Townson looked to protectionism to save the day, telling Mayhew that 'we must have the protection of the government' by means of duties.[54]

With no direction from England, Townson was unable to do more than manage the estate's collapse. A telling example of the situation is provided by the failure of the Burtons to provide any guidance on what he should do with the workers' housing. The new regime allowed for apprentices to lose their rights to houses, lots, and provision grounds, and a refusal to pay rent could result in eviction.[55] Somewhat plaintively, in 1838 Townson asked for decisions to be taken. Would the workers be tenants, or would the houses be given to them? Should he continue spending money on maintaining the houses or let them deteriorate?[56] Since rent for such housing in Jamaica had no real precedent this was a difficult change to manage and potentially fraught with problems but, although the questions related to the preservation of the Burtons' rapidly diminishing capital, answers were not forthcoming. The inaction appears to have emboldened the people of Chiswick and Townson indicated that they felt able to 'cultivate as much land as they please for their own benefit' with no fear of eviction.[57] There is no evidence that the people of Chiswick were ever sold their houses or provision grounds, as happened elsewhere in Jamaica.[58] Instead, over time they abandoned the estate. Contemporary reports noted that settlements were appearing throughout St Thomas-in-the-East, for example, at Bachelor's Hall to the north, and so land was becoming available for the people to move to.[59] It was only in late 1842, four years after Townson sought guidance, that Mayhew asked about the potential for charging rent from the workers. Townson reported that it was now too late and that most of the people had left the estate and moved to nearby Dalvey, where they had 'bought land and built houses'.[60] From 1838 onwards, therefore, the people of Chiswick revealed their view of the land on which they had lived and worked for many years, and the family that owned it; by leaving.

It is unlikely the Burtons ever understood the views of the people of Chiswick, or even considered them. In November 1841 Thomas Burton died, aged sixty-eight. His will

[54] WM/SC/01621, Townson to Mayhew, 18 April 1840.
[55] Curtin, *Two*, p. 129; Higman, *Plantation*, p. 243.
[56] WM/SC/01621, Townson to Mayhew, 24 September 1838.
[57] BLO/MSS.W.Ind.s.19, fol. 123, Steward & Westmoreland to Mayhew, 3 October 1838.
[58] Higman, *Montpelier*, p. 191.
[59] Hall, *Free*, p. 25.
[60] WM/SC/01621, Townson to Mayhew, 7 August 1842.

reveals the great extent of his wealth, virtually all of which came from his Northamptonshire and Devonshire estates. He left, for example, an annuity of £800 per annum to his wife, and £8,000 to his four daughters, while his English estates went to his son Thomas. The will left 'one fourth part of seven fifteenths' of Chiswick to his son-in-law Arthur Steward, who now became the largest shareholder. The rest of Thomas' share in Chiswick was left to his other daughters – Harriet, Augusta, and Louisa.[61]

Steward's newly acquired status as the largest single proprietor proved to be decisive in the next few years. An attorney in Yarmouth, Steward was familiar with the situation in the West Indies, since his brother, J. J. Steward, ran the Burton family's London agents, Steward & Westmoreland.[62] Almost immediately, Steward and his brother took control of the management of Chiswick and began a reassessment of the situation.[63] Mayhew was retained, but his role curtailed, and Townson found himself under real scrutiny. Questions were raised about the level of Townson's expenses and negative comparisons were drawn with Golden Grove. Townson responded by shifting the blame, stating that he had fired the overseer, Stannett, for 'the irregularity of his accounts'. The attorney maintained that costs could not be reduced below the range of £2,100 to £2,200 annually and that wage inflation meant that they would, in fact, continue to rise. He also pointed out that the costs of a cattle mill were far higher than those of a water mill, such as was in use at Golden Grove, and this meant that his expenses were higher than such estates. Townson resisted the opportunity to remind the Burtons that they had refused to invest in a steam engine nearly a decade previously, which would have been paid for by 1840 and would now have been helping with production. He remained, hopeful, however of producing 100 hogsheads in future seasons.[64]

In 1842, however, the crop halved. This time the fault could not be blamed on labour shortages, or the weather, but was clearly a misjudgement by Townson. The dryer weather of the previous few years had seen him decide to shift the cane fields into the 'swamp' to the south of the estate, to take advantage of its higher levels of moisture. This was a calculated risk, but the decision had backfired when the rain returned and flooded the fields, damaging the canes severely. The effects of the flooding, which was made worse by the lack of drainage in the new fields meant that by June Townson had to report that the canes were 'a complete failure', yielding only 36 hogsheads. Moreover, the lack of long-term investment in the capital of Chiswick had severe consequences. The cattle mill roof collapsed and had to be rebuilt, causing a jump in costs. In a final twist of bad luck, the still gave way, interrupting sugar production and adding to costs when its replacement was purchased. As Townson ruefully noted, 'it never rains but it pours'.[65] Even worse for Townson was the fact that the attorney for Golden Grove, Thomas McCornock, who had become the secondary attorney at Chiswick after Forsyth's death, chose this moment to visit his employers in England and informed the

[61] NA/PROB/11/1958/444, Will of Thomas Burton of Great Yarmouth, Norfolk, 11 March 1842; Marriage of Arthur Steward and Mary Burton, *Norfolk Chronicle*, 7 October 1826.
[62] BLO/MSS.W.Ind.s.19, fol. 189, J. J. Steward to Mayhew, Yarmouth, 6 September 1844.
[63] BLO/MSS.W.Ind.s.19, fol. 151, Arthur Steward to Mayhew, 30 July 1841.
[64] WM/SC/01621, Townson to Mayhew, 22 March 1842.
[65] WM/SC/01621, Townson to Mayhew, 5 May 1842; 7 August 1842.

Burtons of all the details, removing any chance of Townson pushing blame elsewhere.[66] Townson explained that his decision resulted from his desire 'get all the sugar I could for the last crop', but his credibility with the family fell considerably.[67] The result of his error was that the Burtons faced a substantial loss.[68]

Table 12 shows the production of the estate for the period from 1838 to 1842, when crop records ceased to be kept, and reveal the extent to which matters at Chiswick deteriorated over the period after apprenticeship. Even in the difficult years of the 1770s and 1780s, Chiswick had produced an average of 223 hogsheads per year. The 1790s had seen an average of 310 hogsheads and during the period to 1820 around 230 hogsheads was the norm. During apprenticeship 118 hogsheads had been averaged and this had now halved. This fall in production was general across the island, but Chiswick had fared worse than Amity Hall where sugar output fell to 156 hogsheads in 1839, 133 in 1840 and 131 in 1846, around 60 per cent of that during apprenticeship.[69] More-over, the production levels from 1838 oscillated markedly, from around 35 hogsheads to 71, meaning that the proprietors faced extremely uncertain cash flows. In contrast, the costs for the estate were steady, averaging around £2,000 to £2,200 per annum. Townson was unable to reduce wage costs below £1,400 and in early 1842 suggested that they might rise as high as £1,600 in the coming year. Likewise, he stated that taxes, salaries, stock, and timber costs would not fall below £700 and might rise to £900.[70]

In the face of growing losses Arthur Steward decided that 'that a change of management in Jamaica should be made' and in July 1842 the owners decided that the next year would see a new attorney, George Wright, appointed.[71] As 1843 opened Townson reported that the workers had not returned to work after the holidays and that 'labourers cannot be obtained when wanted'.[72] Suffering from ill-health, he now travelled to England to see his family and make his will. In his absence, care of the estate was handed to Wright and to McCornock, now returned from England.[73] The letters from Jamaica in Mayhew's files cease to record any commercial details from the estate from this time onwards, suggesting that production had largely ceased. The last letter from Townson to discuss production was in February 1843, where he explained that 'the high rate of wages and scarcity of labour was absolutely more than the proceeds of most estates and would continue to do so until the numbers of labourers increase'.[74] After 1843 Townson's surviving correspondence focused on asking the Burton family to repay him nearly £500 that he claimed to have advanced from his own funds for wages on the estate.[75]

[66] BLO/MSS.W.Ind.s.19, fol. 21, Pitcairn & Amos to Mayhew, 3 August 1836. In 1832 McCor-nock managed seven estates; Higman, *Plantation*, pp. 66–67.

[67] WM/SC/01621, Townson to Mayhew, 24 June 1842.

[68] BLO/MSS.W.Ind.s.19, fol. 155, Steward & Westmoreland to Mayhew, 6 May 1842.

[69] Morgan, 'Labour', p. 461.

[70] WM/SC/01621, Townson to Mayhew, 14 February 1842; 22 March 1842.

[71] BLO/MSS.W.Ind.s.19, fol. 151 Steward to Mayhew, 14 July 1842.

[72] WM/SC/01621, Townson to Mayhew, 16 January 1843.

[73] WM/SC/01621, Townson to Mayhew, 4 February 1843; Townson to McCornock, Kingston, 1 February 1843.

[74] WM/SC/01621, Townson to Mayhew, 4 February 1843.

[75] WM/SC/01621, Townson to Mayhew, 22 June 1844; 23 July 1844; 8 August 1844.

Table 12. *Produce and finances of the Chiswick estate, 1838–1842.*[*]

Crop year	Hogsheads of sugar sold (London and Jamaica)	Estimated gross income from sugar (£ sterling)	Puncheons of rum sold (London and Jamaica)	Gross income from rum (£ sterling)	Expenses (£ sterling)	Net profit (loss) (£ sterling)
1839	70	£2,313			£2,000	£844
1840	33	£1,367	13		£2,142	£ (775)
1841	72	£2,424	30		£2,142	£235
1842	36	£1,122	11		£,2,142	£ (920)

[*] Sugar prices from Hall, *Free*, p. 270. Sources: BLO/MSS.W.Ind.s.18, fol. 126, Townson to Steward & Westmoreland, 3 December 1838; fol. 139, Steward & Westmoreland to Mayhew, 19 June 1839; fol. 149, Steward & Westmoreland to Mayhew, 4 May 1841; fol. 155, Steward & Westmoreland to Mayhew, 6 May 1842; WM/SC/01621, Townson to Mayhew, 7 September 1839; 29 June 1840; 30 September 1840; 14 February 1842; 24 June 1842; 7 August 1842.

The Burtons paid him nothing, largely because they had now seen a way to get rid of Chiswick. In late 1843 George Wright reported to the family that he had found a prospective buyer for Chiswick; William Whitehouse, who had been the overseer in the late 1830s.[76] As has been said already, Whitehouse was a keen innovator who published widely on the way sugar estates could use modern farming techniques to survive in the new era. He perceived, perhaps, that the crucial problem with Chiswick had never been the land, nor even the end of slavery, but poor-quality absentee ownership since 1805. Receiving Whitehouse's offer, Arthur Steward and his brother saw the opportunity, finally, for the family to be rid of the estate and pushed the other members to agree to the sale.[77]

For one final time, getting agreement proved 'a very grand desideratum when they are so numerous and so little united as the Chiswick proprietors.[78] The negotiations for the sale were tortuous and bad-tempered, with the family members arguing amongst themselves, with Mayhew, and with Steward & Westmoreland, about every aspect of the negotiations and complaining about every expense incurred.[79] The negotiations almost collapsed in late 1844 and dragged on into 1845.[80] As Steward put it to Mayhew, 'You cannot be more tired of this matter than I am. Even in petty details everyone seems conspiring to annoy.[81] The final stumbling block was the fact that the family owed £900 to Steward & Westmoreland, which had to be paid from the final sale price. Since the family were reliant upon them to complete the sale, the agents were in the position to enforce their debt and, after more argument, complaint and rancour, the Burtons finally accepted the terms. The Chiswick estate was sold for £1,500, around 12 per cent of its book value in 1829, and perhaps only 6 per cent of its value in 1820. Once the debt to Steward & Westmoreland was paid, it would have left only £600 to be distributed among the Burtons.[82] A small enough sum, but one final twist was left. Whitehouse had intended, no doubt, to buy Chiswick and to implement the forward-thinking approaches to sugar-planting that he had developed and laid out in his written work over the previous decade but, on 9 August 1846 he died from fever at the estate, aged thirty-two.[83] Nonetheless, with the sale already settled his executors made the final payment and, somewhere in late 1846, the Burton family ended their ownership of the Chiswick sugar estate.[84]

[76]   BLO/MSS.W.Ind.s.19, fol. 175, Palmer to Mayhew, 4 November 1843; fol. 177, Steward & Westmoreland to Mayhew, 4 November 1843; fol. 179, Steward to Mayhew, 21 November 1843; WM/SC/01621, Townson to Mayhew, 23 October 1845.

[77]   BLO/MSS.W.Ind.s.19, fol. 179, J. J. Steward to Mayhew, 21 November 1843 and fol. 183, Steward to Mayhew, 22 January 1844.

[78]   BLO/MSS.W.Ind.s.19, fol. 189, Steward to Mayhew, 6 September 1844.

[79]   For example, BLO/MSS.W.Ind.s.19, fol. 181, Dashwood to Mayhew, 27 December 1843; fol. 183, Steward to Mayhew, 22 January 1844; fol. 185, Steward to Mayhew, 31 January 1844.

[80]   BLO/MSS.W.Ind.s.19, fol. 189, J. J. Steward to Mayhew, 6 September 1844.

[81]   BLO/MSS.W.Ind.s.19, fol. 185, J. J. Steward to Mayhew, 31 January 1844.

[82]   BLO/MSS.W.Ind.s.19, fol. 200, Arthur Steward to Mayhew, 6 April 1846.

[83]   *The Gentleman's Magazine* (1846), p. 559; WM/SC/01621, Townson to Mayhew, 22 September 1846.

[84]   WM/SC/01621, Townson to Mayhew, 22 September 1846.

Postscript

'Chiswick, an Abandoned Sugar Estate in the Parish of St Thomas-ye-East'

In 1844, two years before the Burtons sold Chiswick, there were sixty-one sugar estates in St Thomas-in-the-East. By 1854 this number had fallen to twenty-one.[1] Between 1832 and 1847, around 140 of about 670 sugar estates were abandoned and by 1870 only 300 remained. In contrast to this process of abandonment by the absentee owners, the 2,000 Jamaicans who owned freehold land of fifty acres or less in 1838 had increased to 70,000 people by 1870.[2] Exactly how Chiswick fitted into this process after 1846 is uncertain. In August 1845 Whitehouse had married a woman named Mary Ann Isis in Tewkesbury, Worcestershire.[3] Mary died in Cheltenham in 1863, and it is unclear who took ownership after her death, although the 1881 map recorded Chiswick as being owned by the 'heirs of William Whitehouse'.[4] Those heirs, however, seem to have given up on its cultivation since, when the estate was advertised for lease in 1889 it was described as:

> Chiswick, an abandoned sugar estate in the parish of St. Thomas-ye-East, with Rent Roll of about £30 or £40 a year, a large number of Cocoanut Tress, abounding in young Logwood and Logwood Roots. Has also the advantage of a Shipping place.[5]

By 1889, therefore, Chiswick was 'abandoned', and Whitehouse's heirs were looking to get such income as they could from rent. Eventually the owners managed to sell it and at the start of the twentieth century Chiswick was one of the estates in St Thomas – along with Duckenfield, Stokes Hall, Plantain Garden River, Pera, Golden Grove, and Belgium – totalling 8,499 acres, which were owned by Jamaica Sugar Estates Limited, a British syndicate led by Lord Invernairn. By 1937 these estates were producing 64,585 tons of sugar per annum and continued to make substantial profits until the significant changes in the Jamaican sugar industry that occurred from the late 1960s, which lie outside the scope of this study.[6]

---

[1] Hall, *Free*, p. 82.

[2] Higman, *Jamaica*, p. 11; B. W. Higman, *A Concise History of the Caribbean* (Cambridge: Cambridge University Press, 2010), pp. 157 and 169.

[3] *Worcester Journal*, 28 August 1845, p. 3.

[4] *Morning Post*, 8 October 1863, p. 8.

[5] *Colonial Standard and Jamaica Despatch*, 10 October 1889, p. 3.

[6] *The Handbook of Jamaica* (Jamaica: Government Print. Establishment, 1936), p. 389, and *The Handbook of the British West Indies, British Guiana and British Honduras* (London: West India Committee, 1929), p. 177; *The Jamaica Yearbook of Industry and Agriculture*

Looking back across the two centuries before this finale, we can ask what this study of one plantation owned by a family from provincial England has contributed towards our understandings of the wide-ranging historical debates around the history of Jamaica from 1788 onwards? This book has suggested that the story of Chiswick from 1788 to 1846 is, possibly, a typical story of the absentee plantation owner in this period. In 1788 the Burtons inherited their sugar estate. From that date until 1846 the family kept their heads down, ran it, and tried to make money. Nothing more, nothing less. This focus on making money, or as Aquinas puts it an 'immoderate love of possessing', dominated the operation and history of the Chiswick estate thereafter. The first generation of owners, John and Thomas Burton, decided to take ownership of the estate and its enslaved people, although they could have chosen to divest themselves of Chiswick and not become slave-owners. Instead, the brothers chose the opportunity to make money over any other considerations, even though many of their contemporaries in Norwich were asking serious questions about the morality of slavery.

After making this choice in favour of avarice, the brothers focused on managing and improving their plantation and dealt with the economic and social challenges surrounding sugar production as best they could. They were rather successful in doing so, but this success was founded on their active decision to continue to own enslaved people and to buy more of them to keep the estate running, despite the significant discussion surrounding them in Norfolk about the immorality of doing so. Between 1805 and 1833 the second generation of Chiswick's owners continued to ignore the issues of slave-ownership and accepted their ownership of enslaved people. The driving force behind this remained greed, but this second generation of Burtons were not commercially minded. Instead, they left the management of the sugar estate to others and focused instead on spending the profits. The Burtons continued to avoid any interaction with the wider issues surrounding Caribbean slavery, and exhibited no thought for the people of Chiswick, except when they had to consider them to obtain compensation. The third generation of owners, who became involved after slavery had ended, were also content to ignore the situation and people of Chiswick, until Arthur Steward found them a way of getting rid of the estate.

During a period of sixty years, therefore, when significant and important discussions over the future structure of empire, colonial relations, the ending of the slave trade and slavery itself – along with the future nature of colonial labour regimes – were taking place, the Burtons took no apparent part in them. There is no evidence of them writing a single letter to anyone about any of these issues.[7] Indeed, the Burtons appear to have been uninterested, or strategically unaware, of these matters and it is their lack of engagement with these debates that allows the story of the

---

(Jamaica: City Printery, 1962), p. 68; Jamaica Sugar Estate Ltd, Records of Jamaica Sugar Estate Ltd, c1920-c1967, sugar manufacturers, Jamaica, 1924–1968. University of Glasgow Archive Services, GB 248 DC 034/91-132.

[7] The records of the Chiswick contain no such letters, nor are there any letters from the family on the subject in the Norfolk and Suffolk newspapers, nor records of them attending any meetings about the matter.

Burtons and the Chiswick estate to add to our understanding to the wider picture of plantation slavery and absentee ownership. The history of Chiswick does not plunge us into the world of the 'movers and shakers' in Jamaican and colonial politics, men like Simon Taylor, whose life has been so deeply studied, or of the estates like Amity Hall, where the records are copious because of engaged management.[8] The Burtons were not this type of owner, and the story of Chiswick reveals a great deal because of their very lack of active involvement in these questions. The Burtons' involvement in plantation slavery was framed, almost entirely, by their desire to amass wealth, which appears to have trumped any other issues, including the ethical one of slave ownership. Providing they were making money, the Burtons do not seem to have given this matter much thought.

In relation to the 'decline of the planter class', the story of Chiswick under the ownership of the Burton family suggests that, in this one case at least, there was not a situation of decline before the abolition of the slave trade in 1807. We have seen that before 1807 the estate's finances were extremely robust. Chiswick's history concurs, therefore, with other research – such as that of Burnard and Ryden – which has shown that owners of plantations in that period could operate as responsive and innovative businesspeople.[9] On the other hand, Chiswick's story tends to work against Ryden's proposal that while the 1790s had been a successful decade, planters faced a burgeoning financial crisis as the nineteenth century began. While the Burtons' fortunes fluctuated in response to the military and political circumstances of the late eighteenth and early nineteenth centuries, these fluctuations fell within the normal range of business affairs, and the data do not suggest that the Chiswick estate was in terminal decline prior to 1807. Indeed, the Burtons and their managers responded to changes in their business environment in a flexible fashion, and the estate might be characterised as an exemplary case of prudent management during the 1790s and first few years of the nineteenth century. These findings add support to the recent work of Reid that argues for 'the dynamism and efficiency of the plantation system in Jamaica right up to abolition in 1807'.[10]

Chiswick's story shows that the Burton family's fortunes, and their general ability to continue running the estate as the nineteenth century progressed, were dealt significant external blows by the gradual tightening of the noose around slavery as a system. From 1807 onwards, the combination of the abolition of the slave trade, amelioration, and the final abolition of slavery created an ever more difficult environment for the family to operate its sugar estate in. The crucial event was the abolition

---

[8] For example, Petley, 'Slaveholders', p. 54.
[9] See Burnard 'Et in Arcadia', pp. 19–40, David Beck Ryden, '"One of the Fertilest Pleasentest Spotts": An Analysis of the Slave Economy in Jamaica's St Andrew Parish, 1753', *Slavery and Abolition* (2000), pp. 32–55; Ryden, *West Indian Slavery*; Higman, *Plantation*; Veront Satchell, 'Technology and Productivity Change in the Jamaican Sugar Industry, 1760–1830', PhD thesis, University of the West Indies (Mona), 1993; Heather Cateau, 'The New "Negro" Business: Hiring in the British West Indies, 1750–1810', in *In the Shadow of the Plantation: Caribbean History and Legacy*, ed. Alvin O. Thompson (Kingston, Jamaica: Ian Randle, 2002), pp. 100–20.
[10] Ahmed Reid, 'Sugar, Slavery and Productivity in Jamaica, 1750–1807', *Slavery & Abolition* (2016), pp. 159–182, at p. 159.

of the slave trade in 1807, which fundamentally and negatively altered the Burton family's financial and business situation over the next thirty years. It is correct to say that the impact of abolitionist success was made worse by specific commercial issues related to cultivation and sugar prices, which were general to sugar estates in Jamaica. Nonetheless, it was the declining numbers of enslaved people at Chiswick that undermined productivity and profits.

Yet the evidence suggests that these problems could have been overcome had the Burton family run their estate better. The story of Chiswick has shown that the lack of engagement by the owners of Chiswick was the crucial factor in the decline of the estate, and this related in a good measure to their absentee status, which was, in turn, framed by their singular focus on making money. The ending of the slave trade in 1807 inaugurated a long-term decline in the size of the workforce and this was not addressed by the Burtons and their managers. The reason for this was largely that their absentee status allowed them to ignore the gradually changing situation and, also, prevented them from becoming intellectually engaged with the estate other than seeing Chiswick as a profit-making machine. This commercial failure was rooted in the family's disengaged approach to the commercial realities and requirements of absentee ownership and founded upon their primary motivation of extracting maximum profit with as little investment as possible. Hindsight shows that Chiswick was on a slow road to oblivion from 1807. The abolition of slavery in 1833, despite the compensation paid to slave-owners, merely increased the speed of this decline, before the sudden end of apprenticeship finished the Burton family's operations.

None of this was, however, inevitable. The Burtons could have addressed these issues, especially as they were debt-free for most of the period. There were alternative approaches that might have been followed, such as earlier mechanisation, changing techniques of cultivation, or even dispensing with slavery altogether, although this last option was never even considered. Instead, Chiswick's Jamaican managers and English owners remained mired in the 'old' way of doing things, while the world was changing around them. The reasons for this were inertia and absenteeism, both of which sprang from the family's tendency to see Chiswick purely as a producer of wealth for them to spend. Because of these issues the family were unable to deal with the change that occurred after 1807. This was because they were uninterested in the business of the estate and, consequently, because no-one in the family possessed the desire, skills, or temperament to attempt to address the changing commercial situation.

The story of the Burtons and Chiswick suggests that, if we were to use the idea of 'decline' in any meaningful fashion, we would have to say the decline of Chiswick had its roots in 1807 but occurred because the family could not be bothered to address the issues around them and because they did not have the vision to look for alternative approaches. The Jamaican managers like Townson and Forsyth were blinkered by their inability to look past the system of slavery and its racial underpinnings, even after the system was destroyed, but there is little evidence that the Burtons were affected by such ideas. Instead, their inadequacy was founded on their approach to the farming of their land, which saw only profit, and failed to have any sense of responsibility for the way those profits were created. Disconnected from the reality of the situation in Jamaica, the English owners seem to have barely grasped what was going on at their property, especially after 1806. The evidence from Chiswick is unequivocally that the abolition of the slave trade was the key factor in destroying the profitability of Chiswick, but this was only because the family and their managers did not change their commercial operations and ideas about their labour force in response to the newly created ethical environment resulting from the success of Wilberforce and the abolitionists.

The Burton family's story also suggests that we might re-evaluate the idea of 'the planter class' itself. Recent work has provided much data on how absentee planters were connected to the peers in the colonies and has also shown how there were tensions between groupings of planters; especially between those in 'newer' colonies and older ones, such as Jamaica. It has also looked at the differences between wealthier planters and other colonists.[11] The history of Chiswick points us to another line of fissure in what was a small grouping. By 1788, there were about 18,500 white colonists living in Jamaica, outnumbered ten to one by the enslaved population. Although most white male colonists owned enslaved people, only 5 per cent (770) of them owned a sugar estate.[12] This small, but wealthy and politically important, minority of local planters dominated the life of the island, but the ownership of the plantations upon which they relied was shifting rapidly to absentees like the Burtons.

There has been much work done on absentees as a group and the 'West India interest' has, traditionally, been presented as an effective lobbying organisation into the 1820s.[13] Nonetheless, discussion continues about when it ceased to be politically effective. As Osborne has noted, in her excellent study of the membership of the

---

[11] See for example, Jack P. Greene, 'Liberty, Slavery, and the Transformation of British Identity in the Eighteenth-Century West Indies', *Slavery and Abolition* (2000), pp. 1–31; Lambert, *White Creole Culture*, esp. pp. 73–104; Ryden, *West Indian*, esp. pp. 40–82; Ian Barrett, 'Cultures of Pro-Slavery: The Political Defence of the Slave Trade in Britain, c.1787–1807', PhD thesis, University of London, 2009; Draper, *The Price*, esp. pp. 75–113; Christer Petley, '"Devoted Islands" and "that Madman Wilberforce": British Proslavery Patriotism during the Age of Abolition', *Journal of Imperial and Commonwealth History* (2011), pp. 393–495; Burnard, *Mastery*; Petley, *Slaveholders*.

[12] Sheridan, 'The Formation', p. 401; Edward Long, *History of Jamaica*, vol. 2 (London: T. Lowndes, 1774), p. 229; Sheridan, *Sugar and Slavery*, p. 223.

[13] Nicholas Draper, 'Helping to Make Britain Great: The Commercial Legacies of Slave-Ownership in Britain', in *Legacies of British Slave-Ownership: Colonial Slavery and the Formation of Victorian Britain*, ed. Catherine Hall et al. (Cambridge: Cambridge University Press, 2014), pp. 78–126; Michael Taylor, 'The British West India Interest and Its Allies, 1823–1833', *English Historical Review* (2018), pp. 1478–511; Stephen Mullen, 'Proslavery Collaborations Between British Outport and Metropole: The Rise of the Glasgow–West India Interest, 1775–1838', *The Journal of Imperial and Commonwealth History* (2023), pp. 601–43; L. M. Penson, 'The London West India Interest in the Eighteenth Century', *English Historical Review* (1921), pp. 373–92; Williams, *Capitalism*, pp. 85–97; B. W. Higman, 'The West India Interest in Parliament, 1807–1833', *Historical Studies* (1967), pp. 1–19; Sheridan, *Sugar and Slavery*, pp. 58–76; O'Shaughnessy, 'The Formation'; Ryden, 'Sugar, Spirits, and Fodder'; Keith McClelland, 'Redefining the West India Interest; Politics and the Legacies of Slave-Ownership', in *Legacies of British Slave-Ownership: Colonial Slavery and the Formation of Victorian Britain*, edited by Catherine Hall et al. (Cambridge: Cambridge University Press, 2014), pp. 127–62.

West India Committee, estimates of the number of absentee planters in the Houses of Parliament have varied widely, mainly because of what historians have classified as 'a West Indian' in the period. She has argued that the pro-slavery position was not as coherent and unified as has been assumed and highlights a disparate set of views on slavery and emancipation which, she feels, 'fractured consensus among the membership'.[14] Likewise, Douglas Hall has emphasised that the idea of the 'absentee owner' needs to be understood in terms of a multi-faceted group, rather than through ideas of uniformity.[15] Alexandra Franklin examined how merchants and planters resident in England created a 'British' identity, but the Burtons give us sight of a different group of absentees, those who did not have refashion their identity, because they were already members of a local English community.[16] The Burtons did not consciously hide their ownership of a sugar estate, but they do not seem to have had any concept of themselves as 'planters', or as members of a wider group with shared interests, nor were they driven by ingrained racism. Instead, the family remained stubbornly East Anglian in focus and the estate was only one part of a wide-ranging portfolio of assets.[17]

The Burtons take us further, therefore, in the story of the planter class since they seem to have taken no part in engaging with their plantation-owning peers politically or culturally at all. Their story points towards a specific 'fracture' in the 'planter class' that we need to consider. In many ways, the big problem for the Burtons was that they just did not really think very much about the operation of their sugar estate, especially after the death of Thomas Burton in 1805. As I have suggested in considering the history of Africans in East Anglia in the period 1467 to 1833, the culture of the provinces of England in relation to people of African descent was markedly different to that of the colonies, and of the ports such as London, Liverpool, Bristol, and Glasgow.[18] The Burtons appear to have seen their sugar estate as a specific type of asset class, which they needed to manage as best they could in the peculiar circumstance that it was situated in Jamaica, but the ownership of Chiswick does not appear to have drawn them – culturally, intellectually, or emotionally – into that class of people known as 'planters'. This lack of connection to the wider 'planter class' seems to be crucial to the story of Chiswick. Perhaps, therefore, it is also relevant to the wider one concerning the ending of slavery. The Burtons were members of the largest group of owners of colonial estates at the end of the eighteenth century, the absentees, but their cultural setting was firmly not Jamaica. It was East Anglia. The family just do not seem to have engaged with the idea that they were 'planters'. If this was the case for a significant proportion of other absentee families, then it points us to another division that made for their growing political weakness. As

---

[14]   Osborne, 'Power', pp. 2 and 16.
[15]   Hall, 'Absentee', pp. 15–35.
[16]   Alexandra Franklin, 'Enterprise and Advantage: The West India Interest in Britain, 1774–1840', PhD thesis, University of Pennsylvania, 1992, pp. 64 and 91.
[17]   As suggested by Seymour et al., 'Estate', p. 343.
[18]   Maguire, *Africans*, pp. 26–29.

James Townson put it in 1845, 'Our misfortune is that the land is owned by absentees who cannot bring their mind's eye to view the changes going on.'[19]

Finally, this investigation of the story of Chiswick has highlighted the importance of the activity of the enslaved people who lived and worked on the estate from 1788 onwards. As has been argued throughout, the Burtons do not appear to have had any emotional and intellectual connection with the people of Chiswick and the system of slavery. They may, in fact, have subconsciously sought to have avoided thinking about the people and slavery unless forced to. Eventually, this disconnection proved to be a critical weakness in their ownership. This was because it caused the family to ignore the humanity of their workers and their ethical responsibility toward them. Throughout the period of Burton ownership, the family disregarded those workers, even as Chiswick's people resisted the situation in whatever ways they could. In the early years there were runways and, even before 1833, as the financial pressures mounted and the operation of the estate was undercut by the declining number of workers, the people of Chiswick chose their moments to place pressure on the Burtons through low-level disruption.

When the disciplinary regime that held the plantation together was removed after 1833, the workers at Chiswick increasingly, and effectively, altered the situation on the estate. Remarkably, the people of Chiswick were peaceful in their struggle with the regime right until 1838, but their opposition made the estate increasingly difficult to operate as they engaged in wage-bargaining, industrial action, and non-compliance. After 1838, once they were freed fully from the control of the Burtons and their managers, the people of Chiswick just walked away.

It seems reasonable to suggest that this exodus occurred because the Burton family had never truly engaged with Chiswick and never sought to understand, or think about, the people they forced to work there. Consequently, the people of Chiswick had no positive relationship with the Burton family or the land. When coercion ended, there was nothing to keep the people on the estate. For nearly sixty years, the Burtons chose to ignore their status as 'planters' and to disregard the ethical questions that were raised by that status. They chose instead to extract as much wealth as they could from the estate and its workers, without investing in Chiswick, financially or emotionally. In the end, the Burton family's choice in favour of avarice was the fundamental reason the family were forced to sell Chiswick in 1846. Absentee ownership at Chiswick failed, but not simply because it was commercially inefficient, although after 1805 the Burtons largely sought to make money while not actually acting as productive business owners. Nor was failure purely the consequence of the high politics of the British Empire, although the success of the abolitionists had huge impact. In the end, Chiswick was abandoned because absentee status separated the Burtons from the humanity of the workers on which they relied and the ethical consequences of their actions.

---

[19] WM/SC/01621, Townson to Mayhew, 7 January 1845.

BIBLIOGRAPHY

Manuscript material

Bodleian Library Oxford (BLO)

MSS. W. Ind. s. 17, MSS. W. Ind. s. 18 and MSS. W. Ind. s. 19, Letters, documents, and reports to its English owners from the agents in Jamaica managing the Chiswick sugar plantation, 1825 1847. 3 volumes.

William and Mary Libraries, Virginia, Special Collections Research Center Manuscripts & Archives Collection (WM)

SC 01621 James Townson letters regarding Jamaican sugar plantation, 1833–1846

The Jamaican Archives (JA)

1B/11/4 Accounts of the Chiswick Estate, 1778 to 1808
1B/21/24 'Map of St Thomas, East, complied by Thomas Harrison, 1881'

The National Archives, Public Record Office, London (NA)

ADM/106 Navy Board Records
CO/137/28 Correspondence – Board of Trade
PROB 11/1426/242 Will of Thomas Burton of Norwich, Norfolk, 12 June 1805
PROB11/1411/154 Will of John Burton of Jacobstowe, Devon, 13 July 1804
PROB/11/1610/156 Will of Leonard Burton of Ringstead, Northamptonshire, 12 November 1818
PROB/11/1467/206 Will of William Lumsden of Saint Thomas County of Surrey, Jamaica, 17 September 1807
PROB/11/1005/225 Will of Alexander Maitland, merchant of Kings Arm Yard Coleman Street proved 27 February 1775
PROB 11/1103/168 Will of Sir Simon Clarke of Hanover in the County of Cornwall, Island of Jamaica, 10 May 1783
PROB/11/666/379 Will of Lancelot Burton of Saint Anne Westminster, Middlesex, 27 August 1734
T71/865 Claim from Mary Player Smith, as owner-in-fee
T/71/1200 Counterclaims: Jamaica: St Thomas in the East [1835–1841]
T71/867 Registers of Claims: Jamaica, St Thomas in the East
T/71/145 Office of Registry of Colonial Slaves and Slave Compensation Commission: Records

Bank of England

DS/UK/694 'Ebenezer Maitland'
M5/436-437, M5/440 Directors' Annual Lists, 1694–1935, Book 2, ff. 105–127

Norfolk Record Office, Norwich (NRO)

BRA 898 Papers of the East of England Bank, Norwich

COL 9/59–60 On the slave trade, by T. Ransome. With list of local subscribers to anti-slavery cause

COL 9/1 The Colman Manuscript Collection, Society of United Friars, [1666]–1926

FEL 539/31 Fellowes of Shotesham Collection, Estate Papers Estate: Non-Fellowes, Berney Estate

GTN 5/9/43 Letters to and circulars to Lord Suffield (including draft replies) on slavery and prison

MC 1519/1 Transcripts of Letters from William Wright, travelling abroad to his mother in Watton, 1824–26

PD/218/29 Parish of Watton

PD/589/5 Parish Records, Lowestoft

PD/28/14 & 71 Parish Records, Great Yarmouth

RQG/539/493X1 'Account of the emancipation of the Slaves of Unity Valley Pen in Jamaica by David Barclay 1801 2nd edn with appendix' (1811)

RQG/537/493x1 David Barclay's Letter Book 1788–1809, Letter to Alexander Macleod 18 January 1797

Y/WE/1-67 Weekly Register Bills, Great Yarmouth

Suffolk Record Office (SRO)

SRO/994/B/4/12 Lease of two pieces of pasture, 1853

SRO/FAA/23/23/183 Marriage Licence Bond: Jarrett Dashwood and Lorina Farr, 7 November 1771

SRO/HB/26/412/1595 Sale Particulars of Golden Grove Estate, 1891

SRO/HA247/5/96 Pay-list and return of Beccles Troop, 21 May 1822

Other archives

Archbishop of York Marriage Licences Index, 1613–1839

College of Arms, Tynemouth, Vol. I 1607–1703

Middlesex Burials & Memorial Inscriptions, Greater London Burial Index

National Library of Scotland, Shelfmark, EMAM.s.4, 'Maps of Jamaica by James Robertson, 1804'

Oxfordshire History Centre, J/XIX/c/1, Promissory note, 13 February 1707

Southwest Heritage Trust, 4084A/PR/1/1, Burial of John Burton, Jacobstowe, 4 July 1804

City of Westminster Archives Centre, Westminster Burials, St James, Piccadilly

Suffolk Record Office HB/26/412/1595, Golden Grove Estate

Journals of the Assembly of Jamaica, 11 (Scholarly Resources Microfilm, Reel No. 6)

University of Glasgow Archive Services

GB 248 DC 034/91-132 Records of Jamaica Sugar Estate Ltd, c1920–c1960

Published primary sources

Acts of Parliament

The Slavery Abolition Act 1833 (3 & 4 Will. IV c. 73)
House of Commons Parliamentary Papers 1837–8 (215) vol. 48, *Accounts of slave compensation claims*

Other published primary sources

'Account of Rates of Duty on British Plantation Sugar Imported into Great Britain, 1776–1826', *Parliamentary Papers, House of Commons, 1826, XXII (328)*
A True and exact List of the Lords and Commons of Great Britain also a compleat list of His Majesty's Privy-Council, etc. (London: E. Matthews, 1727)
'A Petition of Leonard Burton Esquire, Lord of the Manor of Denford', *Journals of the House of Commons* (London: Order of the House of Commons, 1803)
Agricultural Surveys: Norfolk (Board of Agriculture, 1804)
Annals of Agriculture and Other Useful Arts, Volumes 31–40 (Arthur Young, 1803)
The Annals and History of Leeds, and Other Places in the County of York: From the Earliest Period to the Present Time. United Kingdom (J. Johnson, 1860)
A list of the country banks of England and Wales, private and proprietary; also, of the names of all the shareholders of joint-stock banks [&c.]. (1838)
Anti-slavery Monthly Reporter (London: London Society for the Mitigation and Abolition of Slavery in the British Dominions, 1833)
History of Suffolk. [Collections extracted from J. Raw's 'Suffolk Gentleman's Pocket Book' from 1814 to 1824.] (1814)
Journal of the House of Lords: Volume 63: 1830–1831
Memoirs of the Philadelphia Society for Promoting Agriculture: Containing Communications on Various Subjects in Husbandry & Rural Affairs, Volume 5 (Philadelphia Society for Promoting Agriculture, Johnson & Warner, 1826)
Society for the Conversion and Religious Instruction and Education of the Negro Slaves in the British West India Islands, Report for the year 1829 (1829)
The Poll for the Knights of the Shire for the Western Division of Norfolk, August 1837 (Matchett, Stevenson, & Matchett, 1837)
The Laws of Jamaica: Comprehending all the Acts in Force (St Jago de la Vega, Jamaica: Printed by Alexander Aikman, 1790)
Beckford William, *A descriptive account of the Island of Jamaica* (London: 1788)
Baildon, William Paley, *The Records of the Honourable Society of Lincoln's Inn* (Lincoln's Inn, 1896)
Baines, Edward, *History, Directory & Gazetteer, of the County of York* (London: E. Baines, 1822)
Barclay, Alexander. *Effects of the Late Colonial Policy of Great Britain: Described in a Letter to the Right Hon. Sir George Murray, Showing the Effects Produced in the West India Colonies by the Recent Measures of Government* (London: Smith, Elder, and Company, 1830)
Barrett, Henry, *Great Yarmouth corporation. A report of the investigation before his majesty's municipal commissioners, appointed to examine into the corporate affairs of this borough* (1834)
Burke, Bernard. *Index to Burke's dictionary of the landed gentry of Great Britain & Ireland* (London: Colburn and Company, 1853).

Burke, John. *A Genealogical and Heraldic History of the Landed Gentry; Or Commoners of Great Britain and Ireland Etc.* (1838)

Calendar of Treasury Papers, 1556-7--[1728]: 1702-1707 (London: Longmans, Green, Reader, and Dyer, 1874)

Chambers, John, *A General History of the County of Norfolk*, Volume 2 (J. Stacy, 1829)

Chamberlayne, John, *Magnae Britanniae Notitia* (London, 1710)

Colquhoun, Patrick, *A Treatise on the Wealth, Power, and Resources of the British Empire* (London, 1814)

Cromwell, Thomas Kitson, *History of Norfolk; or excursions in the county* (1819)

Cundall, Frank, *Historic Jamaica: With Fifty-two Illustrations* (London : Institute of Jamaica, 1915)

Dunlap, John A., *Reports of Cases Decided in the High Court of Chancery* (New York: Gould, Banks & Company, 1847)

Druery, John Henry, *Historical and Topographical Notices of Great Yarmouth* (Nichols, 1826)

Edwards, Bryan, *The History, Civil and Commercial, of the British Colonies in the West Indies: Volume II* (London: J. Stockdale, 1793)

Evans, Morgan, 'Notes on the Inoculation of Grassland at Kimbolton', *Journal of the Royal Agricultural Society of England* (1876), pp. 230-36

Farrer, Edmund, *The Church Heraldry of Norfolk: pt. VIII. Part of the Norwich churches. pt. IX. Remainder of the Norwich churches, with those of Lynn, Thetford, and Great Yarmouth, and index, &c., to v. 3.* (A. H. Goose and Company, 1893)

Fuller, Stephen, (agent for the island of Jamaica), *The New Act of Assembly of the Island of Jamaica* (London: R. White, 1789)

Hakewill, James, *A picturesque tour of the island of Jamaica* (London, 1825)

Hargrave, Emily, George Denison Lumb, James, Singleton, *The Registers of the Parish Church of Leeds: Volume 20* (1914)

Lawrence-Archer, James Henry, *Monumental Inscriptions of the British West Indies from the Earliest Date* (London: Chatto & Windus, 1875)

Leslie, Charles, *A new and exact account of Jamaica* (Edinburgh, c. 1741)

Long, Edward, *The History of Jamaica*, 3 vols (London: T. Lowndes, 1774)

Mackie, Charles, *Norfolk Annals: A Chronological Record of Remarkable Events* (1902)

Mathison, Gilbert Farquhar, *Notices Respecting Jamaica, in 1808-1809-1810* (London: J. Stockdale, 1811)

Miège, Guy, *The Present State of Great Britain, and Ireland. The Seventh Edition Corrected [of the Work Originally Compiled by G. Miege]* (London: A. Bettesworth, 1731)

Mogg, Edward, Daniel Paterson, *Paterson's Roads* (London: Longman & Company, 1824)

Palmer, Charles John, *Perlustration of Great Yarmouth Vol. II* (Great Yarmouth: Nall, 1874)

The History of Great Yarmouth (L. A. Meall, 1856)

Perry, Sir Erskine, and Sir Henry Davison, *Reports of Cases Argued and Determined in the Court of Queen's Bench in the Second Year of Victoria* (1840)

Price, Frederick George Hilton, *A Handbook of London Banker* (London: Chatto & Windus, 1876)

Report of the Incorporated Society for the Conversion and Religious Instruction and Education of the Negro Slaves in the British West India Islands (The Society, 1824)

Substance of the Debates on the Bill for Abolishing the Slave Trade (London: W. Phillips, 1808)

Suckling, Alfred, *The History and Antiquities of the County of Suffolk: Volume 1* (Ipswich: W. S. Crowell, 1846)

'Sugar Farm in Jamaica', *The Penny Magazine*, 3 September 1873, pp. 348–49

The Handbook of Jamaica (Jamaica: Government Print Establishment, 1926)

The Handbook of the British West Indies, British Guiana and British Honduras (London: West India Committee, 1929)

The Jamaica Yearbook of Industry and Agriculture (Jamaica: City Printery, 1962)

Thome James Armstrong, Joseph Horace Kimball, *Emancipation in the West Indies* (1838)

Tooke, Thomas. *Details on High and Low Prices of the Thirty Past Years, from 1793 to 1822* (London: John Murray, 1824), Goldsmiths'-Kress Library of Economic Literature, No. 24119.

Tymms, Samuel, *The Family Topographer: The Norfolk circuit: Bedfordshire, Buckinghamshire, Cambridgeshire, Huntingdonshire, Norfolk, Suffolk* (1833)

White, William, *History, Gazetteer, and Directory of Norfolk* (1845)

Whitehouse, W. F., *Agricola's Letters and Essays on Sugar-Farming in Jamaica* (Kingston, Jamaica, 1845)

Whiteley, Henry. *Three Months in Jamaica, in 1832: Comprising a Residence of Seven Weeks on a Sugar Plantation.* Pamphlets printed for the Anti-Slavery Society, 1832

Young, Sir William, *The West Indian Common Place Book* (London, 1807)

Newspapers and magazines

The Barbadian
Morning Herald (London)
Norfolk Chronicle
Norwich Mercury
Bury and Norwich Post
The Farmer's Magazine
The Gentleman's Magazine, and Historical Chronicle
Manchester Mercury
Oxford Journal
The Scots Magazine
Royal Gazette of Jamaica
Colonial Standard and Jamaica Despatch
Yarmouth Independent
Essex Standard
Royal Cornwall Gazette
The London Gazette
The Gentleman's Magazine and Historical Review (1850)
The Athenaeum (1809)
The Legal Examiner (A. Maxwell, 1832)
The Monthly Magazine (United Kingdom: R. Phillips, 1818)
The Universal British Directory of Trade, Commerce, and Manufacture (United Kingdom, 1791)
Warwick and Warwickshire Advertiser

Secondary sources

Ackrill, Margaret, and Leslie Hannah. *Barclays: The Business of Banking, 1690–1996* (Cambridge University Press, 2001)

Allen, Robert C., 'Tracking the Agricultural Revolution in England', *The Economic History Review* New Series, Vol. 52, No. 2 (1999), pp. 209–35

Altink, Henrice, 'Slavery by Another Name: Apprenticed Women in Jamaican Workhouses in the Period 1834–8', *Social History* (2001), pp. 40–59

—— '"To Wed or Not to Wed?": The Struggle to Define Afro-Jamaican Relationships, 1834–1838', *Journal of Social History* (2004), pp. 81–111

—— *Representations of Slave Women in Discourses over Slavery and Abolition, 1780–1838* (London: Routledge, 2007)

Amussen, Susan Dwyer, *Caribbean Exchanges: Slavery and the Transformation of English Society, 1640–1700* (Chapel Hill, NC: The University of North Carolina Press, 2007)

Anstey, Roger, *The Atlantic Slave Trade and British Abolition, 1760–1810* (Atlantic Highlands, NJ: Humanities Press, 1975)

Aravamudan, Srinivas, *Tropicopolitans: Colonialism and Agency, 1688–1804* (Durham, NC: Duke University Press, 1999)

Aufhauser, R. Keith, 'Profitability of Slavery in the British Caribbean', *The Journal of Interdisciplinary History* (1974), pp. 45–67

Barber, Sarah, *Disputatious Caribbean: the West Indies in the Seventeenth Century* (New York:
Palgrave Macmillan, 2014)

Beckles, Hilary McD, 'Freedom and Labour in the Post-Emancipation British Caribbean', *Journal of Social History* (2002), pp. 868–71

—— 'Plantation Production and White "Proto-Slavery": White Indentured Servants and the Colonisation of the English West Indies, 1624–1645', *The Americas* (1985), pp. 21–45

Bent, Morris, 'A "Royal American"', *Journal of the Society for Army Historical Research* Vol. 1, No. 1 (1921), pp. 15–20

—— 'A "Royal American"', *Journal of the Society for Army Historical Research* Vol. 1, No. 3 (1922), pp. 98–104

Berlin, I., and P. D. Morgan (eds), *Cultivation and Culture: Labour and the Shaping of Slave Life in the Americas* (Charlottesville, VA: University of Virginia Press, 1993)

Blackburn, Robin, *The Making of New World Slavery: From the Baroque to the Modern, 1492–1800* (London: Verso, 1997)

Bohstedt, J, *The Politics of Provisions Food Riots, Moral Economy and Market Transition in England, c. 1550–1850* (Farnham: Ashgate, 2010)

Bolland, O. Nigel, 'Systems of Domination after Slavery: The Control of Land and Labour in the British West Indies after 1838', *Comparative Studies in Society and History* (1981), pp. 591–619

Brown, Christopher L., *Moral Capital: Foundations of British Abolitionism* (Chapel Hill, NC: University of North Carolina Press, 2006)

—— 'The Politics of Slavery', in *The British Atlantic World, 1500–1800*, ed. David Armitage and Michael J. Braddick (Basingstoke: Palgrave, 2009), pp. 232–50

Brown, Vincent, *The Reaper's Garden* (Cambridge, MA: Harvard University Press, 2008)

Burn, W. L., *Emancipation and Apprenticeship in the British West Indies* (London: Cape, 1937)

Burnard, Trevor, and John Garrigus, *The Plantation Machine: Atlantic Capitalism in French Saint-Domingue and British Jamaica* (Philadelphia, PA: University of Pennsylvania Press, 2016)

Burnard, Trevor, and Kenneth Morgan, 'The Dynamics of the Slave Market and Slave Purchasing Patterns in Jamaica, 1655–1788', *The William and Mary Quarterly* Vol. 58 (2001), pp. 205–28

Burnard, Trevor, *Mastery, Tyranny, and Desire: Thomas Thistlewood and His Slaves in the Anglo Jamaican World* (Chapel Hill, NC: University of North Carolina Press, 2004)

—— *Planters, Merchants, and Slaves: Plantation Societies in British America, 1650–1820* (Chicago, IL: University of Chicago Press, 2015)

—— 'Powerless Masters: The Curious Decline of Jamaican Sugar Planters in the Foundational Period of British Abolitionism', *Slavery & Abolition* (2011), pp. 185–98

—— '"Prodigious Riches": The Wealth of Jamaica before the American Revolution', *The Economic History Review* New Series, Vol. 54 (2001), pp. 506–24

—— '"The Countrie Continues Sicklie": White Mortality in Jamaica, 1655–1780', *Social History of Medicine* (1999), pp. 45–72

—— 'A Failed Settle Society: Marriage and Demographic Failure in Early Jamaica', *Journal of Social History* (1994), pp. 63–82

—— 'Passengers Only: The Extent and Significance of Absenteeism in Eighteenth-Century Jamaica', *Atlantic Studies* Vol. 1, No. 2 (2004), pp. 178–95

—— 'Harvest Years? Reconfigurations of Empire in Jamaica, 1756–1807', *Journal of Imperial and Commonwealth History* Vol. 40, No. 4 (2012), pp. 533–55

—— 'Et in Arcadia Ego: West Indian Planters in Glory, 1674–1784', *Atlantic Studies* (2012), 19–40

—— '"Wi Lickle but Wi Tallawah": Writing Jamaica into the Atlantic World, 1655–1834', *Reviews in American History* (2021), pp. 168–86

Burnard, Trevor, and Kit Candlin, 'Sir John Gladstone and the Debate over the Amelioration of Slavery in the British West Indies in the 1820s', *Journal of British Studies* Vol. 57 (2018), pp. 760–82

Butler, Kathleen Mary, *The Economics of Emancipation: Jamaica & Barbados, 1823–1843* (Chapel Hill, NC: University of North Carolina Press, 1995)

Candow, J. E., 'A Reassessment of the Provision of Food to Enslaved Persons, with Special Reference to Salted Cod in Barbados', *Journal of Caribbean History* Vol. 43 (2009), pp. 265–81

Carrington, Selwyn H., *The Sugar Industry and the End of the Slave Trade, 1775–1810* (Gainesville, FL: University Press of Florida, 2002)

—— 'Management of Sugar Estates in the British West Indies at the End of the Eighteenth Century', *The Journal of Caribbean History* (1999), pp. 22–53

Cateau, Heather, 'The New "Negro" Business: Hiring in the British West Indies, 1750–1810', in *In the Shadow of the Plantation: Caribbean History and Legacy*, ed. Alvin O. Thompson (Kingston, Jamaica: Ian Randle, 2002), pp. 10020

Checkland, S. G., 'Finance for the West Indies, 1780–1815', *The Economic History Review* New Series, Vol. 10 (1958), pp. 461–69

Chenoweth, Michael, 'The 18th Century Climate of Jamaica: Derived from the Journals of Thomas Thistlewood, 1750–1786', *Transactions of the American Philosophical Society*, New Series, Vol. 93, No. 2 (2003)

—— 'A Reassessment of Historical Atlantic Basin Tropical Cyclone Activity, 1700–1855', *Climatic Change* (2006), pp. 169–240

Colley, Linda, *Britons: Forging the Nation, 1707–1837* (New Haven, CT: Yale University Press, 1992)

Cooper, Frederick, and Laura Ann Stoler (eds), *Tensions of Empire: Colonial Cultures in a Bourgeois World* (Los Angeles, CA and London: University of Los Angeles Press, 1997)

Craton, M., and James Walvin, *A Jamaican Plantation. The History of Worthy Park, 1670–1970* (London and New York: W. H. Allen, 1970)

Craton, M., and Garry Greenland, *Searching for the Invisible Man: Slaves and Plantation Life in Jamaica* (Cambridge, MA: Harvard University Press, 1978)

Craton, Michael, *Testing the Chains: Resistance to Slavery in the British West Indies* (Ithaca, NY: Cornell University Press, 1982)

—— 'Reshuffling the Pack: The Transition from Slavery to other forms of Labour in the British Caribbean, Ca. 1790–1890', *New West Indian Guide* (1994), pp. 23–75

—— 'Proto-Peasant Revolts? The Late Slave Rebellions in the British West Indies, 1816–1832', *Past & Present* (1979), pp. 99–125

—— 'Free Villages in Jamaica', *Social and Economic Studies* (1968), pp. 336–59

Curtin, Philip D., *The Atlantic Slave Trade: A Census* (Madison, WI: University of Wisconsin Press, 1969)

—— *The Rise and Fall of the Plantation Complex: Essays in Atlantic History* (Cambridge: Cambridge University Press, 1990)

—— *Two Jamaicas: The Role of Ideas in a Tropical Colony* (Cambridge, MA: Harvard University Press, 1955)

Da Costa, Emilia Viotti, *Crowns of Glory, Tears of Blood: The Demerara Slave Rebellion of 1823* (Oxford: Oxford University Press, 1997)

Darity, William, 'British Industry and the West Indies Plantations', in *The Atlantic Slave Trade: Effects on Economies, Societies, and Peoples in Africa, the Americas, and Europe*, ed. J. E. Inikori and Stanley L. Engerman (Durham, NC: Duke University Press, 1992), pp. 247–79

Davis, David Brion, *The Problem of Slavery in the Age of Revolution, 1770–1823* (Ithaca, NY: Cornell University Press, 1975)

Davies, Ralph, *The Rise of the Atlantic Economies* (London: Weidenfeld and Nicolson, 1973)

Deerr Noel, *The History of Sugar*, 2 volumes (London: Chapman and Hall, 1949–1950)

Deerr, N., and H. W. Dickinson, 'Sugar Planting in the West Indies at the Beginning of the Nineteenth Century', *Negro History Bulletin* (1947), pp. 20–21

Dierksheide, Christa, *Amelioration and Empire: Progress and Slavery in the Plantation Americas* (Charlottesville, VA: University of Virginia Press, 2014)

Dirks, Nicholas B., *The Scandal of Empire: India and the Creation of Imperial Britain* (Cambridge, MA: Harvard University Press, 2006)

Dobson, David, *Directory of Scottish Settlers in North America, 1625–1825* (Italy: Genealogical Publishing Company, 1984)

Donoghue, John, '"Out of the Land of Bondage": The English Revolution and the Atlantic Origins of Abolition', *The American Historical Review* (2010), pp. 943–74

Draper, Nicholas, *The Price of Emancipation: Slave-Ownership, Compensation and British Society at the End of Slavery* (Cambridge: Cambridge University Press, 2010)

—— 'Helping to Make Britain Great: The Commercial Legacies of Slave-Ownership in Britain', in *Legacies of British Slave-Ownership: Colonial Slavery and the Formation of Victorian Britain*, ed. Catherine Hall et al. (Cambridge: Cambridge University Press, 2014), pp. 78–126

—— '"Possessing Slaves": Ownership, Compensation and Metropolitan Society in Britain at the Time of Emancipation 1834–40', *History Workshop Journal* (2007), pp. 75–102

Drescher, Seymour, *Econocide: British Slavery in the Era of Abolition* (Pittsburgh, PA: University of Pittsburgh Press, 1977)

Duffy, Michael, 'The French Revolution and British Attitudes to the West Indian Colonies', in *A Turbulent Time: The French Revolution and the Greater Caribbean*, ed. David Barry Gaspar and David Patrick (Bloomington, IN: Indiana University Press, 1997), pp. 78–101

Dunn, Richard S., *Sugar and Slaves: The Rise of the Planter Class in the English West Indies, 1624–1713* (Chapel Hill, NC: University of North Carolina Press, 1972)

—— *A Tale of Two Plantations: Slave Life and Labor in Jamaica and Virginia* (Cambridge, MA: Harvard University Press, 2014)

—— 'The Glorious Revolution and America', in *The Oxford History of the British Empire. Volume I, The Origins of Empire*, ed. Nicholas Canny (Oxford: Oxford University Press, 1998), pp. 463–65

Dupuy, Alex, 'French Merchant Capital and Slavery in Saint-Domingue', *Latin American Perspectives* (1985), pp. 77–102

Engerman, Stanley L., and B. W. Higman, 'Europe, the Lesser Antilles and Economic Expansion, 1600–1800', in *The Lesser Antilles in the Age of European Expansion*, ed. Robert L. Paquette and Stanley L. Engerman (Gainesville, FL: University Press of Florida, 1996), pp. 147–64

Eltis, David, and Stanley L. Engerman, 'The Importance of Slavery and the Slave Trade to Industrializing Britain', *The Journal of Economic History* Vol. 60 (2000), pp. 123–44

Eltis, David, Frank D. Lewis, and David Richardson, 'Slave Prices, the African Slave Trade, and Productivity in the Caribbean, 1674–1807', *The Economic History Review* Vol. 58, No. 4 (2005), pp. 673–700

Eltis, David, *Economic Growth and the Ending of the Transatlantic Slave Trade* (New York: Oxford University Press, 1987)

—— *The Rise of African Slavery in the Americas* (Cambridge: Cambridge University Press, 2000)

—— 'The Volume and Structure of the Transatlantic Slave Trade: A Reassessment', *William & Mary Quarterly* (2001), pp. 17–46.

Fergus, Claudius K., *Revolutionary Emancipation: Slavery and Abolitionism in the British West Indies* (Baton Rouge, LA: Louisiana State University Press, 2013)

—— '"Dread of Insurrection": Abolitionism, Security, and Labour in Britain's West Indian Colonies, 1760–1823', *William and Mary Quarterly* (2009), pp. 757–80

French, Christopher J., 'Productivity in the Atlantic Shipping Industry: A Quantitative Study', *Journal of Interdisciplinary History* Vol. 17 (1987), pp. 613–38

—— '"Crowded with Traders and a Great Commerce": London's Domination of Overseas Trade 1700–1775', *London Journal* Vol. 17 (1992), pp. 27–35

Fuentes, Marisa J., *Dispossessed Lives: Enslaved Women, Violence, and the Archive* (Philadelphia, PA: University of Pennsylvania Press, 2016)

Galloway, J. H., *The Sugar Cane Industry: An Historical Geography from Its Origins to 1914* (Cambridge: Cambridge University Press, 1989)

Gauchi, Perry, *William Beckford: First Prime Minister of the London Empire* (New Haven, CT: Yale University Press, 2013)

Goodman, Jordan, *Tobacco in History: The Cultures of Dependence* (London: Routledge, 1993)

Graham, Aaron, *Corruption, Party, and Government in Britain, 1702–1713* (Oxford: Oxford Historical Monographs, 2015)

Grant, Sharon, 'The Reverend Thomas Pennock, Wesleyan Methodist Missionary in Nineteenth Century Jamaica: A Case Study of Acculturation, Enculturation, Or Something Else?', *Wesley and Methodist Studies* (2012), pp. 117–28

Green, William A. *British Slave Emancipation: The Sugar Colonies and the Great Experiment 1830–1865* (Oxford: Clarendon Press, 1976)

Greene, Jack P., 'Liberty, Slavery, and the Transformation of British Identity in the Eighteenth-Century West Indies', *Slavery and Abolition* (2000), pp. 1–31

Gurney, Joseph John, *Familiar Sketch of the Late William Wilberforce* (Norwich: Josiah Fletcher, 1838)

Hall, Douglas, *In Miserable Slavery: Thomas Thistlewood in Jamaica, 1750–86* (Mona, Jamaica: University of the West Indies Press, 1999)

—— 'Absentee Proprietorship in the British West Indies, to about 1850', *The Jamaican Historical Review* (1964), pp. 15–35

—— 'The Apprenticeship Period in Jamaica, 1834–1838', *Caribbean Quarterly* (1953), pp. 142–66

—— 'Bountied European Immigration into Jamaica with Special Reference to the German Settlement at Seaford Town', *Jamaica Journal* (1974), pp. 48–54 and (1975), pp. 2–9

Halliday, Ursula, 'The Slave Owner as Reformer: Theory and Practice at Castle Wemyss Estate, Jamaica, 1800–1823', *Journal of Caribbean History* (1996), pp. 65–82

Handler, Jerome S., and Matthew C. Reilly, 'Contesting "White Slavery" in the Caribbean: Enslaved Africans and European Indentured Servants in Seventeenth-Century Barbados', *New West Indian Guide* (2017), pp. 30–55

Harper, Marjory, *Emigration from North-east Scotland, United Kingdom* (Aberdeen: Aberdeen University Press, 1988)

Heuman, Gad, 'Riots and Resistance in the Caribbean at the Moment of Freedom', *Slavery & Abolition* (2000), pp. 144–45

Herzog, Keith P., 'Naval Operations in West Africa and the Disruption of the Slave Trade during the American Revolution', *American Neptune* (1995), pp. 42–48

Heuman, G., 'Runaway Slaves in Nineteenth-Century Barbados', in *Out of the House of Bondage: Runaways, Resistance and Marronage in Africa and the New World*, ed. G. Heuman (London: Frank Cass, 1986), pp. 95–111

—— 'Riots and Resistance in the Caribbean at the Moment of Freedom', *Slavery & Abolition* (2000), pp. 144–45

Higman, B. W., *Slave Population and Economy in Jamaica, 1807–1834* (Cambridge: Cambridge University Press, 1976)

—— *Montpelier, Jamaica: A Plantation Community in Slavery and Freedom, 1739–1912* (Barbados, Jamaica, Trinidad and Tobago: The University Press of the West Indies, 1998)

—— 'The Sugar Revolution', *Economic History Review* (2000), pp. 213–36

—— *Jamaica Surveyed: Plantation Maps and Plans of the Eighteenth and Nineteenth Centuries* (Kingston, Jamaica: University of the West Indies Press, 2001)

—— *Plantation Jamaica, 1750–1850: Capital and Control in a Colonial Economy* (Kingston, Jamaica: University of the West Indies Press, 2008)

—— 'The West India Interest in Parliament, 1807–1833', *Historical Studies* (1967), pp. 1–19

—— 'The Internal Economy of Jamaican Pens, 1760–1890', *Social and Economic Studies* (1989), pp. 61–86

—— 'The Spatial Economy of Jamaican Sugar Plantations: Cartographic Evidence from the Eighteenth and Nineteenth Centuries', *Journal of Historical Geography* (1987), pp. 17–39

—— 'Jamaican Coffee Plantations, 1780–1860: A Cartographic Analysis', *Caribbean Geography* Vol. 2 (1986), pp. 73–91

—— '"To Begin the World Again": Responses to Emancipation at Friendship and Greenwich Estate, Jamaica', in *Jamaica in Slavery and Freedom*, ed. Kathleen Monteith and Glen Richards (Kingston, Jamaica: University of the West Indies Press, 2002), pp. 291–306

Horowitz, M. R., 'An Early-Tudor Teller's Book', *The English Historical Review* (1989), pp. 103–16

Holt, Thomas C., *The Problem of Freedom: Race, Labor, and Politics in Jamaica and Britain, 1832–1938* (Baltimore, MD: Johns Hopkins University Press, 1992)

Ingram, K. E., *Sources of Jamaican History 1655–1838* (Zug: Inter Documentation, 1976)

Inikori, Joseph E., *Africans and the Industrial Revolution in England* (Cambridge: Cambridge University Press, 2002)

—— 'Slavery and the Development of Industrial Capitalism in England', in *British Capitalism and Caribbean Slavery*, ed. Barbara Solow and Stanley Engerman (Cambridge: Cambridge University Press, 1987), pp. 79–101

Jenkins, Brian, *Henry Goulburn 1784–1856: A Political Biography* (Liverpool: Liverpool University Press, 1996)

Jewson, C. B., *The Jacobin City* (Glasgow: Blackie, 1975)

John Paul II, *Centesimus Annus* (London: Catholic Truth Society, 1991)

Jones, Alice Hanson, *Wealth of a Nation to Be: The American Colonies on the Eve of the Revolution* (New York: Columbia University Press, 1980)

Lambert, David, *White Creole Culture, Politics and Identity During the Age of Abolition* (Cambridge: Cambridge University Press, 2005)

Leo XIII, *Rerum Novarum: Encyclical on the Rights and Duties of Capital and Labour* (London: Catholic Truth Society, 2002)

Lewis, G. K., *Slavery, Imperialism, and Freedom: Studies in English Radical Thought* (New York: Monthly Review Press, 1978)

Livingston, Noël B., *Sketch Pedigrees of Some of the Early Settlers in Jamaica: Comp. from the Records of the Court of Chancery of the Island with a List of the Inhabitants in 1670 and Other Matter Relative to the Early History of the Same* (Tokyo, Japan: Educational Supply Company, 1909)

Maguire, Richard C., *Africans in Norfolk and Suffolk, 1467–1833* (Woodbridge: Boydell Press, 2021)

—— 'Harbord, Edward, Third Baron Suffield (1781–1835)', *Oxford Dictionary of National Biography* (Oxford: Oxford University Press, 2021)

Marshall, Woodville K., 'The Post-Slavery Labour Problem Revisited', in *Slavery, Freedom and Gender: The Dynamics of Caribbean Society*, ed. Brian L. Moore, B. W. Higman, Carl Campbell, and Patrick Bryan (Kingston: University of the West Indies Press, 2001), pp. 115–32

—— '"We be wise to many more tings": Blacks' Hopes and Expectations of Emancipation', in *Caribbean Freedom: Society and Economy from Emancipation to the Present*, ed. Hilary Beckles and Verene A. Shepherd (Kingston, Jamaica: Ian Randle, 1993), pp. 12–20

Mataxas, Eric, *Amazing Grace: William Wilberforce and the Heroic Campaign to End Slavery* (Oxford: Monarch, 2007)

McCahill, M. W. (ed.), *The Correspondence of Stephen Fuller, 1788–1795: Jamaica, the West India Interest at Westminster and the Campaign to Preserve the Slave Trade* (Oxford: Oxford University Press, 2014)

McClelland, Keith, 'Redefining the West India Interest: Politics and the Legacies of Slave Ownership', in *Legacies of British Slave-Ownership: Colonial Slavery and the Formation of Victorian Britain*, ed. Catherine Hall et al. (Cambridge: Cambridge University Press, 2014), pp. 127–62

McCusker, John J., and Russell R. Menard, *The Economy of British America, 1607–1789* (Chapel Hill, NC: University of North Carolina Press, 1985)

McCusker, John, *Money and Exchange in Europe and America, 1600–1775* (Chapel Hill, NC: University of North Carolina Press, 1978)

—— 'The Economy of the British West Indies, 1763–1790: Growth, Stagnation, or Decline?', in *Essays in the Economic History of the Atlantic World*, ed. John McCusker (London: Routledge, 1997), pp. 310–31

McDonald, R. A., *The Economy and Material Culture of Slaves: Goods and Chattels on the Sugar Plantations of Jamaica and Louisiana* (Baton Rouge, LA: Louisiana State University Press, 1993)

McNeill, John Robert, *Mosquito Empires: Ecology and War in the Greater Caribbean, 1620–1914* (New York: Cambridge University Press, 2010)

Mingay, G. E. (ed.), *The Agricultural State of the Kingdom, 1816* (Bath: Adams and Dart, 1970)

—— *English Landed Society in the Eighteenth Century*, new edn (1963; London: Routledge, 2007)

Mintz, Sidney, *Sweetness and Power; The Place of Sugar in Modern History* (New York: Viking, 1985)

Mitchell, Madeleine Enid, *Alphabetical Index to Early Wills of Jamaica, West Indies, 1655–1816: PCC Wills, 1655–1816, Registrar General's Office, Spanish Town, 1662–1750* (Pullman, WA: M. E. Mitchell, 2000)

Morgan, Nicholas J., and Michael Moss. '"Wealthy and Titled Persons" – The Accumulation of Riches in Victorian Britain: The Case of Peter Denny', *Business History* (1989), pp. 28–47

Morgan, Philip D., 'Slaves and Livestock in Eighteenth-Century Jamaica: Vineyard Pen, 1750– 1751', *The William and Mary Quarterly* Vol. 52, No. 1 (1995), pp. 47–76

—— 'Ending the Slave Trade: A Caribbean and Atlantic Context', in *Abolition and Imperialism in Britain, Africa, and the Atlantic*, ed. Derek R. Peterson (Athens, OH: Ohio University Press, 2010), pp. 101–28

Mulcahy, M., *Hurricanes and Society in the British Greater Caribbean, 1624–1783* (Baltimore, MD: The Johns Hopkins University Press, 2006)

Mullen, Stephen, 'Proslavery Collaborations Between British Outport and Metropole: The Rise of the Glasgow–West India Interest, 1775–1838', *The Journal of Imperial and Commonwealth History* (2023), pp. 601–43

Mullin, M., *Africa in America: Slave Acculturation and Resistance in the American South and the British Caribbean* (Urbana, IL: University of Illinois Press, 1992)

Muskett, Paul, 'The East Anglian Agrarian Riots of 1822', *The Agricultural History Review* (1984), pp. 1–13

Nechtman, Tillman W., *Nabobs: Empire and Identity in Eighteenth-Century Britain* (Cambridge: Cambridge University Press, 2010)

Neeson, J. M., *Commoners: Common Right, Enclosure and Social Change in England, 1700–1820* (Cambridge: Cambridge University Press, 1993)

Nelson, Louis P., *Architecture and Empire in Jamaica* (New Haven, CT: Yale University Press, 2016)

Oldfield, J. R., *Popular Politics and British Anti-Slavery: The Mobilisation of Public Opinion against the Slave Trade, 1787–1807* (Manchester: Manchester University Press, 1995)

—— *Transatlantic Abolitionism in the Age of Revolution: An International History of Anti-Slavery, c.1787–1820* (Cambridge: Cambridge University Press, 2013)

O'Shaughnessy, Andrew Jackson, *An Empire Divided: The American Revolution and the British Caribbean* (Philadelphia, PA: University of Pennsylvania Press, 2000)

—— 'The Formation of a Commercial Lobby: The West India Interest, British Colonial Policy and the American Revolution', *The Historical Journal* Vol. 40 (1997), pp. 71–95

Pares, Richard, *A West India Fortune* (London: Longmans, 1950)

—— *Merchants and Planters*, Econ. Hist. Rev. Supplement no. 4 (Cambridge: Cambridge University Press, 1960)

Parry, John H., 'Plantation and Provision Ground: An Historical Sketch of the Introduction of Food Crops into Jamaica', *Revista de Historia de América* (1955), pp. 1–20

Paton, Diana, *No Bond but the Law: Punishment, Race, and Gender in Jamaican State Formation, 1780–1870* (Durham, NC: Duke University Press, 2004)

—— (ed.), *Narrative of Events, since the First of August, 1834, by James Williams, an Apprenticed Labourer in Jamaica* (Durham, NC: Duke University Press, 2001)

Penson, L. M., 'The London West India Interest in the Eighteenth Century', *English Historical Review* (1921), pp. 373–92

Pestana, Carla Gardina, *The English Conquest of Jamaica: Oliver Cromwell's Bid for Empire* (Cambridge, MA: The Belknap Press of Harvard University Press, 2017)

Petley, Christer, *Slaveholders in Jamaica: Colonial Society and Culture during the Era of Abolition* (London: Pickering Chatto, 2009)

—— 'Rethinking the Fall of the Planter Class', *Atlantic Studies* (2012), pp. 1–17

—— 'Slaveholders and Revolution: The Jamaican Planter Class, British Imperial Politics, and the Ending of the Slave Trade, 1775–1807', *Slavery & Abolition* (2018), pp. 53–79

—— 'Managing "Property" The Colonial Order of Things within Jamaican Probate Inventories', *Journal of Global Slavery* (2021), pp. 81–107

—— '"Devoted Islands" and "that Madman Wilberforce": British Proslavery Patriotism during the Age of Abolition', *Journal of Imperial and Commonwealth History* (2011), pp. 393–495

Pettigrew, William A., *Freedom's Debt: The Royal African Company and the Politics of the Atlantic Slave Trade, 1672–1752* (Published for the Omohundro Institute of Early American History and Culture, Williamsburg, VA. Chapel Hill, NC: University of North Carolina Press, 2013)

Phillips, Ulrich B., 'An Antigua Plantation, 1769-1818', *The North Carolina Historical Review* Vol. 3, No. 3 (1926), pp. 439–45

Pilcher, J. M., 'The Caribbean from 1492 to the Present', in *The Cambridge World History of Food, vol. 1*, ed. K. F. Kiple and K. C. Ornelas (Cambridge: Cambridge University Press, 2000), pp. 1278–88

Pincus, Steve, 'Rethinking Mercantilism: Political Economy, the British Empire, and the Atlantic World in the Seventeenth and Eighteenth Centuries', *William and Mary Quarterly* Vol. 69, No. 1 (2012), pp. 3–34

Pitman, Frank W., *The Development of the British West Indies, 1700–1763* (New Haven, CT: Yale University Press, 1917)

Ragatz, L. J., *Statistics for the Study of British Caribbean History* (London: Bryan Edwards Press, 1927)

—— *The Fall of the Planter Class in the British Caribbean, 1763–1833* (New York: Century Company, 1928)

Rawley, James A., and Stephen D. Behrendt, *The Transatlantic Slave Trade: A History* (Lincoln, NE: University of Nebraska Press, 2005)

Rashford, John H., 'The Past and Present Uses of Bamboo in Jamaica', *Economic Botany* Vol. 49, No. 4 (1995), pp. 395–405

Reid, Ahmed, and David B. Ryden, 'Sugar, Land Markets and the Williams Thesis: Evidence from Jamaica's Property Sales, 1750–1810', *Slavery & Abolition* (2013), pp. 401–24

Reid, Ahmed, 'Sugar, Slavery and Productivity in Jamaica, 1750–1807', *Slavery & Abolition* (2016), pp. 159–82

Roberts, Justin, *Slavery and the Enlightenment in the British Atlantic, 1750–1807* (Cambridge: Cambridge University Press, 2013)

Rönnbäck, Klas, 'Governance, Value-added and Rents in Plantation Slavery-based Value-chains', *Slavery & Abolition* (2021), pp. 130–50

Rugemer, Edward B., *Slave Law and the Politics of Resistance in the Early Atlantic World* (Cambridge, MA: Harvard University Press, 2018)

Ryden, David Beck, *West Indian Slavery and British Abolition, 1783–1807* (Cambridge: Cambridge University Press, 2009)

—— 'Sugar, Spirits, and Fodder: The London West India Interest and the Glut of 1807–15', *Atlantic Studies* (2012), pp. 41–64

—— '"One of the Fertilest Pleasentest Spotts": An Analysis of the Slave Economy in Jamaica's St Andrew Parish, 1753', *Slavery and Abolition* (2000), pp. 32–55

Saxby, M. J., 'Ages at Baptism in the Parish of All Saints, Sudbury, 1809–1828: A New Approach to their Interpretation', *Local Population Studies* Vol. 70 (2003), pp. 49–56

Schwartz, L. D., *London in the Age of Industrialisation: Entrepreneurs, Labour Force and Living Conditions, 1700–1850* (Cambridge: Cambridge University Press, 1992)

Schwartz, Stuart, *Sugar Plantations in the Formation of Brazilian Society: Bahia, 1550–1835* (Cambridge: Cambridge University Press, 1985)

Seneca, Lucius Annaeus, *On the Shortness of Life* (translated by John W. Basore) (Loeb Classical Library) (London: William Heinemann, 1932)

Seymour, Susanne, Stephen Daniels, and Charles Watkis, 'Estate and Empire: Sir George Cornewall's Management of Moccas, Herefordshire and La Taste Grenada', *Journal of Historical Geography* (1998), pp. 313–51

Senior, Carl H., 'German Immigrants in Jamaica 1834–8', *Journal of Caribbean History* (1978), pp. 37–38

Shelford, April G., *A Caribbean Enlightenment: Intellectual Life in the British and French Colonial Worlds, 1750–1792* (Cambridge: Cambridge University Press, 2023)

Sheridan, Richard B., *Sugar and Slavery: An Economic History of the British West Indies, 1623–1775* (Kingston, Jamaica: Canoe Press, 1994)

—— *Doctors and Slaves: A Medical and Demographic History of Slavery in the British West Indies, 1680–1834* (Cambridge: Cambridge University Press, 1985)

—— 'The Formation of Caribbean Plantation Society, 1689–1748', in *The Oxford History of the British Empire: The Eighteenth Century*, ed. P. J. Marshall and Judith M. Brown (Oxford: Oxford University Press, 1998), pp. 394–414

—— 'Simon Taylor, Sugar Tycoon of Jamaica, 1740–1813', *Agricultural History* (1971), pp. 285–96

—— 'The Wealth of Jamaica in the Eighteenth Century', *The Economic History Review* New Series (1965), pp. 292–311

—— 'The Crisis of Slave Subsistence in the British West Indies During and After the American Revolution', *William and Mary Quarterly* (1976), pp. 615–41

Smallwood, Stephanie E., 'The Politics of the Archive and History's Accountability to the Enslaved', *History of the Present* Vol. 6, No. 2 (2016), pp. 117–32

Smandych, Russell, '"To Soften the Extreme Rigor of Their Bondage": James Stephen's Attempt to Reform the Criminal Slave Laws of the West Indies, 1813–1833', *Law and History Review* (2005), pp. 537–88

Starkey, O. P., *The Economic Geography of Barbados* (New York: Columbia University Press, 1939)

Steel, M. J., 'A Philosophy of Fear: The World View of the Jamaican Plantocracy in a Comparative Perspective', *The Journal of Caribbean History* (1993), pp. 1–20

Sutch, Richard, 'The Economics of African American Slavery: The Cliometrics Debate', in *Handbook of Cliometrics*, 2nd edn, ed. Claude Diebolt and Michael Haupert (Cham, Switzerland: Springer, 2019)

Swaminathan, Srividhya, *Debating the Slave Trade: Rhetoric of British National Identity, 1759–1815* (Farnham: Ashgate, 2009)

Tadman, Michael, 'The Demographic Cost of Sugar: Debates on Slave Societies and Natural Increase in the Americas', *American Historical Review* Vol. 105 (2000), pp. 1534–75

Taylor, Michael, 'The British West India Interest and Its Allies, 1823–1833', *English Historical Review* (2018), pp. 1478–1511

Thornton, John, *Africa and Africans in the Making of the Atlantic World, 1400–1800*, 2nd edn (Cambridge: Cambridge University Press, 1998)

Turner, Mary, 'Planter Profits and Slave Rewards: Amelioration Reconsidered', in *West Indies Accounts: Essays on the History of the British Caribbean and the Atlantic Economy in Honour of Richard Sheridan*, ed. Roderick A. McDonald (Kingston: University of the West Indies Press, 1996), pp. 232–52

—— 'The Bishop of Jamaica and Slave Instruction', *The Journal of Ecclesiastical History* (1975), pp. 363–78

—— 'Slave Workers, Subsistence and Labour Bargaining: Amity Hall, Jamaica, 1805–1832', in *The Slaves' Economy: Independent Production by Slaves in the Americas*, ed. Ira Berlin and Philip D. Morgan (London: Frank Cass, 1991), pp. 92–106

—— 'Chattel Slaves into Wage Slaves: A Jamaican Case Study', in *From Chattel Slaves to Wage Slaves: The Dynamics of Labour Bargaining in the Americas*, ed. Mary Turner (Kingston, Jamaica: Ian Randle, 1995), pp. 33–47

Venn, John, and John Archibald Venn, *Alumni Cantabrigienses: A Biographical List of All Known Students, Graduates and Holders of Office at the University of Cambridge, from the Earliest Times to 1900* (Cambridge: Cambridge University Press, 2011)

Walsh, Lorena S., 'Liverpool's Slave Trade to the Colonial Chesapeake: Slaving on the Periphery', in *Liverpool and Transatlantic Slavery*, ed. David Richardson, Suzanne Schwarz and Anthony Tibbles (Liverpool: Liverpool University Press, 2007)

Walvin, James, 'Why Did the British Abolish the Slave Trade? Econocide Revisited', *Slavery and Abolition* (2011), pp. 583–88

Ward, John R., 'The Profitability of Sugar Planting in the British West Indies, 1650–1834', *The Economic History Review* (1978), pp. 197–213

—— *British West Indian Slavery, 1750–1834: The Process of Amelioration* (Oxford: Oxford University Pres, 1988)

—— 'The Amelioration of British West Indian Slavery: Anthropometric Evidence', *Economic Historical Review* (2018), pp. 1199–226

Wilberforce, Robert Isaac, and Samuel Wilberforce, *Life of William Wilberforce*, 5 vols (London: J. Murray, 1838)

Williams, Eric, *Capitalism and Slavery* (New York: G. P. Putnam, 1966)

Wilmot, Swithin R., 'Not "Full Free": The Ex-Slaves and the Apprenticeship System in Jamaica, 1834–1838', *Jamaica Journal* (1984), pp. 2–10

—— 'Emancipation in Action: Workers and Wage Conflict in Jamaica 1838–1840', in *Caribbean Freedom: Economy and Society from Emancipation to the Present: A Student Reader*, ed. Hilary Beckles and Verene Shepherd (Princeton, NJ: M. Wiener/London: James Curry Publishers/Kingston, Jamaica: IRP, 1996), pp. 48–53

—— '"We not slave again": Enslaved Jamaicans in Early Freedom, 1838–1865', in *The Faces of Freedom: The Manumission and Emancipation of Slaves in Old World and New World Slavery*, ed. Marc Kleijwegt (Leiden: Brill, 2006), pp. 215–31

Yeh, Sarah E., '"A Sink of All Filthiness": Gender, Family, and Identity in the British Atlantic, 1688–1763', *The Historian* (2006), pp. 66–88

Zahedieh, Nuala, 'Colonies, Copper, and the Market for Inventive Activity in England and Wales, 1680–1730', *Economic History Review* Vol. 66 (2013), pp. 805–25

—— 'Eric Williams and William Forbes: Copper, Colonial Markets, and Commercial Capitalism', *Economic History Review* (2021), pp. 784–808

Unpublished theses

Barrett, Ian, 'Cultures of Pro-Slavery: The Political Defence of the Slave Trade in Britain, c.1787 1807' (PhD thesis, University of London, 2009)

Draper, Nicholas Anthony, 'Possessing Slaves: Ownership, Compensation and Metropolitan British Society at the Time of Emancipation' (PhD thesis, University College London, 2008)

Franklin, Alexandra, 'Enterprise and Advantage: The West India Interest in Britain, 1774–1840' (PhD thesis, University of Pennsylvania, 1992)

Osborne, Angelina, 'Power and Persuasion: The London West India Committee, 1783–1833' (PhD thesis, University of Hull, 2014)

Ramlackhansingh, G. S., 'Amity Hall 1760–1860: The Geography of a Jamaican Plantation' (Master's thesis, University of London, 1966)

Raven, Neil David, and University of Leicester, 'Manufacturing and Trades: The Urban Economies of the North Essex Cloth Towns C1770–1851' (PhD thesis, University of Leicester, 1998)

Satchell, Veront, 'Technology and Productivity Change in the Jamaican Sugar Industry, 1760–1830' (PhD thesis, University of the West Indies (Mona), 1993)

Oxford Dictionary of National Biography

Aylmer, G. E. 'Burton, William (c. 1608–1673), Merchant and Naval Administrator', *Oxford Dictionary of National Biography*, 23 September 2004. Accessed 28 April 2023, www.oxforddnb.com/view/10.1093/ref:odnb/9780198614128.001.0001/odnb-9780198614128-e-66570

Harding, R. 'Vernon, Edward (1684–1757), Naval Officer', *Oxford Dictionary of National Biography*. Accessed 1 December 2022, www.oxforddnb.com/

view/10.1093/ref:odnb/9780198614128.001.0001/odnb-9780198614128-e-28237

Marshall, Alan, 'Vernon, James (bap. 1646, d. 1727), Government Official and Politician', *Oxford Dictionary of National Biography*, 23 September 2004. Accessed 30 November 2022, www.oxforddnb.com/view/10.1093/ref:odnb/9780198614128.001.0001/odnb-9780198614128-e-28243

Price, Jacob M., and Leslie Hannah, 'Barclay, David (1729–1809), Banker and Brewer', *Oxford Dictionary of National Biography,* 23 September 2004. Accessed 20 October 2023, www.oxforddnb.com/view/10.1093/ref:odnb/9780198614128.001.0001/odnb-9780198614128-e-37150

New English Translation of St. Thomas Aquinas's Summa Theologiae (Summa Theologica) (trans. Alfred J. Freddoso, University of Notre Dame), st2-2-ques118.pdf (nd.edu)

The History of Parliament Online, www.historyofparliamentonline.org/

Fisher, David. R. and Stephen Farrell, 'Fuller Maitland (formerly Maitland), Ebenezer (1780–1858), of Park Place; Shinfield Park, Berks.; Stansted Mountfitchet, Essex and 11 Bryanston Square, Mdx', *The History of Parliament: The House of Commons 1820–1832*, ed. D. R. Fisher (Woodbridge: Boydell, 2009)

Gauci, Perry, 'Vernon, James II (1677–1756), of Westminster, Mdx', *The History of Parliament: The House of Commons 1690–1715*, ed. D. Hayton, E. Cruickshanks, S. Handley, 2002. Accessed 1 December 2022, www.historyofparliamentonline.org/volume/1690-1715/member/vernon-james-ii-1677-1756

Legacies of British Slavery Online

'Andrew Arcedeckne', *Legacies of British Slavery* database, accessed 20 October 2023, http:// wwwdepts-live.ucl.ac.uk/lbs/person/view/24517

'Andrew Arcedeckne of Jamaica', *Legacies of British Slavery* database, accessed 27 October 2023, http://wwwdepts-live.ucl.ac.uk/lbs/person/view/2146640843

'Alexander Barclay', *Legacies of British Slavery database, accessed 20 October 2023,* http://wwwdepts-live.ucl.ac.uk/lbs/person/view/15549

'Thomas Burton II', *Legacies of British Slavery database,* accessed 20 October 2023, http://wwwdepts-live.ucl.ac.uk/lbs/person/view/21886

'Ambrose Carter', *Legacies of British Slavery database, accessed 20 October 2023,* http:// wwwdepts-live.ucl.ac.uk/lbs/person/view/2146653439

'Chaloner Arcedeckne', *Legacies of British Slavery database, accessed 27 October 2023,* http://wwwdepts-live.ucl.ac.uk/lbs/person/view/2146640845

'Friendship Castle / Dalvey [Jamaica | St Thomas-in-the-East, Surrey]', *Legacies of British Slavery database, accessed 7 November 2023,* http://wwwdepts-live.ucl. ac.uk/lbs/estate/view/19527

'James Forsyth', *Legacies of British Slavery database, accessed 20 October 2023,* http:// wwwdepts-live.ucl.ac.uk/lbs/person/view/13987

'James Townson', *Legacies of British Slavery database, accessed 20 October 2023,* http:// wwwdepts-live.ucl.ac.uk/lbs/person/view/21751

'John Mackenzie or McKenzie', *Legacies of British Slavery database, accessed 15 March 2023,* http://wwwdepts-live.ucl.ac.uk/lbs/person/view/2146653167.

'Samuel Poole', *Legacies of British Slavery database, accessed 8 March 2023,* http:// wwwdepts-live.ucl.ac.uk/lbs/person/view/21001

'Dr James Vernon', *Legacies of British Slavery database,* accessed 20 October 2023, http://wwwdepts-live.ucl.ac.uk/lbs/person/view/2146649207

'Jamaica Trelawney 127 (Stone Henge Estate)', *Legacies of British Slavery database,* accessed 20 October 2023, http://wwwdepts-live.ucl.ac.uk/lbs/claim/view/21942

'Jamaica St Thomas-in-the-East, Surrey 439 (Middleton Estate)', *Legacies of British Slavery database, accessed 18 October 2023,* http://wwwdepts-live.ucl.ac.uk/lbs/claim/view/12043

Other electronic sources

Deed Books for Jamaica, 1669–1797, Vol. 245; Folio 181, and Vol. 341, www.jamaican-familysearch.com/Members/j/James_deeds.htm

1811 Jamaica Almanac, Givings-In for the Different Parishes, 1810, Surrey, St Thomas-in-the-East, accessed 13 December 2022, www.jamaicanfamilysearch.com/Members/a/AL11STIE.htm.

Kingsley, Nicolas, '(162) Arcedeckne of Glevering Hall', *Landed Families of Britain and Ireland,* accessed 28 August 2023, https://landedfamilies.blogspot.com/2015/04/162-arcedeckne-of-glevering-hall.html

Suckling, Alfred, 'North Cove', in *The History and Antiquities of the County of Suffolk: Volume 1* (Ipswich: W. S. Crowell, 1846), pp. 47–52. *British History Online,* accessed 25 November 2022, www.british-history.ac.uk/no-series/suffolk-history-antiquities/vol1/pp47-52

INDEX

Printed and bound by CPI Group (UK) Ltd, Croydon, CR0 4YY

24/04/2025

14661367-0001